CHINA IN THE 21ST CENTURY

MILITARY AND SECURITY DEVELOPMENTS IN CHINA

CHINA IN THE 21ST CENTURY

Additional books in this series can be found on Nova's website under the Series tab.

Additional E-books in this series can be found on Nova's website under the E-books tab.

DEFENSE, SECURITY AND STRATEGIES

Additional books in this series can be found on Nova's website under the Series tab.

Additional E-books in this series can be found on Nova's website under the E-books tab.

CHINA IN THE 21ST CENTURY

MILITARY AND SECURITY DEVELOPMENTS IN CHINA

ANTHONY G. LEEHY
AND
JOHN J. WILDSTEIN
EDITORS

Nova Science Publishers, Inc.
New York

For permission to use material from this book please contact us:
Telephone 631-231-7269; Fax 631-231-8175
Web Site: http://www.novapublishers.com

Library of Congress Cataloging-in-Publication Data

Military and security developments in China / editors, Anthony G. Leehy and John J. Wildstein.
p. cm.
Includes index.
ISBN 978-1-61942-009-0 (hbk.)
1. China--Military policy. 2. China--Armed Forces. 3. National security--China. 4. National security--Taiwan. 5. Chinese reunification question, 1949- 6. China--Strategic aspects. I. Leehy, Anthony G. II. Wildstein, John J. III. Schiffer, Michael, 1965- IV. United States. Dept. of Defense. Office of the Secretary of Defense.
UA835.M54 2011
355'.033051--dc23

2011042414

Published by Nova Science Publishers, Inc. † New York

CONTENTS

PREFACE

China's rise as a major international actor is likely to stand out as a defining feature of the strategic landscape of the early 21st century. Sustained economic development has raised the standard of living for China's citizens and elevated China's international profile. This development, coupled with an expanding science and technology base, has also facilitated a comprehensive and ongoing military modernization program. The United States welcomes a strong, prosperous, and successful China that reinforces international rules and norms and enhances security and peace both regionally and globally. This book examines China's expanding military capabilities which can facilitate cooperation in pursuit of shared objectives with the United States. Strengthening our military-to-military relationship is a critical part of our strategy to shape China's choices as we seek to capitalize on opportunities for cooperation while mitigating risks.

Chapter 1 – China's rise as a major international actor is likely to stand out as a defining feature of the strategic landscape of the early 21st century. Sustained economic development has raised the standard of living for China's citizens and elevated China's international profile. This development, coupled with an expanding science and technology base, has also facilitated a comprehensive and ongoing military modernization program. The United States welcomes a strong, prosperous, and successful China that reinforces international rules and norms and enhances security and peace both regionally and globally.

China is steadily assuming new roles and responsibilities in the international community. In 2004, Chinese President Hu Jintao articulated new guidance for the People's Liberation Army (PLA), including missions extending beyond China's immediate territorial interests. This catalyzed

China's growing involvement in international peacekeeping efforts, counter-piracy operations, humanitarian assistance and disaster relief, and the evacuation of Chinese citizens from overseas trouble spots. China's 2010 Defense White Paper asserts that China's —future and destiny have never been more closely connected with those of the international community. Nonetheless, China's modernized military could be put to use in ways that increase China's ability to gain diplomatic advantage or resolve disputes in its favor.

Although the PLA is contending with a growing array of missions, Taiwan remains its —main strategic direction.China continued modernizing its military in 2010, with a focus on Taiwan contingencies, even as cross-Strait relations improved. The PLA seeks the capability to deter Taiwan independence and influence Taiwan to settle the dispute on Beijing's terms. In pursuit of this objective, Beijing is developing capabilities intended to deter, delay, or deny possible U.S. support for the island in the event of conflict. The balance of cross-Strait military forces and capabilities continues to shift in the mainland's favor.

Over the past decade, China's military has benefitted from robust investment in modern hardware and technology. Many modern systems have reached maturity and others will become operational in the next few years. Following this period of ambitious acquisition, the decade from 2011 through 2020 will prove critical to the PLA as it attempts to integrate many new and complex platforms, and to adopt modern operational concepts, including joint operations and network-centric warfare.

China has made modest, but incremental, improvements in the transparency of its military and security affairs. However, there remains uncertainty about how China will use its growing capabilities.

The United States recognizes and welcomes PRC contributions that support a safe and secure global environment. China's steady integration into the global economy creates new incentives for partnership and cooperation, particularly in the maritime domain. Although China's expanding military capabilities can facilitate cooperation in pursuit of shared objectives, they can also increase the risk of misunderstanding and miscalculation. Strengthening our military-tomilitary relationship is a critical part of our strategy to shape China's choices as we seek to capitalize on opportunities for cooperation while mitigating risks. To support this strategy, the United States must continue monitoring PRC force development and strategy. In concert with our friends and Allies, the United States will also continue adapting our forces, posture, and operational concepts to maintain a stable and secure East Asian environment.

Chapter 2 - This is an edited, reformatted and augmented version of a Department of Defense Briefing.

In: Military and Security Developments in China ISBN 978-1-61942-009-0
Editors: A. Leehy and J. Wildstein

Chapter 1

MILITARY AND SECURITY DEVELOPMENTS INVOLVING THE PEOPLE'S REPUBLIC OF CHINA*

Office of the Secretary of Defense

GLOSSARY OF ACRONYMS

AAV	Amphibious Assault Vehicle
AEW&C	Airborne Early Warning and Control
APCSS	Asia Pacific Center for Security Studies
ASAT	Anti-Satellite
ASBM	Anti-Ship Ballistic Missile
ASCM	Anti-Ship Cruise Missile
Bcm	billion cubic meters
b/d	barrels per day
C4ISR	Command, Control, Communications, Computers, Intelligence, Surveillance, and Reconnaissance
CCP	Chinese Communist Party
CMC	Central Military Commission

* This is an edited, reformatted and augmented version of an Office of the Secretary of Defense of the Department of Defence of the United States, a Report to Congress Pursuant to the National Defense Authorization Act for Fiscal Year 2000 publication , dated 2011.

CNO	Computer Network Operations
COMSAT	Communications Satellite
CONUS	Continental United States
DCT	Defense Consultative Talks
DDG	Guided-Missile Destroyer
DPCT	Defense Policy Coordination Talks
DSS	Defense Security Service
DSTL	Developing Sciences and Technologies List
EEZ	Exclusive Economic Zone
EU	European Union
FAO	Foreign Affairs Office
FFG	Guided-Missile Frigate
GDP	Gross Domestic Product
GPS	Global Positioning System
HA/DR	Humanitarian Assistance/Disaster Relief
ICBM	Intercontinental-Range Ballistic Missile
IJO	Integrated Joint Operations
LACM	Land Attack Cruise Missile
MIRV	Multiple Independently Targeted Re-entry Vehicles
MMCA	Military Maritime Consultative Agreement
MND	Ministry of National Defense
MR	Military Region
MRBM	Medium-Range Ballistic Missile
MRL	Multiple Rocket Launcher
NCO	Non-Commissioned Officer
NDU	National Defense University
NFU	No First Use
OMTE	Outline of Military Training and Evaluation
OTH	Over-the-Horizon
PLA	People's Liberation Army
PLAAF	People's Liberation Army Air Force
PRC	People's Republic of China
R&D	Research and Development
S&ED	Strategic and Economic Dialogue
SAM	Surface-to-Air Missile
SCO	Shanghai Cooperation Organization
SLBM	Submarine-Launched Ballistic Missile
SLOC	Sea Lines of Communication
SRBM	Short-Range Ballistic Missile

SS	Diesel-Electric Attack Submarine
SSBN	Nuclear-Powered Ballistic Missile Submarine
SSN	Nuclear-Powered Attack Submarine
UAV	Unmanned Aerial Vehicle
UCAV	Unmanned Combat Aerial Vehicle UN: United Nations
UNCLOS	UN Convention on the Law of the Sea
USCG	United States Coast Guard
USMC	United States Marine Corps

EXECUTIVE SUMMARY

China's rise as a major international actor is likely to stand out as a defining feature of the strategic landscape of the early 21st century. Sustained economic development has raised the standard of living for China's citizens and elevated China's international profile. This development, coupled with an expanding science and technology base, has also facilitated a comprehensive and ongoing military modernization program. The United States welcomes a strong, prosperous, and successful China that reinforces international rules and norms and enhances security and peace both regionally and globally.

China is steadily assuming new roles and responsibilities in the international community. In 2004, Chinese President Hu Jintao articulated new guidance for the People's Liberation Army (PLA), including missions extending beyond China's immediate territorial interests. This catalyzed China's growing involvement in international peacekeeping efforts, counter-piracy operations, humanitarian assistance and disaster relief, and the evacuation of Chinese citizens from overseas trouble spots. China's 2010 Defense White Paper asserts that China's —future and destiny have never been more closely connected with those of the international community. Nonetheless, China's modernized military could be put to use in ways that increase China's ability to gain diplomatic advantage or resolve disputes in its favor.

Although the PLA is contending with a growing array of missions, Taiwan remains its —main strategic direction.China continued modernizing its military in 2010, with a focus on Taiwan contingencies, even as cross-Strait relations improved. The PLA seeks the capability to deter Taiwan independence and influence Taiwan to settle the dispute on Beijing's terms. In pursuit of this objective, Beijing is developing capabilities intended to deter, delay, or deny possible U.S. support for the island in the event of conflict. The balance of cross-Strait military forces and capabilities continues to shift in the mainland's favor.

Over the past decade, China's military has benefitted from robust investment in modern hardware and technology. Many modern systems have reached maturity and others will become operational in the next few years. Following this period of ambitious acquisition, the decade from 2011 through 2020 will prove critical to the PLA as it attempts to integrate many new and complex platforms, and to adopt modern operational concepts, including joint operations and network-centric warfare.

China has made modest, but incremental, improvements in the transparency of its military and security affairs. However, there remains uncertainty about how China will use its growing capabilities.

The United States recognizes and welcomes PRC contributions that support a safe and secure global environment. China's steady integration into the global economy creates new incentives for partnership and cooperation, particularly in the maritime domain. Although China's expanding military capabilities can facilitate cooperation in pursuit of shared objectives, they can also increase the risk of misunderstanding and miscalculation. Strengthening our military-tomilitary relationship is a critical part of our strategy to shape China's choices as we seek to capitalize on opportunities for cooperation while mitigating risks. To support this strategy, the United States must continue monitoring PRC force development and strategy. In concert with our friends and Allies, the United States will also continue adapting our forces, posture, and operational concepts to maintain a stable and secure East Asian environment.

ANNUAL UPDATE

> "In the next five years, our economy and society will develop faster, boosting comprehensive national power. The developments will provide an even more stable material base to our defense and military buildup."
>
> – PRC Defense Minster Liang Guanglie.

Several significant developments in China over the past year relate to the questions Congress posed in Section 1246 of the National Defense Authorization Act for Fiscal Year 2010 (Public Law 111-84).

China's Challenges and Opportunities in 2010

The government of China remained focused on maintaining economic development and enhancing China's security interests in 2010. The Chinese Communist Party (CCP) has built its legitimacy on the promise of economic growth, stability, and national unity. To ensure its position, the CCP closely monitors potential sources of domestic unrest, from unemployment and rising income disparities to pro-democracy movements and ethnic tensions. Additionally, Beijing is seeking to balance a more confident assertion of its growing interests in the international community with a desire to avoid generating opposition and countervailing responses from regional and major powers. An example of this could be seen in Beijing's recalibrated rhetorical approach to regional territorial disputes such as the South China Sea following the June 2010 Association of Southeast Asian Nations Regional Forum (ARF).

The 11th Five Year Plan concluded in 2010 and was marked by new milestones in PLA force development and technology acquisition. Motivated by expanding economic and security interests, the PLA is now venturing into the global maritime domain, a sphere long dominated by the U.S. Navy. Relations with Taiwan have continued to improve, but the PLA shows no sign of slowing its efforts to develop plans and capabilities for a cross-Strait contingency.

Much of the PLA's success over the next decade will be determined by how effectively it integrates emerging capabilities and platforms into the force. By most accounts, the PLA is on track to achieve its goal of building a modern, regionally-focused military by 2020.

In tandem with the PLA's improved capacities for regional military operations, PRC officials in recent years have emphasized China's sovereignty and territorial interests with greater frequency. Citing a violation of these —core interests, the PLA suspended military-to-military relations with the United States in January 2010, following U.S. approval of arms sales to Taiwan.

Developments in China's National Security Leadership

Vice President Xi Jinping became a vice chairman of the CCP Central Military Commission (CMC) at the 5th Plenum of the 17th Central Committee in October 2010. Based on historical precedent, this move could be the penultimate step to Xi becoming the General Secretary of the CCP and

Chairman of the Central Military Commission (CMC). During the leadership transition process that is expected to unfold around the 18th Party Congress in the fall of 2012, it is not clear if President Hu Jintao will relinquish the Party General Secretary and CMC Chairman positions, or if he will follow the precedent set by Jiang Zemin in 2002 and retain the CMC Chairmanship for a number of months, or even years, to facilitate the power transition.

Developments in the Security Situation in the Taiwan Strait

Since the election in Taiwan of President Ma Ying-jeou in March 2008, Beijing and Taipei have made significant progress in improving cross-Strait relations. Both Beijing and Taipei have emphasized expanding economic and cultural ties as a means of reducing tension and sustaining the current positive cross-Strait atmosphere.

Beijing and Taipei signed the Economic Cooperation Framework Agreement (ECFA) in 2010. Beijing has at times demonstrated flexibility on the issue of Taiwan's participation in international forums, but has also continued to pressure players in the international community to restrict this participation.

Despite the warming of cross-Strait ties, China continued its military modernization in 2010, including specific efforts to provide a credible range of military options in a Taiwan contingency. In the current decade to 2020, the PLA is likely to steadily expand its military options for Taiwan, including those to deter, delay, or deny third party intervention.

Developments in the Size, Location, and Capabilities of PRC Military Forces

China's long-term, comprehensive military modernization is improving the PLA's capacity to conduct high-intensity, regional military operations, including —anti-access and area denial (A2AD) operations. The terms —anti-access and area denial refer to capabilities that could be employed to deter or counter adversary forces from deploying to, or operating within, a defined space.

Consistent with a near-term focus on preparing for Taiwan Strait contingencies, China continues to base many of its most advanced systems in the military regions (MRs) opposite Taiwan. Although these capabilities could be employed for a variety of regional crisis or conflict scenarios, China has made less progress on capabilities that extend global reach or power projection. Outside of peacetime counter-piracy missions, for example, China's Navy has little operational experience beyond regional waters. Although the PLA's new roles and missions in the international domain reflect China's expanding set of interests, regional contingencies continue to dominate resources and planning.

Ballistic and Cruise Missiles

China has prioritized land-based ballistic and cruise missile programs. It is developing and testing several new classes and variants of offensive missiles, forming additional missile units, upgrading older missile systems, and developing methods to counter ballistic missile defenses.

- The PLA is acquiring large numbers of highly accurate cruise missiles, many of which have ranges in excess of 185 km. This includes the domestically-produced, ground-launched DH-10 land-attack cruise missile (LACM); the domestically produced ground- and ship-launched YJ62 anti-ship cruise missile (ASCM); the Russian SS-N-22/SUNBURN supersonic ASCM, which is fitted on China's SOVREMENNY-class DDGs acquired from Russia; and, the Russian SS-N27B/SIZZLER supersonic ASCM on China's Russian-built, KILO-class diesel-electric attack submarines.
- By December 2010, the PLA had deployed between 1,000 and 1,200 short-range ballistic missiles (SRBM) to units opposite Taiwan. To improve the lethality of this force, the PLA is introducing variants of missiles with improved ranges, accuracies, and payloads.
- China is developing an anti-ship ballistic missile (ASBM) based on a variant of the CSS-5 medium-range ballistic missile (MRBM). Known as the DF-21D, this missile is intended to provide the PLA the capability to attack large ships, including aircraft carriers, in the western Pacific Ocean. The DF-21D has a range exceeding 1,500 km and is armed with a maneuverable warhead.
- China is modernizing its nuclear forces by adding more survivable delivery systems. In recent years, the road mobile, solid propellant CSS-10 Mod 1 and CSS-10 Mod 2 (DF-31 and DF-31A) intercontinental-range ballistic missiles (ICBMs) have entered service. The CSS10 Mod 2, with a range in excess of 11,200 km, can reach most locations within the continental United States.

- China may also be developing a new road-mobile ICBM, possibly capable of carrying a multiple independently targetable re-entry vehicle (MIRV).

Naval Forces

Since the 1990s, the PLA Navy has rapidly transformed from a large fleet of low-capability, single-mission platforms, to a leaner force equipped with more modern, multi-mission platforms. In contrast to the fleet just a decade ago, many PLA Navy combatants are equipped with advanced air-defense systems and modern ASCMs, with ranges in excess of 185 km. These capabilities not only increase the lethality of PLA Navy platforms, particularly in the area of anti-surface warfare (ASuW), but also enable them to operate beyond the range of land-based air defenses.

The PLA Navy possesses some 75 principal surface combatants, more than 60 submarines, 55 medium and large amphibious ships, and roughly 85 missile-equipped small combatants. The PLA has now completed construction of a major naval base at Yulin, on the southernmost tip of Hainan Island. The base is large enough to accommodate a mix of attack and ballistic missile submarines and advanced surface combatants, including aircraft carriers. Submarine tunnel facilities at the base could also enable deployments from this facility with reduced risk of detection.

- China's aircraft carrier research and development program includes renovation of the ex-VARYAG, which could begin sea trials in 2011, although without aircraft. It will likely serve initially as a training and evaluation platform, and eventually offer a limited operational capability. China could begin construction of a fully indigenous carrier in 2011, which could achieve operational capability after 2015. China likely will build multiple aircraft carriers with support ships over the next decade.
- China currently has a land-based training program for carrier pilots; however, it will still take several additional years for China to achieve a minimal level of combat capability on an aircraft carrier.
- The PLA Navy is improving its over-thehorizon (OTH) targeting capability with sky wave and surface wave OTH radars. In combination with early-warning aircraft, unmanned aerial vehicles (UAVs), and other surveillance and reconnaissance equipment, the sky wave OTH radar allows the PRC to carry out surveillance and reconnaissance over the western Pacific. The OTH radars can be used

in conjunction with reconnaissance satellites to locate targets at great distances from the PRC, thereby supporting long-range precision strikes, including employment of ASBMs.

- China continues to produce a new class of nuclear-powered ballistic missile submarine (SSBN). JIN-class (Type 094) SSBNs will eventually carry the JL-2 submarine-launched ballistic missile with an estimated range of some 7,400 km. The JIN and the JL-2 will give the PLA Navy its first credible sea-based nuclear capability. Although DoD initially forecast the JL-2 would reach IOC by 2010, the program has faced repeated delays.
- China has expanded its force of nuclear-powered attack submarines (SSN). Two second-generation SHANG-class (Type 093) SSNs are already in service and as many as five third-generation Type 095 SSNs will be added in the coming years. When complete, the Type 095 will incorporate better quieting technology, improving its capability to conduct a range of missions from surveillance to the interdiction of surface vessels with torpedoes and ASCMs.
- The current mainstay modern diesel powered attack submarines (SS) in the PLA Navy's submarine force are the 13 SONG-class (Type 039) units. Each can carry the YJ-82 ASCM. The follow-on to the SONG is the YUAN-class SS; as many as four of which are already in service. The YUAN-class SS might also include an air-independent power system. The SONG, YUAN, SHANG and the still-to-be-deployed Type 095 all will be capable of launching the long-range CHSS-NX-13 ASCM, once the missile completes development and testing.
- China has deployed some 60 of its new HOUBEI-class (Type 022) wave-piercing catamaran hull missile patrol boats. Each boat can carry up to eight YJ-83 ASCMs. These ships have increased the PLA Navy's littoral warfare capabilities.
- The PLA Navy has acquired a new generation of domestically produced surface combatants. These include at least two LUYANG II-class (Type 052C) DDGs fitted with the indigenous HHQ-9 long-range surface-to-air missile (SAM) with additional hulls under construction; two LUZHOU-class (Type 051C) DDGs equipped with the Russian SA-N-20 long-range SAM; and as many as eight JIANGKAI II-class (Type 054A) guided-missile frigates (FFG) fitted with the medium-range HHQ-16 vertically launched naval SAM. These ships significantly improve the PLA Navy's area air defense

capability, which will be critical as the PLA Navy expands its operations into —distant seas, beyond the range of shore-based air defense.

Air and Air Defense Forces

China bases 490 combat aircraft within unrefueled operational range of Taiwan and has the airfield capacity to expand that number by hundreds. Newer and more advanced aircraft make up a growing percentage of the inventory.

- The January 2011 flight test of China's next generation fighter prototype, the J-20, highlights China's ambition to produce a fighter aircraft that incorporates stealth attributes, advanced avionics, and super-cruise capable engines over the next several years.
- China is upgrading its B-6 bomber fleet (originally adapted from the Soviet Tu16) with a new, longer-range variant that will be armed with a new long-range cruise missile.
- The PLA Air Force has continued expanding its inventory of long-range, advanced SAM systems and now possesses one of the largest such forces in the world. Over the past five years, China has acquired multiple SA-20 PMU2 battalions, the most advanced SAM system Russia exports. It has also introduced the indigenously designed HQ-9.
- China's aviation industry is developing several types of airborne early warning and control system (AWACS) aircraft. These include the KJ-200, based on the Y8 airframe, for AWACS as well as intelligence collection and maritime surveillance, and the KJ-2000, based on a modified Russian IL-76 airframe.

Ground Forces

The PLA has about 1.25 million ground forcepersonnel, approximately 400,000 of whom are based in the three military regions (MRs) opposite Taiwan. China continues to gradually modernize its large ground force. Much of the observed upgrade activity has occurred in units with the potential to be involved in a Taiwan contingency. Examples of ground unit modernization include the Type 99 third-generation main battle tank, a new-generation amphibious assault vehicle, and a series of multiple rocket launch systems.

In October 2010, the PLA conducted its first Group Army-level exercise, which it called —MISSION ACTION (SHIMING XINGDONG).The primary participants from the Beijing, Lanzhou, and Chengdu Military Regions practiced maneuver, ground-air coordination, and long-distance mobilization via military and commercial assets as they transited between MRs. Given that these MRs are located along China's land borders, the exercise scenario was likely based on border conflict scenarios. In addition to providing large-scale mobility and joint experience, the exercise allowed PLA command staff to test their ability to plan and execute a large joint campaign while practicing communication between command elements across dispersed forces. This skill is critical to responding to crises along China's periphery.

Developments in China's Space and Cyber Capabilities

Space and Counterspace Capabilities

In 2010, China conducted a national record 15 space launches. It also expanded its space-based intelligence, surveillance, reconnaissance, navigation, meteorological, and communications satellite constellations. In parallel, China is developing a multidimensional program to improve its capabilities to limit or prevent the use of space-based assets by adversaries during times of crisis or conflict.

- During 2010, Beijing launched five BeiDou navigation satellites. China plans to complete a regional network by 2012 and a global network by 2020.
- China launched nine new remote sensing satellites in 2010, which can perform both civil and military applications.
- In 2010, Beijing also launched two communications satellites (one military and one civil), a meteorological satellite, two experimental small satellites, and its second lunar mission during the year.
- China continues to develop the Long March V (LM-V) rocket, which is intended to lift heavy payloads into space. LM-V will more than double the size of the Low Earth Orbit and Geosynchronous Orbit payloads China is capable of placing into orbit. To support these rockets, China began constructing the Wenchang Satellite Launch Center in 2008. Located on Hainan Island, this launch facility is expected to be complete by 2012, with the initial LM-V launch scheduled for 2014.

Cyberwarfare Capabilities

In 2010, numerous computer systems around the world, including those owned by the U.S. Government, were the target of intrusions, some of which appear to have originated within the PRC. These intrusions were focused on exfiltrating information. Although this alone is a serious concern, the accesses and skills required for these intrusions are similar to those necessary to conduct computer network attacks. China's 2010 Defense White Paper notes China's own concern over foreign cyberwarfare efforts and highlighted the importance of cyber-security in China's national defense.

Cyberwarfare capabilities could serve PRC military operations in three key areas. First and foremost, they allow data collection through exfiltration. Second, they can be employed to constrain an adversary's actions or slow response time by targeting network-based logistics, communications, and commercial activities. Third, they can serve as a force multiplier when coupled with kinetic attacks during times of crisis or conflict.

Developing capabilities for cyberwarfare is consistent with authoritative PLA military writings. Two military doctrinal writings, *Science of Strategy,* and *Science of Campaigns* identify information warfare (IW) as integral to achieving information superiority and an effective means for countering a stronger foe. Although neither document identifies the specific criteria for employing computer network attack against an adversary, both advocate developing capabilities to compete in this medium.

The Science of Strategy and *Science of Campaigns* detail the effectiveness of IW and computer network operations in conflicts and advocate targeting adversary command and control and logistics networks to impact their ability to operate during the early stages of conflict. As the *Science of Strategy* explains, —In the information war, the command and control system is the heart of information collection, control, and application on the battlefield. It is also the nerve center of the entire battlefield.

In parallel with its military preparations, China has increased diplomatic engagement and advocacy in multilateral and international forums where cyber issues are discussed and debated. Beijing's agenda is frequently in line with the Russian Federation's efforts to promote more international control over cyber activities. China has not yet agreed with the U.S. position that existing mechanisms, such as International Humanitarian Law and the Law of Armed Conflict, apply in cyberspace.

China's thinking in this area is evolving as it becomes more engaged.

Developments in China's Defense Technology Acquisition

China relies on foreign technology, acquisition of key dual-use components, and focused indigenous research and development (R&D) to advance military modernization.

The PRC also utilizes a large, well-organized network of enterprises, defense factories, affiliated research institutes, and computer network operations to facilitate the collection of sensitive information and export-controlled technology, as well as basic research and science that supports U.S. defense system modernization.

Many of the organizations comprising China's military-industrial complex have both military and civilian research and development functions. This network of government-affiliated companies and research institutes often enables the PLA to access sensitive and dual-use technologies or knowledgeable experts under the guise of civilian research and development. The enterprises and institutes accomplish this through technology conferences and symposia; legitimate contracts and joint commercial ventures; partnerships with foreign firms; and joint development of specific technologies.

In the case of key national security technologies, controlled equipment, and other materials not readily obtainable through commercial means or academia, the PRC has utilized its intelligence services and employed other illicit approaches that violate U.S. laws and export controls.

- In August 2010, Noshir Gowadia was convicted of providing the PRC with classified U.S. defense technology. Gowadia assisted the PRC in developing a low-signature cruise missile exhaust system capable of rendering a cruise missile resistant to detection by infrared missiles.
- In September 2010, Chi Tong Kuok was convicted for conspiracy to illegally export U.S. military encryption technology and smuggle it to Macau and Hong Kong. The relevant technology included encryption, communications equipment, and Global Positioning System (GPS) equipment used by U.S. and NATO forces.

Challenges to Taiwan's Deterrent Forces

There were no armed incidents in the vicinity of the Taiwan Strait in 2010 and the overall situation remained stable. However, the PRC's military modernization and the deployment of advanced capabilities opposite the island have not eased, and the balance of military force continues to shift in Beijing's favor.

Taiwan President Ma Ying-jeou's defense reforms designed to streamline and professionalize the military continue, but budget shortfalls and escalating costs will lengthen the time necessary for implementation.

Taiwan plans to cut its military force to 215,000 troops and transition to an all-volunteer military by 2015, but recruitment and cost challenges may require a reevaluation of the scope or implementation schedule. It will also reorganize several support commands and looks to civilianize its key defense research and development facilities to improve efficiency and productivity.

Consistent with the provisions of the Taiwan Relations Act, Public Law 96-8 (1979), the United States continues to make available defense articles and defense services to enable Taiwan to maintain a sufficient self-defense capability. Toward this end, in January 2010, the Obama Administration announced its intent to sell to Taiwan $6.4 billion in defensive arms and equipment, including UH60 utility helicopters; PATRIOT PAC-3 air and missile defense systems; HARPOON training missiles; Multifunctional Information Distribution Systems technical support for Taiwan's Syun An command, control, communications, computers, intelligence, surveillance, and reconnaissance (C4ISR) system; and OSPREY-class minehunting ships.

China's Foreign Military Engagement

China's military engages with foreign militaries to build relationships, improve functional capabilities, and shape foreign perceptions of China. PLA engagement activities support China's military modernization goals through acquisition of advanced weapons systems; increased operational experience both within and beyond Asia; and access to foreign military practices, operational doctrine, and training methods.

- China continues to conduct counter-piracy operations in the Gulf of Aden. PLA Navy ships have remained in the Gulf of Aden since January 2009. In July 2011 the PLA Navy deployed its ninth escort formation. Outside of foreign —goodwill cruises,|| this represents the PLA Navy's only series of operational deployments beyond the immediate western Pacific region.
- China's Ministry of National Defense (MND) announced that by December 2010, it had comprehensively expanded foreign military

relations through establishment of military relations with over 150 countries, including attaché offices in 112 countries. 102 countries have military attaché offices in China. The PLA continues sending over 170 military delegations overseas every year and receiving over 200 foreign military delegations as part of high-level strategic consultations and professional and technical exchanges.

- In April 2010, China introduced its —August First aerial demonstration team to the international media and discussed the PLA Air Force's intention for the team to perform in foreign countries.

Combined Exercises

PLA participation in bilateral and multilateral exercises is increasing. The PLA derives political benefit through increased influence and enhanced ties with partner states and organizations. Such exercises provide the PLA opportunities to improve capabilities and gain operational insights by observing tactics, command decision-making, and equipment used by more advanced militaries.

- During the recently completed 11th Five-Year Plan, the PLA held 32 joint exercise and training events with foreign militaries. These activities covered issues such as counter-terrorism, maritime drills, ground forces training, peacekeeping, and search and rescue.
- In July, PLA and Brazilian special operations forces conducted FRIENDSHIP-2010, a joint counterterrorism exercise, which included live fire exercises supported by fighter/bombers, transport aircraft, and attack and transport helicopters.
- China and Peru conducted —PEACE ANGEL 2010,‖ a humanitarian medical rescue exercise in November.
- In early November, the PLA conducted FRIENDSHIP ACTION-2010 with Albanian forces. This marked the PLA's third exercise with foreign troops within China and the first with a European military.
- The PLA Air Force participated in two major international events in 2010; a bilateral air exercise with Turkey and subsequently, PEACE MISSION 2010, which was conducted under the auspices of the Shanghai Cooperation Organization. This latter exercise involved launching air operations from PRC bases to fly missions over Kazakhstan.

Peacekeeping and Humanitarian Assistance/ Disaster Relief Operations

China's participation in UN peacekeeping operations increased six-fold during the six-year period from January 2004 to January 2010. China is now the leading contributor of peacekeeping personnel among the five permanent members of the UN Security Council. China's contributions have included engineering, logistics, medical troops, civilian police, and observers. In January 2004, China had 359 peacekeepers deployed to eight UN peacekeeping missions, with no single contingent larger than 70 troops. As of January 2010, China had 2,131 peacekeepers supporting 10 UN missions, with five separate contingents larger than 200 troops.

- In September 2010, China co-hosted its first UN peacekeeping senior commanders training course at the PRC MND Peacekeeping Center.
- China has maintained a force of 125 riot police in Haiti, in support of the UN stabilization force. After Haiti suffered a devastating earthquake in January 2010, these riot police provided escorts to the PRC medical team Beijing dispatched to the country for humanitarian support.
- China's civilian and military leaders have identified humanitarian assistance and disaster relief as an area for China to cooperate with foreign partners and advance PRC interests.
- As of early 2011, China had pledged 250 million U.S. dollars to Pakistan for flood relief. This pledge of aid, which came after international criticism of China's initial response, constituted China's largest-ever humanitarian aid package to a foreign nation. Beijing dispatched two of its international search-and-rescue teams to aid Pakistan, and the PLA sent a medical team. In another first for China, the PLA deployed four military helicopters out of China to support the relief effort.
- In July 2010, China's Ministry of National Defense announced that the PLA had participated in at least 20 international humanitarian rescue missions since 2002, and that its international rescue team had joined six international rescue missions since its creation in 2001.

UNDERSTANDING CHINA'S STRATEGY

Overview

China's leaders characterize the initial two decades of the 21st century as a —strategic window of opportunity. They assess that during this period, both domestic and international conditions will be conducive to expanding China's —comprehensive national power (*zonghe guoli*—综合国力), a term that encapsulates all elements of state power including economic capacity, military might, and diplomacy. Speaking in December 2010, PRC Defense Minister Liang Guanglie asserted that —making the country prosperous and making the armed forces strong are two major cornerstones for realizing the great rejuvenation of the Chinese nation. China's leaders anticipate that a successful expansion of comprehensive national power will serve China's overriding strategic objectives, which include perpetuating CCP rule; sustaining economic growth and development; maintaining domestic political stability; defending national sovereignty and territorial integrity; and securing China's status as a great power.

In the near term, the PRC regards stable relations with the U.S. and China's neighbors as essential to stability and critical to maximizing this window of opportunity. At the same time, China's growing economic and military confidence and capabilities occasionally manifest in more assertive rhetoric and behavior when Beijing perceives threats to its national interests or feels compelled to respond to public expectations.

The PRC is particularly concerned that regional actors might counterbalance China's rise through military development and coalitions. China publicly states that its rise is —peaceful and that it harbors no —hegemonic designs or aspirations for territorial expansion. However, China's lack of transparency surrounding these growing capabilities has increased concerns in the region about China's intentions.

Understanding Chinese Strategy

China uses white papers, speeches, and articles as the principal mechanisms to publicly communicate policy and strategy.

Published on March 31, 2011, China's Defense White Paper for 2010 summarizes four national defense —goals as:

- Safeguarding national sovereignty, security and interests of national development;
- maintaining social harmony and stability;
- accelerating the modernization of national defense and the armed forces; and,
- maintaining world peace and stability.

Military Decision Making Structures and Processes in China

The PLA is the armed instrument of the Chinese Communist Party (CCP) and organizationally, is subordinate to the Party apparatus. Career military officers are CCP members, and units at the company level and above have political officers responsible for personnel decisions, propaganda, and counterintelligence. Major decisions at all levels are made by CCP committees, also led by the political officers and commanders.

The PLA's highest decision-making body, the Central Military Commission (CMC), is technically a department of the CCP Central Committee, but is staffed primarily by military officers.

The Chairman is a civilian, usually the General Secretary of the CCP and the President. Other members include the commanders of the service arms and the four general headquarters departments, and a number of Vice Chairmen.

Vice President Xi Jinping, the anticipated successor to PRC President Hu Jintao, is one of three Vice Chairmen and the only other civilian on the CMC. China's Ministry of National Defense is a relatively small office specializing in military-related tasks that are the responsibility of the civilian government rather than the armed forces, including foreign military relations, mobilization, recruitment, and civil support to military operations. The Minister of Defense is a uniformed military officer and CMC member.

The PLA currently has less representation in key party decision-making bodies than in the mid-1990s or even the mid-2000s. With the passing of China's revolutionary generation, fewer national leaders hail from a military background. However, PLA leaders are increasingly inclined to voice their thoughts and opinions on international affairs in the public domain.

The Defense White Paper for 2010 notes that China continues to implement the military strategy of —Active Defense and is enhancing —national strategic capabilities while maintaining China's —no first use policy on nuclear weapons. China's stated defense strategy is focused on fostering a security environment conducive to China's comprehensive development.

While addressing many of the themes presented in previous PRC Defense White Papers, the latest version conveys some important differences. The new document expresses confidence that the China's position relative to other major powers has improved substantially. Relations with the United States are portrayed with a degree of concern, while the current state of cross-Strait relations is presented in a favorable light. The latest version highlights the PLA's growing focus on military operations other than war, but overall, the document presents only incremental new insights into the PLA's structure, doctrine and capabilities. Overall, the transparency of China's military and security affairs has improved gradually in recent years, highlighted by its publication of Defense White Papers, establishment of a MND spokesperson, the launch of an official MND website, wider media coverage of military issues, and growing availability of books and professional journals on military and security topics.

The Chinese High Command

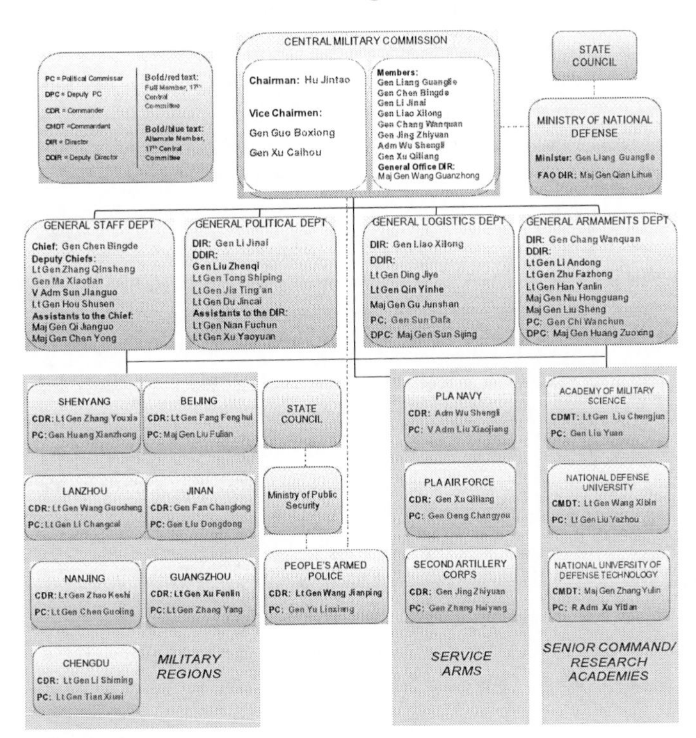

The PRC Military Structure

China's Upcoming Military Leadership Transition

China's civilian and military leadership are expected to undergo extensive changes during the 18th Party Congress, likely to be held in the fall of 2012. Vice President Xi Jinping was appointed Vice Chairman of the Central Military Commission (CMC) in October 2010. It is unclear whether Hu will follow in the footsteps of his predecessor Jiang Zemin and remain CMC chairman for some period of time after relinquishing his other leadership roles.

The uniformed CMC membership is also expected to experience a major transition during the 18th Party Congress. Seven of the ten uniformed CMC members will almost certainly retire based on age limits. In December 2010, Defense Minister Liang highlighted the PLA's shift towards a —more rational force structure as the Navy, Air Force, and Second Artillery Corps take on a larger and more prominent place in the PLA. *The three uniformed members expected to retain their CMC posts beyond 2012 are:*

General Chang Wanquan, Director of the General Armament Department (GAD), is the only ground forces officer eligible by age to serve an additional term. A former commander of the Shenyang Military Region (MR) and chief of staff of the Beijing MR, General Chang spent most of his career in operations and training posts in the Lanzhou MR. He also served as director of the campaign teaching and research office at the National Defense University in the late 1990s. In his current post as GAD director, Chang oversees foreign weapon procurement and domestic production, military testing, and the space and satellite programs. Two current senior CMC members, Chief of the General Staff Chen Bingde and director of the General Political Department Li Jinai, are also former GAD chiefs, underscoring the emphasis the Party has placed on these elements of the PLA's modernization program.

Admiral Wu Shengli, the Commander of the PLA Navy, has presided over a substantial increase in the Navy's international engagement, including its ongoing counter-piracy deployment to the Gulf of Aden. A former destroyer captain in China's East Sea Fleet and later commandant of the Dalian Naval Vessels Academy who rose to become commander of the South Sea Fleet, Wu also served as a deputy chief of the general staff in the mid-2000s. He is the second naval officer to serve on the CMC since the Navy, Air Force and 2nd Artillery Corps commanders were added to its membership in 2004.

General Xu Qiliang, the Commander of the PLA Air Force is a former pilot who served much of his career in the Nanjing MR opposite Taiwan. He rose to Chief of Staff of the Beijing MR Air Force and then Commander of the Shenyang MR Air Force. Along with Wu Shengli, his promotion to Commander of his service followed a tour as a Deputy Chief of the General Staff in the mid-2000s.

China's Strategic Priorities

Since China launched its —reform and opening, in 1978, the essential elements of China's strategy have remained relatively constant. Rather than challenge the existing global order, China has adopted a pragmatic approach to international relations and economic development that seeks to strengthen the economy, modernize the military, and solidify the CCP's hold on power. This approach reflects Beijing's assumption that great power status over the long-term is best achieved by avoiding confrontation in the near-term. China's leaders routinely emphasize the goal of reaching critical economic and military benchmarks by 2020 and eventually becoming a world-class economic and military power by 2050.

China's leaders appear to make decisions based on an array of interrelated and sometimes competing strategic priorities, which include perpetuating CCP rule; sustaining economic growth and development; maintaining domestic political stability; defending national sovereignty and territorial integrity; and securing China's status as a great power. Although evolving security challenges and growing capabilities have prompted adjustments over the past three decades, the overarching strategic vision has remained largely intact.

During 2010, China continued on a path toward its long-term strategic objectives. Despite domestic concerns over inflation, growing income disparities, and a possible housing bubble, to date China's economy appears to have weathered the global economic turmoil with relative success. In 2010, the PRC economy surpassed that of Japan to become the world's second largest. Although PRC leaders remain concerned over a number of economic challenges, many analysts have suggested that China's economic performance in recent years has endowed Beijing with greater confidence in its economic model and in its relative strength.

Militarily, China's sustained modernization program is paying visible dividends. During 2010, China made strides toward fielding an operational anti-ship ballistic missile, continued work on its aircraft carrier program, and finalized the prototype of its first stealth aircraft. Despite continued gaps in some key areas, large quantities of antiquated hardware, and a lack of operational experience, the PLA is steadily closing the technological gap with modern armed forces.

China's leaders speak about their strategic priorities in terms of what they call China's —core interests.

In a December 2010 exposition on China's foreign policy, State Councilor Dai Bingguo enumerated China's core interests as:

- The state system, political system, and political stability of China; that is the leadership of the CCP, the socialist system, and the path of socialism with Chinese characteristics.
- The sovereignty and security, territorial integrity, and national unity of China.
- The basic guarantee for the sustained development of the economy and society of China.
- The PRC leadership is also focused on the many potential problems that could complicate or derail China's growth trajectory or its strategy of —peaceful development.

These include the following:

- Economics: Continued economic development remains the bedrock of social stability and underwrites China's military power. A wide range of economic factors could disrupt this trajectory, including the rapid contraction of a potentially overheated economy. China's leaders have already scaled back GDP targets for 2011-2015 to mitigate risk of overheating and to manage expectations. Other potential economic risks for China include shifting global trade patterns, resource constraints, or attempts to challenge access to resources.
- Nationalism: Communist Party leaders and military officials continue to exploit nationalism to bolster the legitimacy of the Party and deflect domestic criticism. However, this approach is inherently risk-laden, as these forces could easily turn against the state or complicate China's policy process. Nationalistic appeals for a more muscular PRC posture, particularly during times of crisis, effectively constrain more moderate, pragmatic elites in China's foreign policy establishment. Alternatively, PRC elites may point to nationalism as a justification for their own inflexibility in dialogues with foreign interlocutors.
- Growing Expectations: China'sdevelopment has translated into greater expectations both at home and abroad for involvement in the international arena. Other nations have called on Beijing to shoulder a greater role in solving international problems, to a point at which some Chinese leaders worry about taking on more than they can

handle. At the same time, the domestic perception of China's growing status is producing popular demands for a more assertive pursuit of China's international interests.

- Regional Balancing: China's growing economic, diplomatic and military presence and influence in Asia and globally is raising concerns among many countries about China's ultimate aims –and the threats this could present to them. These regional concerns could catalyze regional or global balancing efforts.
- Domestic Political Pressures: Regime survival shapes the strategic outlook of China's leaders and drives decision making. The Communist Party continues to face long-term popular demands for improved government responsiveness, transparency and accountability. If unmet, these factors weaken CCP legitimacy.
- Demographic Pressures: Demographic stresses will increase in the future,creating a structural constraint on China's ability to sustain high economic growth rates as well as a social challenge for the CCP.
- Environment: China's economic development has come at a high environmental cost. China's leaders are increasingly concerned that environmental degradation could undermine regime legitimacy by threatening economic development, public health, social stability, and China's international image.
- Cross-Strait Dynamics:Despite a reduction in tensions following the March 2008 election of Taiwan President Ma Ying-jeou, the possibility of a military conflict with Taiwan, including U.S. military intervention, remains a pressing, long-term focus for the PLA. In the absence of a peaceful cross-Strait resolution or long-term non-aggression pact, the Taiwan mission will likely continue to dominate PLA modernization and operational planning.

The New Historic Missions

In 2004, Hu Jintao articulated a mission statement for the armed forces titled, the —Historic Missions of the Armed Forces in the New Period of the New Century (*xin shiji xin jieduan wojun lishi shiming*—). These —new historic missions focus primarily on adjustments in the PRC leadership's assessment of the international security environment and the expanding definition of national security.

China's Territorial Disputes

China faces extensive territorial disputes along its land and maritime periphery. Next to the status of Taiwan, these disputes play a central role in PLA planning. Although China has generally adopted a less confrontational posture towards its regional disputes since the late 1990s (China has settled eleven land disputes with six of its neighbors since 1998), some regional actors fear China's growing military and economic weight is beginning to produce a more assertive posture, particularly in the maritime domain.

In addition to a longstanding and contentious border dispute with India, China has maritime boundary disputes with Japan over the East China Sea and throughout the South China Sea with Vietnam, Malaysia, the Philippines, Brunei, and Taiwan.

These have sparked occasional armed conflict, including a 1962 border conflict with India and a 1979 ground invasion of Vietnam. In the South China Sea, China fought Vietnamese forces in the Paracel Islands in 1974 and near Fiery Cross Reef in 1988. In 1995, China occupied Mischief Reef, also in the Spratly Islands, amid protest from the Philippines. In 2002, Beijing and ASEAN brokered a Declaration on Conduct in the South China Sea. While non-binding, the declaration was followed by a period of relative stability.

China's broad claim to potentially all of the South China Sea remains a source of regional contention. Beginning in the 1930s and 1940s, the Republic of China began publishing regional maps with a dashed line around the perimeter of South China Sea. After taking power in 1949, the CCP maintained this claim. Both the PRC and Taiwan continue to base their South China Sea claims on that broad delineation. China increasingly regards the South China Sea as a vital commercial and security corridor for East and Southeast Asia.

In recent years, some of China's neighbors have questioned Beijing's long-term commitment to peacefully and cooperatively resolve the remainder of its disputes. PLA Navy assets have repeatedly circumnavigated the South China Sea since 2005, and civilian enforcement ships, sometimes supported by the PLA Navy, have occasionally harassed foreign vessels. Underscoring the volatility of these various disputes, a PRC-flagged fishing boat collided with Japanese Coast Guard vessels near the disputed Senkaku Islands in the East China Sea, triggering a highly charged political standoff between Tokyo and Beijing in September 2010.

These missions were further codified in a 2007 amendment to the CCP Constitution. The missions, as currently defined, include:

- Provide an important guarantee of strength for the party to consolidate its ruling position.
- Provide a strong security guarantee for safeguarding the period of strategic opportunity for national development.
- Provide a powerful strategic support for safeguarding national interests.
- Play an important role in safeguarding world peace and promoting common development.

According to official writings, the driving factors behind the articulation of these missions were: changes in China's security situation, challenges and priorities regarding China's national development, and a desire to realign the tasks of the PLA with the CCP's objectives. Politburo member and CMC Vice Chairman Xu Caihou in 2005 asserted —the historic missions embody the new requirements imposed on the military by the Party's historic tasks, accommodate new changes in our national development strategy, and conform to the new trends in global military development.

In a point reiterated in the latest PRC Defense White Paper, economic development remains a central task and the PLA is expected to support China's economic interests and security. This poses new challenges for a military that, until recently had virtually no operational experience outside of its region.

President Hu Jintao's strategic guidance to the military reflects this view, calling on the PLA to play a broader role in securing China's strategic interests, including those beyond its territorial boundaries. In a March 2009 speech to military delegates to China's National People's Congress, President Hu urged the military to concentrate on —building core military capabilities, but also —the ability to carry out military operations other than war (*fei zhanzheng junshi xingdong*—非战争军事行动). Hu maintained, —with the prerequisite of satisfactorily completing all missions—taking preparation for military struggle as the lead—the armed forces must participate actively in and support national economic construction and public welfare.

China's 2010 Defense White Paper highlights the PLA's evolving roles and missions, noting that:

> They organize preparations for military operations other than war (MOOTW) in a scientific way, work out pre-designed strategic programs against nontraditional security threats, reinforce the building of specialized forces for emergency response, and enhance capabilities in counter-terrorism and stability maintenance, emergency rescue, and the protection of security.

Authoritative PRC media describe these —military operations other than war as including: counter-terrorism, maintaining social stability, disaster relief and rescue, and international peacekeeping operations.

China's leaders have mentioned other —non-war military activities including protecting sea lanes, cyber warfare, security of space-based assets, conducting military diplomacy, and preparing for unexpected conditions and events.

- The PLA Navy's ongoing deployment to conduct counter-piracy escort missions in the Gulf of Aden is one example of China's pursuit of its new historic missions.
- Another example was the 2010 voyage of China's first large hospital ship, which made stops in Asia and Africa. The ship is able to support combat operations, but PRC official press reporting stresses the humanitarian aspects of the ship's mission.
- Most recently, the PLA employed lift assets to assist in the evacuation of PRC citizens from Libya. This marked the PLA's first noncombatant evacuation operation (NEO).

Debates on Future Strategy

China's current strategy remains one of managing the external environment to ensure conditions are conducive to China's economic development and military modernization. This approach serves the paramount goal of preserving the survival and leadership of the CCP. Although this strategy appears to enjoy widespread acceptance among Beijing's foreign and security policy establishment, military and academic writings reveal differences of opinion concerning the means of achieving China's broad national objectives.

China Debates its National Security Strategy in 2010

Throughout 2010, a line of commentary in Western and Chinese media and academic circles, suggested that China has grown stronger relative to the United States, particularly as a result of the global financial crisis. Some commentators asserted that a more powerful China should more proactively pursue its national interests. While this increasingly public debate indicates the CCP is allowing discussion of competing strategic priorities, there is little indication that its senior leaders are abandoning Deng Xiaoping's foreign policy legacy in the near term.

The tension between managing China's image and advancing China's interests was revealed on several occasions in 2010. This included discussions of how Beijing should respond to South China Sea tensions and U.S.-South Korea joint exercises in the Yellow Sea. Much of the resulting commentary hailed perceptions that Beijing had taken a stronger stand on these issues in line with its growing international weight.

Some commentators argued that China needed to take a still stronger stand or asserted that on the contrary, Beijing lacked sufficient power to sustain a more assertive position, despite a relative U.S. decline.

An increasingly public debate in China regarding the exercise of national power reflects the fact that both assertive and accommodating behaviors come with a set of costs for Beijing. Many in China feel that the steady expansion of comprehensive national power entitles China to greater respect and deference. However, during the current —strategic window of opportunity, the Chinese leadership remains wary of undermining their long-term objectives.

By autumn 2010, commentary on security relations with the United States had moderated, probably due to efforts to smooth the way for President Hu Jintao's planned early 2011 visit to the United States. The official communiqué of the 5th Plenum of the 17th CCP Central Committee held from October 15-18, 2010: —stressed that our country is still in the important strategic opportunity period. We judge this to be a re-affirmation of Deng's strategy of carefully preserving a stable environment for China's development as opposed to a call for Beijing to take a more assertive stance.

Although the view is increasingly articulated that the time has come for China to discuss more candidly and pursue its national interests, the prevailing voices within China's leadership have supported former paramount leader Deng Xiaoping's dictum from the early 1990s that China should, —observe calmly; secure our position; cope with affairs calmly; hide our capabilities and bide our time; be good at maintaining a low profile; and never claim leadership.This guidance reflected Deng's belief that PRC interests are best served by focusing on internal development and stability while steering clear of direct confrontation or antagonism with major powers. In December 2010, State Councilor Dai Bingguo specifically cited Deng's guidance, insisting China adhered to a —path of peaceful development|| and would not seek expansion or hegemony. He asserted that the —bide and hide rhetoric was not a —smokescreen employed while China builds its strength, but rather an admonition to be patient and not stand out.

Some PRC scholars question whether Deng's policy approach will continue to win support as China's interests and power expand. China's perceived security interests have changed considerably since Deng's era to include a heavy reliance on maritime commerce. China's improving naval capabilities enable roles and missions that would have been impossible for the PLA to pursue just a decade ago. Proponents of a more active and assertive PRC role on the world stage have suggested that China would be better served by a firm stance in the face of U.S. or other regional pressure.

There has also been an active debate among military and civilian theorists in China concerning future capabilities the PLA should develop to advance China's interests beyond traditional requirements. Some senior officers and civilian theorists advocate an expansion of the PLA's power projection capabilities to facilitate missions well beyond Taiwan and regional disputes. Publicly, PRC officials contend that increasing the scope of China's maritime capabilities is intended to build capacity for international peacekeeping, humanitarian assistance, disaster relief, and protection of sea lanes.

Military and Security Aspects of Beijing's Regional Energy Strategy

China's engagement, investment, and foreign construction related to energy continue to grow. Beijing has constructed or invested in energy projects in more than 50 countries, spanning nearly every continent. This ambitious investment in energy assets is driven primarily by two factors. First, Beijing is increasingly dependent upon imported energy to sustain its economy. A net oil exporter until 1993, China still lacks trust in international energy markets. Second, energy projects present a viable option for investing China's vast foreign currency holdings.

In addition to ensuring reliable energy sources, Beijing hopes to diversify both producers and transport options. Although energy independence is no longer realistic for China, given population growth and increasing per capita energy consumption, Beijing still seeks to maintain a supply chain less susceptible to external disruption.

In 2009, China imported approximately 56 percent of its oil and conservative estimates project that China will import almost two-thirds of its oil by 2015 and three-quarters by 2030. Beijing looks primarily to the Persian Gulf, Central Asia, and Africa to satisfy its growing demand for oil. Imported oil contributes to approximately 10% of China's total energy consumption.

A second goal of Beijing's foreign energy strategy is to alleviate China's heavy dependence on Sea Lines of Communication (SLOCs), particularly the South China Sea and Strait of Malacca. In 2010, over 80 percent of China's oil imports transited the South China Sea and Strait of Malacca. A crude oil pipeline from Kazakhstan to China illustrates efforts to increase overland supply. In January 2011, a 300,000 b/d spur pipeline from Siberia to Daqing began delivering crude to China. China also commenced construction on a pipeline designed to transport crude oil and natural gas from Kyuakpya, Burma, to Kunming, China, bypassing the Strait of Malacca.

China's Top Crude Oil Suppliers 2009

Country	Volume	%
Saudi Arabia	843	21
Angola	646	16
Iran	465	11
Russia	307	8
Sudan	245	6
Oman	234	6
Iraq	144	4
Kuwait	142	3
Libya	127	3
Kazakhstan	121	3
Other	818	19
TOTAL	4,092	

Volumes are in 1,000 barrels per day
Figures have been rounded

Given China's growing energy demand, new pipelines will only slightly alleviate China's maritime dependency in either the Strait of Malacca or the Strait of Hormuz. The sheer volume of oil and liquefied natural gas imports to China from the Middle East will make strategic SLOCs increasingly important to Beijing.

In 2009 a pipeline that will deliver up to 40 billion cubic meters (bcm) of natural gas per year from Turkmenistan to China via Kazakhstan and Uzbekistan commenced operation. Another natural gas pipeline designed to deliver 14 bcm per year from Burma is in the initial stages of construction and estimated for completion in 2013. Additionally Beijing is negotiating with Moscow for two pipelines that could supply China with up to 69 bcm of gas.

China's Military Strategy

PLA theorists have developed a framework for doctrine-driven reform with the long-term goal of building a force capable of fighting and winning —local wars under conditions of informatization.Drawing upon foreign military experiences, particularly U.S.-led campaigns up to and including Operation ENDURING FREEDOM and Operation IRAQI FREEDOM, Soviet and Russian military theory, and the PLA's own combat history, China is transforming across the whole of its armed forces.

China relies on a body of overall principles and guidance known as the —National Military Strategic Guidelines for the New Period (*xin shiqi guojia junshi zhanlüe fangzhen*—期国家军事战略方針) to plan and manage the development and use of the armed forces. This is the closest equivalent in China of the U.S. —National Military Strategy.

The current operational component of China's National Military Strategic Guidelines for the New Period is known as —Active Defense (*jiji fangyu*—积极防御). Active Defense is the highest-level strategic guidance for all PLA activities and applies to all services. Tenets of Active Defense include the following:

- Overall, our military strategy is defensive. We attack only after being attacked. But our operations are offensive.
- Space or time will not limit our counter-offensive.
- We will not put boundaries on the limits of our offenses.
- We will wait for the time and conditions that favor our forces when we do initiate offensive operations.
- We will focus on the opposing force's weaknesses.

Academic research suggests that the current guidelines most likely date to 1993, reflecting the impact of the 1991 Persian Gulf War and the collapse of the Soviet Union on PRC military-strategic thinking. The guidelines were revised in 2002 and 2004, likely reflecting China's perceptions of its evolving security environment and the changing character of modern warfare.

In practice, this strategic evolution has prompted a major shift toward investments in asymmetric, network-centric warfare and A2AD capabilities that are intended to deny elements of the modern battle space to potential enemies. According to the 2008 Defense White Paper, these guidelines emphasize fighting and winning local wars under conditions of informatization and building toward integrated joint operations, with a stress on asymmetric warfare to —make the best use of our strong points to attack the enemy's weak points.

Citing the need to ensure —close coordination between military struggle and political, diplomatic, economic, cultural, and legal endeavors, the guidelines also emphasize the importance of integrating multiple instruments of state power to ensure deterrence and prevent conflict.

Naval Warfare

During the mid 1980s, the CMC approved a specific naval component of —Active Defense called —Offshore Defense (*jinhai fangyu*—近海防御), which is sometimes translated more literally as, —Near Seas Defense. Offshore Defense is an overarching strategic concept that directs the PLA Navy to prepare for three essential missions including:

- keeping the enemy within limits and resisting invasion from the sea;
- protecting the nation's territorial sovereignty; and,
- safeguarding the motherland's unity and maritime rights.

The so-called —near seas, which remain a primary focus for the Navy, include the Yellow Sea, East China Sea, and South China Sea. Increasingly, the PLA is taking on missions that reflect China's expanding commercial and diplomatic interests beyond the near seas, into the —far seas which include the Philippine Sea and beyond. PLA Navy doctrine for maritime operations focuses on six offensive and defensive campaigns: blockade, anti-sea lines of communication, maritime-land attack, anti-ship, maritime transportation protection, and naval base defense.

Senior civilian officials and PLA officers have argued that China's economic and political power is contingent upon access to, and use of the sea, and that a strong Navy is required to safeguard such access. Despite an increasingly public discussion concerning missions farther from China, the Navy appears primarily focused on contingencies within the —first and second island chains|| (see map), with emphasis on a potential conflict with U.S. forces over Taiwan or a territorial dispute.

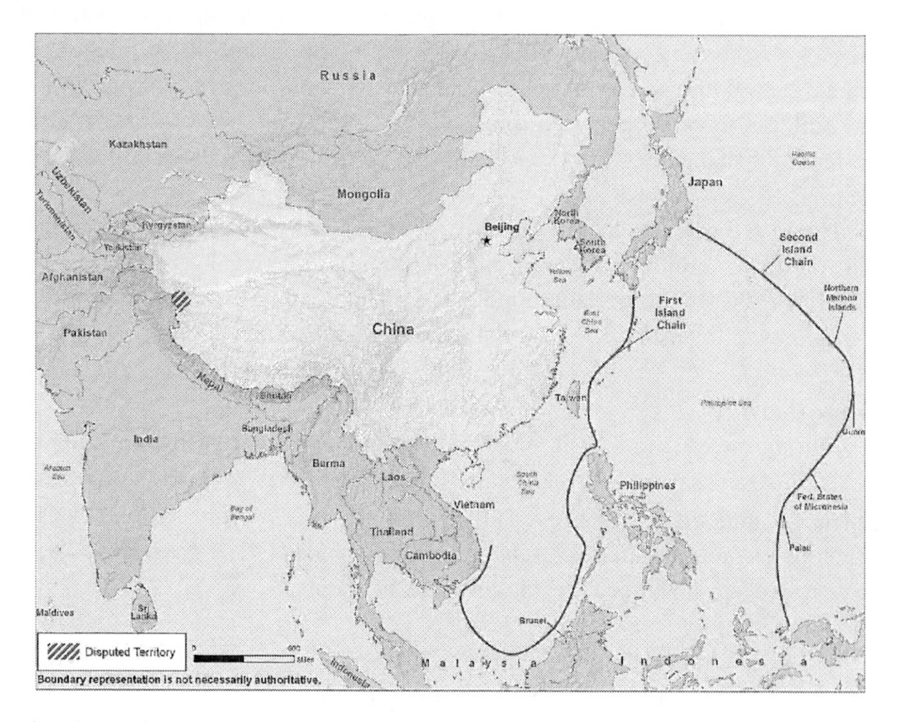

The First and Second Island Chains. PRC military theorists refer to two "island "chains" along China" s maritime perimeter. The First Island Chain includes Taiwan and the Ryuku Islands, the Second Island Chain extends from Japan to Guam.

Ground Warfare

Under —Active Defense, ground forces are tasked with defending China's borders, ensuring domestic stability, and exercising regional power projection. PLA ground forces are transitioning from a static defensive force allocated across seven internal MRs, oriented for positional, mobile, urban, and mountain offensive campaigns; coastal defense campaigns; and landing campaigns, to a more offensive and maneuver-oriented force organized and equipped for operations along China's periphery.

The 2010 Defense White Paper asserts that the ground force has:

> emphasized the development of new types of combat forces, optimized its organization and structure, strengthened military training in conditions of informatization, accelerated the digitized upgrading and retrofitting of main battle weaponry, organically deployed new types of weapon platforms, and significantly boosted its capabilities in long-distance maneuvers and integrated assaults.

The ground forces appear to be leading the PLA's effort to experiment with *ad hoc*, multi-service, joint tactical formations to execute integrated joint operations.

Air Warfare

The PLA Air Force continues its conversion from a force for limited territorial defense to a more flexible and agile force able to operate off-shore in both offensive and defensive roles, using the U.S. and Russian air forces as models. Mission focus areas include: strike, air and missile defense, early warning and reconnaissance, and strategic mobility. The PLA Air Force also has a leading role in China's planning for anti-access and area denial operations.

The PLA's new missions are also driving discussions about the future of the PLA Air Force, where a general consensus has emerged that protecting China's global interests requires an increase in the Air Force's long-range transportation and logistics capabilities. In September 2010, the PLA Air Force conducted an unprecedented deployment of Su-27 fighter aircraft to Turkey to participate in joint air exercises with the Turkish Air Force. China has also been investing in stealth technology, as evidenced by the appearance of its first stealth aircraft prototype in January 2011. However, as with the Navy, it is likely that the Air Force's primary focus for the coming decade will remain on building the capabilities required to pose a credible military threat to Taiwan and U.S. forces in East Asia, deter Taiwan independence, or influence Taiwan to settle the dispute on Beijing's terms.

Space Warfare

PLA strategists regard the ability to utilize space and deny adversaries access to space as central to enabling modern, informatized warfare. Although PLA doctrine does not appear to address space operations as a unique operational —campaign, space operations form an integral component of other PLA campaigns. Publicly, Beijing attempts to dispel any skepticism over its military intentions for space. In 2009, the commander of the PLA Air Force, General Xu Qiliang, publically retracted his earlier assertion that the militarization of space was a —historic inevitability after President Hu Jintao swiftly contradicted him.

The PLA is acquiring a range of technologies to improve China's space and counterspace capabilities. A PLA analysis of U.S. and Coalition military operations reinforced the importance of operations in space to enable informatized warfare, claiming that —space is the commanding point for the information battlefield.

Offense as Defense

PRC military strategists characterize —Active Defense" as inherently defensive, suggesting that China strikes only —after the enemy has struck. Taken alone, this statement, which was reiterated in China's 2010 Defense White Paper, seems clear. However, more detailed Chinese writings leave the actual significance far more ambiguous. In particular, it remains unclear what actions taken by an adversary might cross the threshold of an initial strike.

The Science of Military Strategy, which is published by the PLA's Academy of Military Science, asserts that the definition of an enemy strike is not limited to conventional, kinetic military operations. Rather, an enemy —strike may also be defined in political terms. Thus:

> Striking only after the enemy has struck does not mean waiting for the enemy" s strike passively... It doesn" t mean to give up the "advantageous chances" in campaign or tactical operations, for the "first shot" on the plane of politics must be differentiated from the "first shot" on that of tactics.
>
> [This section continues] if any country or organization violates the other country" s sovereignty and territorial integrity, the other side will have the right to „fire the first shot" on the plane of tactics.

If China loosely defines a —strike to encompass some political action, this significantly alters the purportedly —defensive nature of this strategic construct. This implies that PLA forces might be employed preemptively in the name of defense.

PLA writings emphasize the necessity of—destroying, damaging, and interfering with the enemy's reconnaissance...and communications satellites, suggesting that such systems, as well as navigation and early warning satellites, could be among initial targets of attack to —blind and deafen the enemy. The same PLA analysis of U.S. and Coalition military operations also states that —destroying or capturing satellites and other sensors... will deprive an opponent of initiative on the battlefield and [make it difficult] for them to bring their precision guided weapons into full play.

Integrated Network Electronic Warfare

PRC military writings highlight the seizure of electromagnetic dominance in the early phases of a campaign as among the foremost tasks to ensure battlefield success. PLA theorists have coined the term —integrated network electronic warfare (*wangdian yitizhan*—网电一体战) to describe the use of electronic warfare, computer network operations, and kinetic strikes to disrupt battlefield information systems that support an adversary's warfighting and power projection capabilities. PLA writings identify —integrated network electronic warfare as one of the basic forms of —integrated joint operations,‖ suggesting the centrality of seizing and dominating the electromagnetic spectrum in PLA campaign theory.

Secrecy and Deception

PRC military writings point to a working definition of strategic deception as —[luring] the other side into developing misperceptions... and [establishing for oneself] a strategically advantageous position by producing various kinds of false phenomena in an organized and planned manner with the smallest cost in manpower and materials. In addition to information operations and conventional camouflage, concealment, and denial, the PLA draws from China's historical experience and the traditional role that stratagem and deception have played in Chinese statecraft.

There is an inherent tension in Chinese strategic culture today, pitting a deep-seated tendency to conceal military capabilities and force development against a partial acceptance that excessive secrecy inflames regional and global anxiety about China's rising power. For over a decade PRC leaders have identified the so called —China threat theory as a serious hazard to the country's international standing and reputation, threatening the development of a persistent alignment of regional and global powers in opposition to China. In addition, extreme secrecy is increasingly difficult to reconcile with China's role in the integrated global economy, which depends upon transparency and the free flow of information for success.

There is perhaps another source of tension between the emerging reality of Chinese military power and China's tradition of secrecy, and that is the fact that many of China's new military capabilities are difficult or impossible to hide. Examples of such capabilities include advanced aircraft, long range missiles, and modern naval assets. Furthermore, missiles, space-based, and counterspace systems must be tested and exercised before being operationally deployed with confidence. The PLA's growing inventory of these new assets and the ranges at which they operate effectively prevents their concealment.

FORCE MODERNIZATION GOALS AND TRENDS

Overview

Since the early 1990s PRC leaders have sustained an ambitious and broad-based military modernization program intended to transform the PLA into a modern force. Although the PLA currently retains a large number of legacy platforms and weapons, the percentage of modern equipment in the force is growing rapidly. China has closed important technological gaps and achieved some capabilities that are on par with or exceed global standards. Motivated by a growing set of economic and security interests, China's leaders have given the PLA a new and more externally focused direction, as evidenced by China's growing naval presence on the global maritime domain.

For the PLA, this modernization effort remains a work in progress. The first decade of the 21st century can be characterized as a period of ambitious PLA acquisition and development. Although this trend will continue in the years ahead, the more dominant theme of the 2010- 2020 decade is likely to be training and integration. Senior PRC leaders recognize that this period will prove critical to meeting the PLA's modernization objectives, and they have demanded that the military engage in more realistic training and organizational reform.

Throughout the PLA's modernization drive, Taiwan contingency planning has largely dominated the agenda. Even though cross-Strait tensions have subsided since 2008, Taiwan remains a critical mission, and the PLA continues building capabilities aimed not only at Taiwan, but also to deter, delay or deny possible U.S. or allied intervention in a cross-Strait conflict. At the same time, a diminished sense of urgency over Taiwan has enabled the PLA to devote attention to an expanding set of regional and global missions. This includes a focus on —safeguarding China's expanding national interests and protecting —sovereignty as outlined in the New Historic Missions, described in the previous chapter By the latter half of the current decade, China will likely be able to project and sustain a modest-sized force, perhaps several battalions of ground forces or a naval flotilla of up to a dozen ships, in low-intensity operations far from China.

This evolution will lay the foundation for a force able to accomplish a broader set of regional and global objectives. However, it is unlikely that China will be able to project and sustain large forces in high-intensity combat operations far from China prior to 2020.

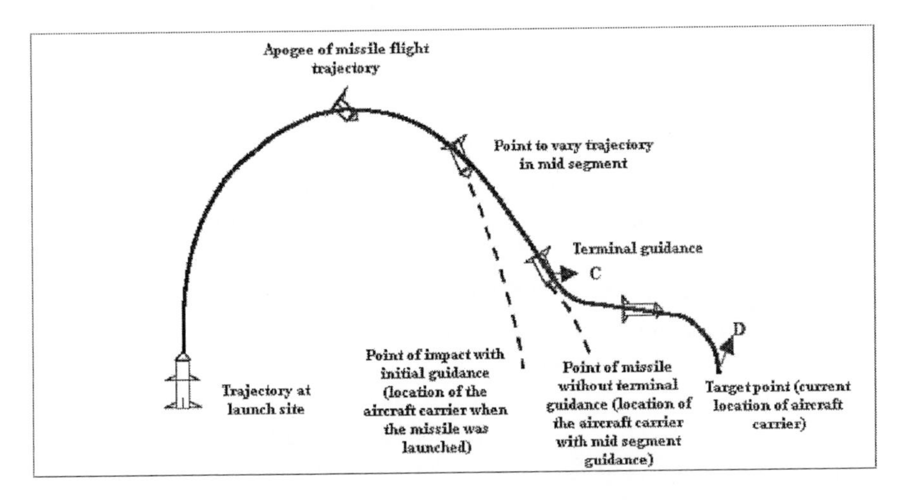

Missile Flight Trajectory with Terminal Guidance. This graphic of an anti-ship ballistic missile" s use of midcourse and terminal guidance to strike an aircraft carrier appeared in a 2006 article from the Second Artillery Engineering College.

Despite significant improvements, the PLA continues to face deficiencies in inter-service cooperation and actual experience in joint exercises and combat operations. Recognizing these shortcomings, China's leaders continue to stress asymmetric strategies to leverage China's advantages while exploiting the perceived vulnerabilities of potential opponents. The PLA has also embarked on human capital reform, intended to attract and retain talented personnel.

Anti-Access/Area Denial Capability Developments

As part of its planning for a regional contingency, China is developing measures to deter or counter third-party intervention, including by the United States. Although many of these capabilities were developed with a focus on Taiwan, they have broad applications and implications extending beyond a Taiwan scenario. China's approach to this challenge, which it refers to as —counter-intervention, is manifested in a sustained effort to develop the capability to attack, at long ranges, military forces that might deploy or operate within the western Pacific. The U.S. Department of Defense characterizes these as —anti-access and —area denial capabilities. China is pursuing a variety of air, sea, undersea, space, counterspace, information warfare systems, and operational concepts to achieve this capability, moving toward an array of overlapping, multilayered offensive capabilities extending from China's coast into the western Pacific.

An essential element of China's emerging A2AD regime is the ability to control and dominate the information spectrum in all dimensions of the modern battlespace. PLA authors often cite the need in modern warfare to control information, sometimes termed —information blockade or —information dominance, and gain an information advantage in the early phases of a campaign to achieve air and sea superiority. China is improving information and operational security to protect its own information structures, and is also developing electronic and information warfare capabilities, including denial and deception, to defeat those of its adversaries. China's —information blockade likely envisions employment of military and non-military instruments of state power across the battlespace, including in cyberspace and outer space. China's investments in advanced electronic warfare systems, counterspace weapons, and computer network operations, combined with more traditional forms of control historically associated with the PLA and CCP systems, such as propaganda, deception, and denial through opacity, reflect the emphasis and priority China's leaders place on building capability for information advantage.

In more traditional domains, China's A2AD focus appears oriented toward restricting or controlling access to the land, sea, and air spaces along China's periphery, including the western Pacific. For example, China's current and projected force structure improvements will provide the PLA with systems that can engage adversary surface ships up to 1,850 km from the PRC coast.

These include:

- Anti-Ship Ballistic Missiles: Medium Range Ballistic Missiles (MRBMs) designed to target forces at sea, combined with overhead and over-the-horizon targeting systems to locate and track moving ships.
- Conventional and nuclear-powered attack submarines: KILO, SONG, YUAN, and SHANG-class attack submarines capable of firing advanced ASCMs.
- Surface combatants: LUZHOU, LUYANG I/II, SOVREMENNY-II-class guided missile destroyers with advanced long-range anti-air and anti-ship missiles.
- Maritime Strike Aircraft: FB-7 and FB7A, B-6G, and the SU-30 MK2, armed with ASCMs to engage surface combatants.

Similarly, current and projected systems such as the J-20 stealth fighter and longer-range conventional ballistic missiles could improve the PLA's ability to strike regional air bases, logistical facilities, and other ground-based infrastructure. PRC military analysts have concluded that logistics and power projection are potential vulnerabilities in modern warfare, given the requirements for precision in coordinating transportation, communications, and logistics networks. China is fielding an array of conventionally armed ballistic missiles, modern aircraft, UAVs, ground- and air-launched land-attack cruise missiles, special operations forces, and cyber-warfare capabilities to hold targets at risk throughout the region.

The air and air defense component of China's regional strategy includes long-range, advanced SAMs, such as the Russian SA-10 and SA-20 PMU1/PMU2, as well as the indigenous HQ-9. Beijing will also use Russian-built and domestically produced fourth-generation aircraft (e.g., Su-27/F-11 and Su-30 variants) as well as the indigenous F-10 to compete for local air dominance. The PLA Navy would employ Russian Su-30MK2 fighters, armed with AS-17/Kh-31A anti-ship missiles, B-6G bombers, and FB-7 fighter-bombers for maritime interdiction. Additionally, acquisition and development of longer-range UAVs and UCAVs will expand China's options for long-range reconnaissance and strike.

Building Capacity for Conventional Precision Strike

Short-Range Ballistic Missiles (< 1,000 km). As of December 2010, the PLA had somewhere between 1,000-1,200 SRBMs. The total number of SRBMs represents little to no change over the past year. However, the PLA continues to field advanced variants with improved ranges and more sophisticated payloads that are gradually replacing earlier generations that do not possess true —precision strike|| capability.

Medium-Range Ballistic Missiles (1,000-3,000 km). The PLA is acquiring and fielding conventional MRBMs to increase the range at which it can conduct precision strikes against land targets and naval ships, including aircraft carriers, operating far from China's shores out to the first island chain.

Land-Attack Cruise Missiles. The PLA continues to field air- and ground-launched LACMs, such as the YJ-63, KD-88, and DH-10 systems for stand-off, precision strikes.

Ground Attack Munitions. The PLA Air Force has a small number of tactical air-tosurface missiles as well as precision-guided munitions including all-weather, satellite-guided bombs, anti-radiation missiles, and laser-guided bombs.

Anti-Ship Cruise Missiles. The PLA Navy has or is acquiring nearly a dozen ASCM variants, ranging from the 1950s-era CSS-N-2 to the modern Russian-made SS-N-22 and SS-N-27B. The pace of ASCM research, development, and production within China has accelerated over the past decade.

Anti-Radiation Weapons. The PLA imported Israeli-made HARPY unmanned combat aerial vehicles (UCAVs) during the 1990s and Russian-made anti-radiation missiles. China continues development of an indigenous version of the Russian Kh-31P (AS-17) known as the YJ-91 and is starting to integrate this system into its fighter-bomber force.

Artillery-Delivered High Precision Munitions. The PLA is developing or deploying artillery systems with the range to strike targets within or even across the Taiwan Strait, including the PHL-03 300 mm multiple-rocket launcher (MRL) (100+ km range) and the WS-2 400 mm MRL (200 km range).

In January 2011, initial images of China's 5th generation J-20 stealth fighter were posted on the Internet. Although the appearance of this prototype underscores the level of PRC investment in advanced defense systems, the

Defense Department does not expect the J-20 to achieve an effective operational capability prior to 2018. China faces several hurdles as it moves toward J-20 production, including the mastery of high performance jet engine production.

Ballistic Missile Defense

China's existing long-range advanced SAM inventory offers limited capability against ballistic missiles, but advertises a capability against cruise missiles. The SA-10 was originally designed to counter low-flying cruise missiles, a capability enhanced in the later model SA-20 systems. The SA-20 PMU2, the most advanced SAM Russia offers for export, also has the advertised capability to engage ballistic missiles with ranges of 1000km and speeds of 2,800 m/s.

China's HQ-9 long-range SAM system is also advertised (through its export variant FD-2000) to protect against low-altitude cruise missiles and is expected to have a limited capability to provide point defense against tactical ballistic missiles with ranges up to 500 km. China is proceeding with the research and development of a missile defense —umbrella|| consisting of kinetic energy intercept at exo-atmospheric altitudes (>80 km), as well as intercepts of ballistic missiles and other aerospace vehicles within the upper atmosphere. In January 2010, China successfully intercepted a ballistic missile at mid-course, using a ground-based missile.

Extended Operational Reach

In addition to preparing for a Taiwan contingency, the PLA has been developing new platforms and capabilities that will extend its operational reach to address other concerns within the East and South China Seas, and possibly to the Indian Ocean and beyond the second island chain in the western Pacific.

In describing the modernization tasks for each of the service arms, China's Defense White Papers in 2008 and 2010 emphasized mobility and operations at greater distances from China's mainland. The main avenues for the PLA to realize these capabilities are through its naval, ballistic missile, and air forces.

The PLA Navy

The PLA Navy is at the forefront of efforts to extend operational reach beyond China's regional waters. China's 2010 Defense White paper asserts that —recent emergency rescue and disaster relief operations, counter-terrorism exercises, and... training [demonstrate]... a notable improvement in the PLA's capabilities of equipment support in long-distance and trans-regional maneuvers, escort operations in distant waters, and complex battlefield environments.

The PLA Navy has demonstrated the capability to conduct limited deployments of modern surface platforms outside the second island chain, including nine separate deployments to the Gulf of Aden to support sustained counter-piracy operations from 2009 through mid 2011. The PLA Navy also has acquired new classes of ships to support conventional military operations as well as humanitarian assistance and disaster relief missions, including the Type 071 amphibious transport dock and the hospital ship, which the Chinese call the —Peace Ark.

The PLA Navy's Investment in Platforms such as nuclear-powered submarines and its first aircraft carrier suggest China is seeking to support additional military missions beyond a Taiwan contingency.

China has invested in several civilian port projects throughout Asia and along the Indian Ocean. Although such investments may improve peacetime logistical support options for the PLA Navy, not to mention enhancing PRC soft power in the region, they are not a substitute for military bases. Without overseas military bases, China will be constrained in its ability to project and sustain power beyond the immediate region. A decision in Beijing to abandon its longstanding and self-imposed policy against overseas basing would signal that China seeks a greater blue water combat capability.

Second Artillery Corps

As detailed elsewhere in this report, China's ballistic missile force is acquiring conventional medium-range and intermediate-range ballistic missiles, extending the distance from which it can threaten other countries with conventional precision or near-precision strikes.

The PLA Air Force

The PLA Air Force is developing longer-range versions of the B-6/BADGER bomber that, when equipped with a long-range land-attack cruise missile, will enable strikes as far as the second island chain. The J-20 will eventually give the PLA Air Force a platform capable of long range, penetrating strikes into complex air defense environments.

During the Shanghai Cooperation Organization's Peace Mission exercise in September 2010, PLA Air Force B-6s conducted long-range bombing missions in Kazakhstan while operating out of Urumqi in western China. The PLA Air Force reached another milestone in out-of-area operations in 2010 by deploying Su-27 fighter aircraft to Turkey for joint exercises. Although the PLA Air Force has encountered some difficulty in expanding its fleet of long-range heavy transport aircraft, it marked a new milestone in February 2011, when it employed four IL-76 long-haul transport aircraft to assist with evacuating Chinese citizens from Libya. This mission marked the PLA Air Force's first overseas deployment to evacuate PRC citizens.

PLA Ground Force

Although the PLA's large ground force has not experienced the same dramatic modernization as other branches of the PLA, it has steadily improved capabilities in certain areas. Much, but not all, of this effort has focused on units garrisoned nearest Taiwan. For example, a new amphibious assault vehicle has entered service in key units, improving the PLA's capability to conduct amphibious attacks. Throughout the PLA, small numbers of modern main battle tanks, armored vehicles, self-propelled artillery, and air defense weapons have entered service in selected units. Concurrent with this modernization, PLA ground force training has begun to emphasize combined arms operations and long-range mobility.

Strategic Capabilities

China has made steady progress in recent years to develop offensive nuclear, space, and cyber warfare capabilities—the only aspects of China's armed forces that are currently global in nature. In the case of cyber and spaceweapons, however, there is little evidence thatChina's military and civilian leaders have fully thought through the global and systemic effects that would be associated with the employment of these strategic capabilities. Additionally, China is both qualitatively and quantitatively improving its strategic missile forces.

Nuclear Forces

China's nuclear arsenal currently consists of approximately 55-65 intercontinental ballistic missiles (ICBMs), including the silo-based CSS-4 (DF-5); the solid-fueled, road-mobile CSS-10 Mods 1 and 2 (DF-31 and DF-31A); and the more limited range CSS-3 (DF-3). This force is complemented by liquid-fueled CSS-2 intermediate-range ballistic missiles and road-mobile, solid-fueled CSS-5 (DF-21D) MRBMs for regional deterrence missions. The operational status of China's single XIAclass ballistic missile submarine (SSBN) and medium-range JL-1 submarine-launched ballistic missiles (SLBM) remain questionable.

By 2015, China's nuclear forces will include additional CSS-10 Mod 2s and enhanced CSS-4s. The first of the new JIN-class (Type 094) SSBN appears ready, but the associated JL-2 SLBM has faced a number of problems and will likely continue flight tests. The date when the JIN-class SSBN/JL-2 SLBM combination will be fully operational is uncertain.

China is also currently working on a range of technologies to attempt to counter U.S. and other countries' ballistic missile defense systems, including maneuvering re-entry vehicles, MIRVs, decoys, chaff, jamming, thermal shielding, and anti-satellite (ASAT) weapons. PRC official media also cites numerous Second Artillery Corps training exercises featuring maneuver, camouflage, and launch operations under simulated combat conditions, which are intended to increase survivability. Together with the increased mobility and survivability of the new generation of missiles, these technologies and training enhancements strengthen China's nuclear force and enhance its strategic strike capabilities.

The introduction of more mobile systems will create new command and control challenges for China's leadership, which now confronts a different set of variables related to deployment and release authorities. For example, the PLA has only a limited capacity to communicate with submarines at sea, and the PLA Navy has no experience in managing a SSBN fleet that performs strategic patrols with live nuclear warheads mated to missiles. Land-based mobile missiles may face similar command and control challenges in wartime, although probably not as extreme as with submarines.

Beijing's official policy towards the role of nuclear weapons continues to focus on maintaining a nuclear force structure able to survive an attack, and respond with sufficient strength to inflict unacceptable damage on the enemy. The new generation of mobile missiles, maneuvering and MIRV warheads, and penetration aids are intended to ensure the viability of China's strategic deterrent in the face of continued advances in U.S. and, to a lesser extent,

Russian strategic intelligence, surveillance, and reconnaissance; precision strike; and missile defense capabilities.

Beijing has consistently asserted that it adheres to a —no first use|| (NFU) policy, stating it would use nuclear forces only in response to a nuclear strike against China. China's NFU pledge consists of two stated commitments: China will never use nuclear weapons first against any nuclear-weapon state, and China will never use or threaten to use nuclear weapons against any non-nuclear-weapon state or nuclear-weapon-free zone. However, there is some ambiguity over the conditions under which China's NFU policy would apply, including whether strikes on what China considers its own territory, demonstration strikes, or high altitude bursts would constitute a first use. Moreover, some PLA officers have written publicly of the need to spell out conditions under which China might need to use nuclear weapons first; for example, if an enemy's conventional attack threatened the survival of China'snuclear force, or of the regime itself. However, there has been no indication that national leaders are willing to attach such nuances and caveats to China's —no first use doctrine.

Beijing will likely continue to invest considerable resources to maintain a limited nuclear force, also referred to by some PRC writers as —sufficient and effective, to ensure the PLA can deliver a damaging retaliatory nuclear strike.

Space and Counterspace

China's space activities and capabilities, including ASAT programs, have significant implications for anti-access/area denial efforts in Taiwan Strait contingencies and beyond.

Reconnaissance

China is deploying imagery, reconnaissance, and Earth resource systems with military utility. Examples include the Yaogan satellites, the Haiyang-1B, and the Huanjing disaster/environmental monitoring satellite constellation. China is planning eight satellites in the Huanjing program that are capable of visible, infrared, multi-spectral, and synthetic aperture radar imaging. In the next decade, even as Beijing fields a larger and more capable array of reconnaissance satellites, it probably will continue to employ commercial satellite imagery to supplement its coverage. China currently accesses high-resolution, commercial electro-optical and synthetic aperture radar imagery from all of the major providers including Spot Image (Europe), Infoterra (Europe), MDA (Canada), Antrix (India), GeoEye (United States), and Digital Globe (United States).

Manned Space

China's most recent manned mission, Shenzhou-7, concluded in September 2008. Shenzhou-7 included China's first spacewalk as well as the launch and rendezvous with an autonomous microsatellite. China will continue its manned space program, including both manned and unmanned docking, with the goals of establishing a permanently manned space station by 2020 and landing a human on the moon by 2030.

Position, Navigation, and Timing (PNT): Since the 1990s, China has used the U.S. Global Positioning System (GPS) for a wide variety of military, civil, and commercial applications. Building on this foundation, China is pursuing several avenues to reduce its dependence on GPS and become a major supplier of PNT services and user equipment. Currently, the PRC is increasing its use of Russia's GLONASS, deploying its own BeiDou-2 (Compass) system as well as a second independent satellite system called CAPS, while augmenting these overhead systems with a variety of ground-based signals.

The experimental BeiDou-1 system consisted of just three satellites, providing both civil and military services to China. China is replacing BeiDou-1 with the much larger BeiDou-2 constellation, intended to eventually provide a worldwide PNT service, independent of foreign control. By 2012, the BeiDou 2 constellation is expected to provide regional services with approximately 10 satellites. The PRC plans to complete the BeiDou-2 system by 2020, with 35 a satellite constellation offering global coverage.

Communications

China uses communications satellites for both regional and international telecommunications in support of civil and military users, including satellite television, Internet, and telephony. China also maintains a single data-relay satellite launched in mid-2008, the TianLian1. China has recently entered the world market by exporting satellites and infrastructure to Venezuela and Nigeria. Although the satellite built and launched for Nigeria failed, China continues to market its services worldwide, to customers such as Pakistan, Bolivia, Laos, and Vietnam.

ASAT Weapons

In January 2007, China successfully tested a direct-ascent ASAT weapon against a PRC weather satellite, demonstrating its ability to attack satellites in low-Earth orbit. China continues to develop and refine this system, which is one component of a multi-dimensional program to limit or prevent the use of space-based assets by potential adversaries during times of crisis or conflict.

In addition to the direct-ascent ASAT program, China is developing other kinetic and directed-energy (e.g., lasers, high-powered microwave, and particle beam weapons) technologies for ASAT missions. Foreign and indigenous systems give China the capability to jam common satellite communications bands and GPS receivers.

PLA Underground Facilities

Since the early 1950s, the PLA has employed underground facilities (UGFs) to protect and conceal its vital assets. China's strategic missile force, the Second Artillery Corps (SAC), has developed and utilized UGFs since deploying its oldest liquid-fueled missile systems and continues to utilize them to protect and conceal their newest and most modern solid-fueled mobile missiles. As early as the mid 1990's Chinese media vaguely acknowledged the existence of UGFs that support the SAC. Since December 2009, several PRC and foreign media reports offered additional insight into this obscure tunnel network, which reportedly stretches for over 5,000 km.

Given China's nuclear policy of —no first use and until recently its limited ballistic missile early warning capability, Beijing had assumed it might have to absorb an initial nuclear blow prior to engaging in —nuclear counterattack. Nuclear survivability was particularly critical given China's relatively small number of nuclear weapons and the development by potential adversaries of modern, precision munitions. In recent years, advanced construction design has allowed militaries to go deeper underground to complicate adversarial targeting. Although secrecy and ambiguity remain China's predominant approach in the nuclear realm, occasional disclosure of information on some missile-related UGFs is consistent with an effort to send strategic signals on the credibility of its limited nuclear arsenal.

These public disclosures include images of tunnels, modern network-based security and control centers, and advanced camouflage measures. Categories of military facilities which make good candidates for UGFs include: command posts; communications sites; storage for important weapons and equipment; and protection for personnel.

China's nuclear arsenal has long provided Beijing with an inherent ASAT capability, although a nuclear explosion in space would also damage China's own space assets, along with those of whomever it was trying to target.

Citing the requirements of its manned and lunar space programs, China is improving its ability to track and identify satellites—a prerequisite for effective, precise counterspace operations.

Information Warfare

PRC military thinkers have written extensively on information warfare, reflecting a strong conceptual understanding of its methodology and potential utility. For example, a November 2006 Liberation Army Daily commentary outlines:

> [The] mechanism to get the upper hand of the enemy in a war under conditions of informatization finds prominent expression in whether or not we are capable of using various means to obtain information and of ensuring the effective circulation of information; whether or not we are capable of making full use of the permeability, sharable property, and connection of information to realize the organic merging of materials, energy, and information to form a combined fighting strength; [and,] whether or not we are capable of applying effective means to weaken the enemy side" s information superiority and lower the operational efficiency of enemy information equipment.

The PLA is investing in electronic countermeasures, defenses against electronic attack (e.g., electronic and infrared decoys, angle reflectors, and false target generators), and computer network operations (CNO).

China's CNO concepts include computer network attack, computer network exploitation, and computer network defense. The PLA has established information warfare units to develop viruses to attack enemy computer systems and networks, as well as tactics and measures to protect friendly computer systems and networks. These units include elements of the militia, creating a linkage between PLA network operators and China's civilian information technology professionals. Under the rubric of Integrated Network Electronic Warfare, the PLA seeks to employ both computer network operations and electronic warfare to deny an adversary access to information essential to conduct combat operations.

Power Projection beyond Taiwan

China continues to invest in military programs designed to improve extended-range operations. Current trends in China's military capabilities could provide China with a force capable of conducting a range of military operations in Asia well beyond Taiwan.

China's political leaders have also charged the PLA with developing capabilities for military operations other than war such as peacekeeping, disaster relief, and counterterrorism operations. These capabilities hold the potential to make positive contributions in the delivery of international public goods, but also increase Beijing's options for military coercion to gain diplomatic advantage, advance interests, or resolve disputes in its favor.

Analysis of China's weapons development and deployment patterns suggests Beijing is already looking at contingencies beyond Taiwan as it builds its force. For example, new missile units outfitted with conventional, theater-range missiles at various locations in China could be used in a variety of non-Taiwan contingencies. Given the fact that Taiwan can be reached by land-based aviation, China's aircraft carrier program would offer very limited value in a Taiwan scenario and would require additional naval resources for protection. However, it would enable China to extend its naval air capabilities elsewhere. Airborne Early Warning and Control (AEW&C) and aerial-refueling programs would also facilitate extended air operations. Advanced destroyers and submarines could protect and advance China's maritime interests up to and beyond the second island chain. China's expeditionary forces (three airborne divisions, two amphibious infantry divisions, two marine brigades, and about seven special operations groups) are improving with the introduction of new equipment, better unit-level tactics, and greater coordination of joint operations. Over the long-term, improvements in China's C4ISR, including space-based and over-the-horizon sensors, could enable Beijing to identify, track, and target military activities deep into the western Pacific Ocean.

China's increasing focus on humanitarian assistance and disaster relief (HA/DR) missions will require a unique set of technological developments, including large ships and strategic airlift, to support these missions. Of course, many of these HA/DR capabilities would also enhance the PLA ability to support military operations along and beyond China's borders.

India

China deepened its ties with India through increased trade and high-level dialogues in 2010, though border tensions remained an irritant in the bilateral relationship. Bilateral trade in 2010 reached nearly $60 billion. The two neighbors have held several rounds of dialogue over disputed territorial claims. Sino-Indian defense ties were institutionalized in 2007 with the establishment of an Annual Defense Dialogue. Though India cancelled high-level military exchanges following China's denial of a visa to a senior Indian general in 2010, both sides agreed to resume exchanges in April 2011. During his December 2010 trip to New Delhi, Premier Wen Jiabao attempted to smooth over differences following a year of uneasy relations, but he did not address serious irritants. A high degree of mistrust continues to strain the bilateral relationship. To strengthen its deterrent posture relative to India, the PLA has replaced liquid-fueled, nuclear-capable CSS-2 IRBMs with more advanced and survivable solid-fueled CSS-5 MRBM systems. China is also investing in road development along the Sino-Indian border. Although this construction is primarily aimed at facilitating economic development in western China, improved roads could also support PLA border defense operations. India is also improving infrastructure along its northeastern border.

New Delhi remains concerned by China's close military relationship with Pakistan and Beijing's growing footprint in the Indian Ocean, Central Asia, and Africa.

Russia

Beijing continues to view Moscow as a useful international partner. Despite awareness that some Russian interests are not consistent with those of China, Moscow and Beijing share many overlapping interests, and China benefits greatly from a more stable and peaceful northern border. Sino-Russia bilateral cooperation continues on a range of international issues, especially in Central Asia where the two jointly manage the Shanghai Cooperation Organization (SCO).

Despite this cooperation, Russia has concerns about China's rise, while PLA strategists continue to regard Russia as a potential long- term security challenge. China shifted its strategic orientation to the south and east following the collapse of the Soviet Union, but Beijing retains significant force structure in the Lanzhou, Beijing, and Shenyang Military Regions, in addition to its conventional and strategic missile forces, to maintain deterrence.

Central Asia

China has several important interests in Central Asia. Most notably, China is interested in acquiring energy and natural resources. Beijing has pursued multiple agreements with energy-rich Central Asian states. This includes a pipeline deal that will extend from Turkmenistan through Uzbekistan and Kazakhstan into China.

Beijing is also interested in Central Asia from a domestic security perspective. From the domestic security standpoint, Beijing hopes to undermine support for China's Uighur separatists, who share religious, ethnic, and linguistic connections to groups in Central Asia. Beijing believes that

Islamic radicalism and competing political ideologies could destabilize an already fragile security situation in Western China.

China has used the multilateral Shanghai Cooperation Organization, which it cofounded, to address border security, counterterrorism, and regional security. Beijing has also conducted bilateral and multilateral exercises with SCO member states to enhance China's regional influence and build cohesive opposition to Uighur activities.

South China Sea

Before the CCP took power in 1949, the Chinese government regarded the South China Sea as a region of geostrategic interest and a part of China's —historical waters. As early as the 1930's, the Republic of China was considering a broad line delineating the South China Sea as Chinese territory. The —U-shaped dashed line that began appearing on Chinese maps in 1947 continues to define PRC claims to the South China Sea. Until recently, however, the PLA Navy's limited operational reach constrained Beijing's military options in the South China Sea.

Over the past five years, China has begun demonstrating a more routine naval and civilian enforcement presence in the South China Sea. In several instances, particularly in 2009, China's use of force and coercion to push it disputed maritime territorial claims elicited concern among many of its Asian neighbors.

Although the PRC remains wary of triggering regional opposition and may have adjusted certain tactics, Beijing appears eager to strengthen its claim to the disputed region over the long-term. This includes legal efforts as well as the deployment of more capable naval and civilian law enforcement ships. A more robust presence would position China for force projection, blockade, and surveillance operations to influence the critical sea lanes in the region, through which some 50 percent of global merchant traffic passes.

Competition for resources, including oil, gas, and fishing rights, coupled with strong nationalistic sentiments continues to drive territorial disputes among several South China Sea claimants. Although tensions in this hotly disputed region subsided after the-1990s, signs of friction re-emerged in 2007, particularly between China and Vietnam.

In response to the 2004 articulation of the PLA's —New Historic Missions, China's senior military leaders began developing concepts for an expanded regional maritime strategy and presence. For example, in 2006, PLA Navy Commander Wu Shengli called for a —powerful navy to protect fishing, resource development and strategic passageways for energy. Many of these ideas echo the debates in the late 1980s and early 1990s over building PLA naval capabilities. However, the rise of Taiwan contingency planning as the dominant driver of PLA force modernization in the mid-1990s, and especially after 2001, largely sidelined these discussions. The 2008 and 2010 Defense White Papers reflect greater attention to the PLA's expanding mission set.

As part of its military modernization effort, China has increasingly shifted resources away from the PLAN's North Sea Fleet to the South Sea Fleet, greatly expanding the latter's capabilities. China's ability to deploy a more robust strategic and conventional military presence off its southern coast is having a growing impact on regional rivalries and power dynamics.

Resources for Force Modernization

Overview

The PLA has decreased reliance on foreign weapons acquisitions as China's defense-industrial and research bases mature. However, the PLA still looks to foreign assistance to fill some critical near-term capability gaps. China continues to leverage foreign investments, commercial joint ventures, academic exchanges, the experience of repatriated PRC students and researchers, and state-sponsored industrial/technical espionage to increase the level of technologies and expertise available to support military research, development, and acquisition. Beijing's long-term goal is to create a wholly indigenous defense industrial sector, augmented by a strong commercial sector, to meet the needs of PLA modernization and to compete as a top-tier producer in the global arms market. China's leaders can draw from diverse sources to support PLA modernization, including: domestic defense investments, indigenous defense industrial development, a growing research and development and science and technology base, dual-use technologies, and foreign technology acquisition.

Military Expenditure Trends

On March 4, 2011, Beijing announced a 12.7 percent increase in its military budget to approximately $91.5 billion. This increase continues more than two decades of sustained annual increases in China's announced military budget. Analysis of 2000-2010 data indicates China's officially disclosed military budget grew at an average of 12.1 percent in inflation-adjusted terms over the period. Although the military budget increases are slightly larger than the percentage increases of its overall economic growth of 10.2 percent over the same period, the actual change in the implied burden of the official defense budget on the economy appears negligible.

Estimating China's Actual Military

The Department of Defense estimates China's total military-related spending for 2010 was over $160 billion, using 2010 prices and exchange rates.

Estimating actual PLA military expenditures is a difficult process due to the lack of accounting transparency and China's still incomplete transition from a command economy. Moreover, China's published military budget does not include major categories of expenditure, such as foreign procurement. China's legislature has not made public any details of the role, if any, that it plays in exercising oversight of the PLA budget. However, public calls within China for greater budget transparency, generally in response to sustained and systemic official corruption, suggest that improvement in government transparency as a whole could develop over time.

The United States and other countries continue to urge China to increase transparency in military spending. In August 2010, China submitted a report on its military expenditures to the UN Secretary General, the third such report in as many years. China's report was submitted in the UN Simplified Reporting Form, which provides minimal information on major budget categories, in contrast to the more detailed Standardized Reporting Form used by countries practicing greater defense transparency.

China's Advancing Defense Industries

Since the late 1990s, China's state-owned defense and defense-related companies have undergone a broad-based transformation. Beijing continues to improve its business practices, streamline bureaucracy, broaden incentives for its factory workers, shorten developmental timelines, improve quality control, and increase overall defense industrial production capacity. Beijing is also emphasizing integration of defense and nondefense sectors to leverage the latest dual-use technologies and the output from China's expanding science and technology base. Augmented in part by direct acquisition of foreign weapons and technology, these reforms have enabled China to incorporate mid-1990s technology into the development and production of most of its advanced weapon systems. Some systems, particularly ballistic missiles, incorporate cutting-edge technologies in a manner that rivals even the world's most modern systems.

Civil-Military Integration

Developing innovative dual-use technology and an industrial base that serves both military and civilian needs is a high priority for China's leadership. President Hu expressed in his political report to the CCP's 17th Party Congress in October 2007:

> We must establish sound systems of weapons and equipment research and manufacturing... and combine military efforts with civilian support, build the armed forces through diligence and thrift, and blaze a path of development with Chinese characteristics featuring military and civilian integration.

China's defense industry has benefited from integration with a rapidly expanding civilian economy and science and technology sector, particularly elements that have access to foreign technology. Progress within individual defense sectors appears linked to the relative integration of each, through China's civilian economy, into the global production and research and development (R&D) chain. For example, the shipbuilding and defense electronics sectors, benefiting from China's leading role in producing commercial shipping and information technologies, have witnessed the greatest progress over the last decade. Information technology companies in particular, including Huawei, Datang, and Zhongxing, maintain close ties to the PLA.

In contrast, enterprises producing high-performance computers, advanced applications software, and specialized top-end semiconductors/micro-processors—key to the evolution of increasingly advanced and capable defense microelectronics and applications, but with limited counterparts in the PRC civil-industrial sector—have experienced slower progress. The aviation and ordnance sectors have similarly suffered from a limited number of spin-off benefits, despite partnerships between foreign multinational corporations and domestic industry.

Sector-by-Sector Analysis

Progress across China's defense industry sectors has been uneven. Production trends and resource allocation appear to favor missile and space systems, followed by maritime assets (both surface and sub-surface), aircraft, and ground force materiel. In all areas, China is increasing the quality of its output and surge production capabilities, if not capacities. However, many of China's most advanced systems are still based heavily on foreign designs copied through reverse engineering, highlighting a persistent weakness in China's capability for overall system design and integration.

Missile and Space Industry

China produces a broad range of sophisticated ballistic, cruise, air-to-air, and surface-to-air missiles. Many of China's primary final assembly and rocket motor production facilities have received upgrades over the past few years, likely increasing production capacity. In addition to supplying China's military, complete systems and missile technologies could also be marketed for export. Surge production for these systems could result in a significantly higher output of SRBMs and perhaps double the number of MRBMs per year. China's space launch vehicle industry is expanding to support satellite launch services and the manned space program.

Shipbuilding Industry

China operates a vibrant and globally competitive shipbuilding industry. By some measures, China is the largest shipbuilder in the world. Shipyard expansion and modernization have increased China's shipbuilding capacity and capability, generating benefits for all types of military projects, including: submarines; surface combatants; naval aviation, including aircraft carriers; and lift assets. China continues relying on foreign suppliers for some propulsion units and to a much lesser degree, fire control systems, cruise missiles, surface-to-air missiles, torpedo systems, sensors, and other advanced electronics. Modular shipbuilding techniques will allow China to spread production across multiple locations, increasing both efficiency and output. China has already demonstrated an ability to surge submarine and amphibious production.

Armament Industry

China's ground force modernization includes production of new tanks, armored personnel carriers, and artillery pieces. There have been advances in almost every area of PLA ground forces with new production capacity to accommodate surge requests. China's reliance on foreign partners to fill gaps in critical technical capabilities could still limit actual surge output.

Aviation Industry

China's commercial and military aviation industries have advanced from producing direct copies of early Soviet models to developing and producing indigenous aircraft. These include improved versions of older aircraft and modern fourth generation fighters. China's commercial aircraft industry has imported high-precision and technologically advanced machine tools, electronics, and other components that can also be used in the production of military aircraft. However, China's ability to surge production in the aircraft industry will be limited by its reliance on foreign sourcing for aircraft engines and avionics, as well as the lack of skilled personnel and facilities.

Foreign Technology Acquisition

Key areas where China continues to rely most heavily on foreign technologies include: guidance and control systems, engine technology, and enabling technologies such as precision machine tools, advanced diagnostic and forensic equipment, applications and processes essential to rapid prototyping, and computer-assisted design/manufacturing. China often pursues these foreign technologies for the purpose of reverse engineering or to supplement indigenous military modernization efforts.

Russia has been China's primary weapons and materiel provider, selling Beijing advanced fighter aircraft, helicopters, missile systems, submarines, and destroyers. Relying on Russian components for several of its production programs, China purchased production rights to Russian weapon designs. However, this trend is changing as China becomes more self-sufficient in development and production.

Israel previously supplied advanced military technology to China, but has reformed its export control regime through the passage of a Defense Export Control Act in July 2007 and the adoption of implementing regulations in December 2007.

Since 2003, China has pressured European Union (EU) Member States to lift the embargo on lethal military sales to China that the EU imposed in response to China's 1989 crackdown on demonstrators. In their Joint Statement following the 2004 EU-China Summit, European and PRC leaders committed to work towards lifting the Tiananmen embargo. Although the issue remains on the EU agenda, there is no consensus among the EU Member States on lifting the embargo in the near future.

In addition, economic espionage, supported by extensive open source research, computer network exploitation, and targeted intelligence operations also enables China to obtain technologies to supplement indigenous military modernization efforts.

In its 2008 report, *Targeting U.S. Technologies: A Trend Analysis of Reporting From Defense Industry*, the Defense Security Service (DSS) found that in the previous year, foreign collectors, including the PRC, attempted to obtain information and technologies from each of the 20 categories of the Developing Sciences and Technologies List (DSTL). The DSTL is a compendium of scientific and technological capabilities being developed worldwide that have the potential to enhance or degrade U.S. military capabilities significantly in the future.

The DSS report described China's science and technology collection priorities as: guidance and control systems, advanced energy technologies, nanotechnology, space and counterspace systems, nuclear forces, innovative materials, aeronautics and astronautic mechanisms, computer-aided manufacturing and design, and information technologies. The PRC continues to target these technologies.

The U.S. Department of Commerce's Bureau of Industry and Security and the Department of Justice identified at least 26 major cases since 2006 linking China to the acquisition of technologies and applications cited above, as well as to current and future warship technology, electronic propulsion systems, controlled power amplifiers with military applications, space launch technical data and services, C-17 aircraft, Delta IV rockets, infrared cameras, information related to cruise missile design, and military-grade accelerometers. Additional technologies cited in these cases consisted of microwave integrated circuits; weapon scopes; restricted night-vision equipment and data; satellite/missile thermal insulation blankets; controlled electronic components; traveling wave tubes used with satellite and radar systems; microwave amplifiers with radar applications; export controlled technical data related to plasma technology for UAVs; carbon fiber material for aircraft, rockets, spacecraft, and the uranium enrichment process; and, extended range programmable logic devices.

The PRC's continuing efforts to acquire U.S. military and dual-use technologies are enabling the PRC science and technology base to diminish the U.S. technological edge in areas critical to the development of military weapons and communications systems. Additionally, the technologies China has acquired could be used to develop more advanced technologies by shortening PRC R&D cycles.

Trends and Projections

China's National Medium- and Long-Term Program for Science and Technology Development (2006-2020), issued by the State Council in February 2006, seeks to transform China into an —innovation-oriented society by 2020. The plan defines China's science and technology focus in terms of —basic research,—leading-edge technologies, —key fields and priority subjects, and —major special items, all of which have military applications.

Basic Research

As part of a broad effort to expand basic research capabilities, China identified five areas that have military applications as major strategic needs or science research plans requiring active government involvement and funding:

- material design and preparation;
- manufacturing in extreme environmental conditions;
- aeronautic and astronautic mechanics; information technology development; and, nanotechnology research.

In nanotechnology, China has progressed from virtually no research or funding in 2002 to being a close second to the United States in total government investment.

Leading-Edge Technologies

China is focusing on the following technologies for rapid development:

- Information Technology: Priorities include intelligent perception technologies, ad hoc networks, and virtual reality technologies;
- New Materials: Priorities include smart materials and structures, high-temperature superconducting technologies, and highly efficient energy materials technologies;
- Advanced Manufacturing: Priorities include extreme manufacturing technologies and intelligent service advanced machine tools;
- Advanced Energy Technologies:
- Priorities include hydrogen energy and fuel cell technologies, alternative fuels, and advanced vehicle technologies;

- Marine Technologies: Priorities include three-dimensional maritime environmental monitoring technologies, fast, multi-parameter ocean floor survey technologies, and deep-sea operations technologies; and,
- Laser and Aerospace Technologies are also high priorities.

Key Fields and Priority Subjects

China has identified certain industries and technology groups with potential to provide technological breakthroughs, remove technical obstacles across industries, and improve international competitiveness.Specifically, China's defense industries are pursuing advanced manufacturing, information technology, and defense technologies. Examples include radar, counterspace capabilities, secure C4ISR, smart materials, and low-observable technologies.

Major Special Items

China has also identified 16 —major special items for which it plans to develop or expand indigenous capabilities. These include core electronic components, high-end universal chips and operating system software, very large-scale integrated circuit manufacturing, next- generation broadband wireless mobile communications, high-grade numerically controlled machine tools, large aircraft, high- resolution satellites, manned spaceflight, and lunar exploration.

FORCE MODERNIZATION AND SECURITY IN THE TAIWAN STRAIT

Overview

China's acute focus on Taiwan has served for two decades as the dominant force shaping PLA modernization. Although China's other emerging interests increasingly compete for attention and resources, defense planners continue to regard Taiwan as the PLA's primary mission. Beijing seeks the military capability to deter Taiwan moves toward independence. This mission has catalyzed efforts to deter, delay, or deny the possible intervention of U.S. forces in a cross-Strait conflict. Although cross-Strait ties have improved steadily since 2008 and the prospect of a near-term crisis appears low, the PRC remains focused on developing the prerequisite military capabilities to eventually settle the dispute on Beijing's terms.

Status of Aircraft Carrier Developments

During the next decade China is likely to fulfill its carrier ambitions, becoming the last permanent member of the UN Security Council to obtain a carrier capability. In April 2011, China's Xinhua state news agency posted the newspaper's first pictures of the former Soviet carrier (Kuznetsov-class Hull-2) under renovation in Dalian, proclaiming that China will soon fulfill its —70-year aircraft carrier dreams. In June 2011, PLA Chief of the General Staff, Chen Bingde, finally confirmed China's carrier program.

Throughout 2010, the PRC continued refurbishing Kuznetsov Hull-2 (the ex-VARYAG), which China purchased from Ukraine in 1998. This carrier will likely begin sea trials in 2011, and the ship could become operationally available, although without aircraft, by the end of 2012. However, it will take several years for an operationally viable air group of fixed and rotary wing aircraft to achieve even a minimal level of combat capability. The PLA Navy has initiated a land-based program to begin training navy pilots to operate fixed-wing aircraft from an aircraft carrier. This program will probably be followed in about three years by full-scale ship-borne training aboard Kuznetsov Hull-2.

China has demonstrated an interest in foreign carrier-borne fighters and carrier aviation, but it appears that a domestic carrier aircraft production program is progressing. Currently in flight testing, the carrier aircraft, known as the J-15, is reportedly an unlicensed copy of a Russian Su-33, which China obtained from Ukraine in 2004.

China is also looking abroad for operational expertise. In May 2009, Brazilian Defense Minister Nelson Jobim announced that the Brazilian Navy would provide training to PLA Navy officers in aircraft carrier operations.

However, Brazil's limited capabilities in this area and the extensive problems associated with Brazil's own carrier program raise some questions as to the implications of the offer.

In addition to the Kuznetsov-class carrier, the PLA Navy will likely build several additional carriers in Chinese shipyards. In March 2009, PLA Navy Admiral Wu Huayang affirmed, —China is capable of building aircraft carriers... Given the level of development in our country, I think we have such strength. Construction of China's first indigenous carrier, which would likely have a similar displacement and design of the Kuznetsov Hull-2, could begin as early as 2011. If China commences construction in 2011, the PLA Navy could have its first indigenous carrier achieving operational capability as early as 2015.

Since the election of Taiwan President Ma Ying-jeou in March 2008, China and Taiwan have embarked on a period of improved economic and political ties. The two sides have expanded trade and economic links, such as direct shipping, flights, and mail across the Strait. The United States welcomes and encourages this trend as a means to reduce tensions and bridge differences between the two sides. Nevertheless, there is no indication that China's long-term objectives have changed.

In October 2010, senior PRC officials indicated that the two sides were in no rush to address thorny political or military issues, but would focus on improving economic cooperation. Consistent with that statement, the PRC has not taken steps to reduce its military forces facing Taiwan. China has continued to develop a wide range of weapons and capabilities designed to provide credible military options in a Taiwan contingency. This includes efforts to deter or limit the effectiveness of potential U.S. intervention.

Security in the Taiwan Strait is largely a function of dynamic interactions between and among mainland China, Taiwan, and the United States. Although the PLA probably lacks the necessary military power to successfully conduct a full-scale amphibious invasion of Taiwan, it is working to close perceived capability gaps in the coming years.

Furthermore, Taiwan's relatively modest defense spending has failed to keep pace with ambitious military developments on the mainland.

Taiwan has historically relied upon multiple factors to deter PLA aggression: the PLA's inability to project sufficient power across the 185 km Taiwan Strait; the Taiwan military's technological superiority; the inherent geographic advantages of island defense; and the possibility of U.S. intervention. China's increasingly modern weapons and platforms (over a thousand ballistic missiles, an anti-ship ballistic missile program, increasingly modern ships and submarines, combat aircraft, and improved C4ISR capabilities) threaten to negate many of those factors upon which Taiwan has depended.

Taiwan has taken important steps to build its war reserve stocks, grow its defense industrial base, improve joint operations and crisis response capabilities, and increase its officer and noncommissioned officer (NCO) corps. These improvements have partially addressed Taiwan's eroding defensive advantages. Taiwan released its first Quadrennial Defense Review in March 2009, and is following through on that report by creating an all-volunteer military and reducing its active military end-strength from 275,000 to 215,000 personnel to create a —small but smart and strong force. Under this plan, which is slated for completion by December 2014, the cost savings from a smaller force will free up resources to increase volunteer salaries and benefits. However, the additional personnel costs needed to initially attract and retain personnel under the volunteer system could divert funds from foreign and indigenous acquisition programs, as well as near-term training and readiness.

U.S. policy toward Taiwan is based on our one China policy, based on the three Joint Communiqués and the Taiwan Relations Act [Public Law 96-8 (1979)]. U.S. policy opposes any unilateral changes to the status quo in the Taiwan Strait by either side. The United States continues to support peaceful resolution of cross-Strait differences in a manner acceptable to the people on both sides.

Consistent with the Taiwan Relations Act, the United States has helped to maintain peace, security, and stability in the Taiwan Strait by providing defense articles and services to enable Taiwan to maintain a sufficient self defense capability. To this end, the Obama Administration announced in January 2010 its intent to sell to Taiwan US$6.4 billion worth of defensive arms and equipment, including:

- UH-60 utility helicopters;
- PATRIOT PAC-3 air and missile defense systems;
- HARPOON anti-ship cruise missile training;
- Multifunctional Information Distribution
- Systems technical support for Taiwan's
- Syun An C4ISR system; and, OSPREY-class minehunting ships.

In addition, the U.S. Department of Defense, through transformation of the U.S. Armed Forces and global force posture realignments, is maintaining the capability and capacity of the United States to defend against Beijing's use of force or coercion against Taiwan.

Beijing's Taiwan Strategy

Through the employment of both —carrots and sticks Beijing apparently seeks to deter Taiwan moves toward independence and achieve eventual unification. The PRC strives to integrate the two economies while advancing cultural and historic ties. Politically, China has sought to expand ties with the KMT Party on Taiwan while attempting to isolate political entities with more overtly pro-independence leanings. The PRC employs economic enticement, propaganda, and political engagement in pursuit of these objectives.

The military component of China's Taiwan strategy is likely intended to create an impression on Taiwan that accommodation with China is ultimately in the island's best interest. This approach appears to include a heavy focus on amphibious operations, long range strike, and anti-access and area denial capabilities, which are intended to alter Taiwan's threat calculus as well as that of any party considering intervention in a cross-Strait crisis.

Beijing appears prepared to defer the use of force as long as it believes long term reunification remains possible and the costs of conflict outweigh the benefits. Although Beijing often emphasizes its preference for—peaceful unification|| under the principle of —one country, two systems, it has never renounced the possibility of using force to achieve this end. Beijing likely calculates that the prospect of employing military force is an important point of leverage in this relationship.

Historically, the PRC has alluded to several events or conditions that might prompt it to employ military force in pursuit of its Taiwan policy. These conditions have evolved over time in response to political developments on Taiwan, the evolution of PLA capabilities, and Beijing's perception of Taiwan's foreign relations. These circumstances have included:

- Formal declaration of Taiwan independence;
- undefined moves toward Taiwan independence;
- internal unrest on Taiwan;
- Taiwan's acquisition of nuclear weapons;
- indefinite delays in the resumption of cross-Strait dialogue on unification;
- foreign intervention in Taiwan's internal affairs; and,
- foreign troops stationed on Taiwan.

Article 8 of China's March 2005 —AntiSecession Law states that Beijing may use —non-peaceful means if —secessionist forces... cause the fact of Taiwan's secession from China; if —major incidents entailing Taiwan's secession occur; or, if —possibilities for peaceful reunification are exhausted. The ambiguity of these —redlines preserves Beijing's flexibility.

Beijing's Courses of Action against Taiwan

The PLA is capable of increasingly sophisticated military action against Taiwan. Should Beijing resolve to employ military force against Taiwan, some analysts assert the PLA would mobilize forces in a manner that optimizes speed of engagement over strategic deception. Others contend that Beijing would sacrifice preparations in favor of tactical surprise, with the goal of forcing rapid military and/or political resolution before other countries could respond. If a quick resolution is not possible, Beijing would seek to:

- deter potential U.S. intervention by highlighting the potential cost to the U.S. and targeting the resolve of the U.S. public and leadership;
- failing that, delay intervention and seek victory in an asymmetric, limited, quick war; or,
- fight to a standstill and pursue a political settlement after a protracted conflict.

Maritime Quarantine or Blockade

Although a traditional maritime quarantine or blockade would have a short-term impact on Taiwan, such an operation would tax PLA Navy capabilities. PRC military writings describe potential alternative solutions including air blockades, missile attacks, and mining to obstruct harbors and approaches.

Beijing could declare that ships en route to Taiwan must stop in mainland ports for inspection prior to transiting to Taiwan ports. Beijing could also attempt the equivalent of a blockade by declaring exercise or missile closure areas in approaches to ports, effectively closing port access and diverting merchant traffic. The PLA employed this method during the 1995-96 missile firings and live-fire exercises. However, there is a risk that Beijing would underestimate the degree to which any attempt to limit maritime traffic to and from Taiwan would trigger countervailing international pressure and military escalation. Currently, China probably could not effectively enforce a full military blockade, particularly in the face of intervention by a major naval power. However, its ability to execute a blockade will improve steadily through 2020.

Limited Force or Coercive Options

Beijing might use a variety of disruptive, punitive, or lethal military actions in a limited campaign against Taiwan, likely in conjunction with overt and clandestine economic and political activities. Such a campaign could include computer network or limited kinetic attacks against Taiwan's political, military, and economic infrastructure to induce fear in Taiwan and degrade the populace's confidence in the Taiwan leadership. Similarly, PLA special operations forces could infiltrate Taiwan and conduct attacks against infrastructure or leadership targets.

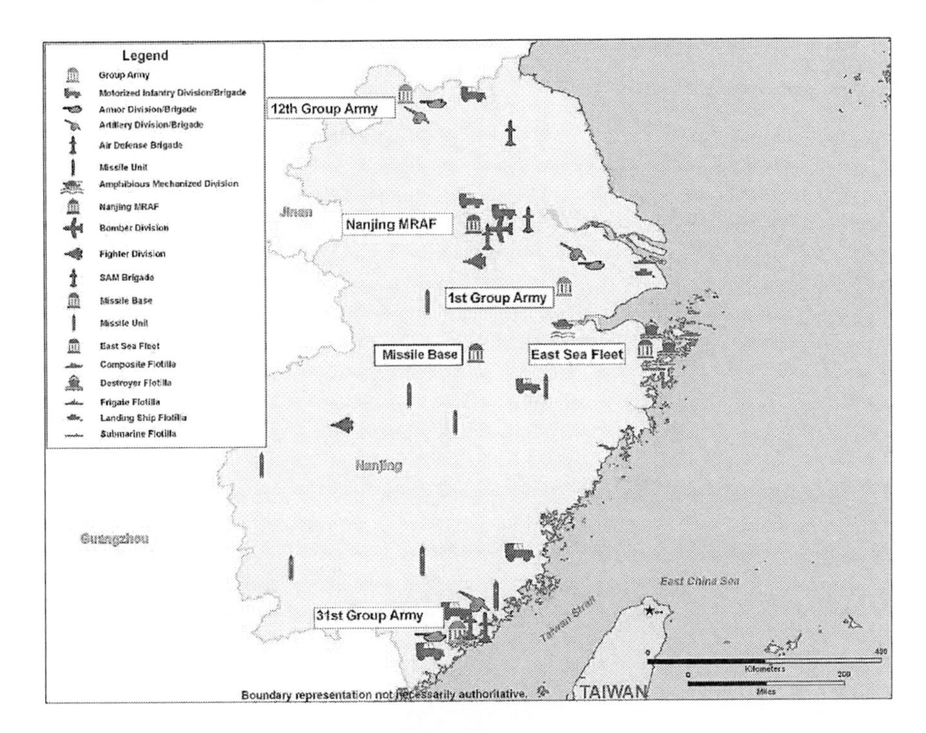

Disposition of PLA Forces in Nanjing Military Region.

Air and Missile Campaign

Limited SRBM attacks and precision strikes against air defense systems, including air bases, radar sites, missiles, space assets, and communications facilities, could be conducted in an attempt to degrade Taiwan's defenses, neutralize Taiwan's leadership, or break the public's will to fight.

Amphibious Invasion

Publicly available PRC writings describe different operational concepts for amphibious invasion. The most prominent of these, the Joint Island Landing Campaign, envisions a complex operation relying on coordinated, interlocking campaigns for logistics, air and naval support, and electronic warfare. The objective would be to break through or circumvent shore defenses, establish and build a beachhead, transport personnel and materiel to designated landing sites in the north or south of Taiwan's western coastline, and launch attacks to seize and occupy key targets and/or the entire island.

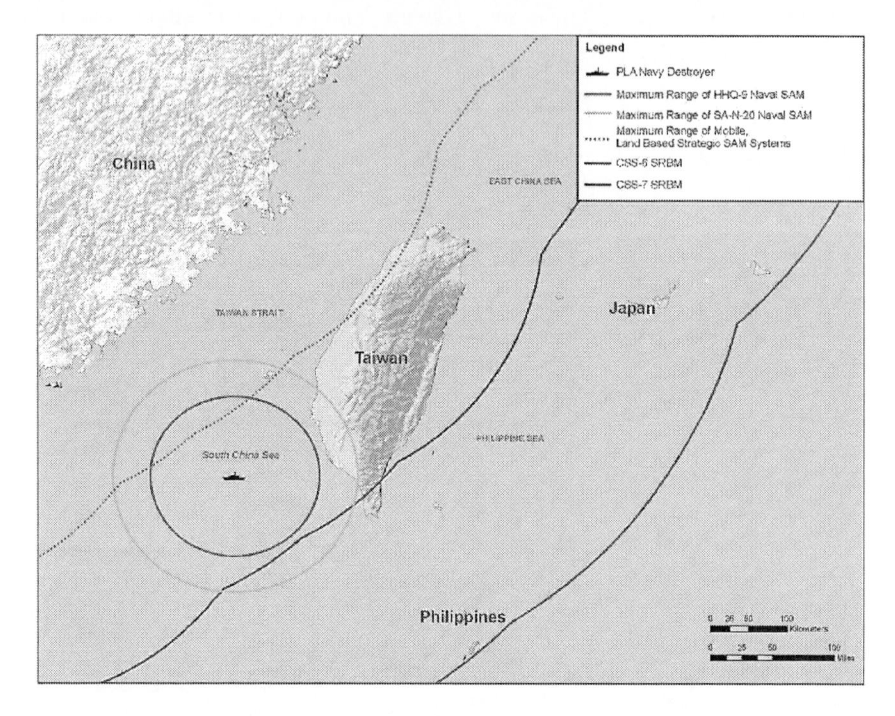

Taiwan Strait SAM & SRBM Coverage. This map depicts notional coverage based on the range of land and sea based missile systems, including advanced SAMs that China would likely employ in a Taiwan conflict. A single PLA Navy Destroyer is used to illustrate the range of sea-based SAM coverage. Actual air defense coverage would be non-contiguous and dependent upon precise deployment sites. If deployed near the Taiwan Strait, the PMU2" s extended range provides the PLA" s SAM force with an offensive capability against Taiwan aircraft.

The PLA is capable of accomplishing various amphibious operations short of a full-scale invasion of Taiwan. With few overt military preparations beyond routine training, China could launch an invasion of small, Taiwan-held islands such as Pratas Reef or Itu Aba. A PLA invasion of a medium-sized, defended, offshore island such as Mazu or Jinmen is within China's capabilities. Such an invasion would demonstrate military capability and political resolve while achieving tangible territorial gain and simultaneously showing some measure of restraint. However, this type of operation involves significant operational and political risk. It could galvanize the Taiwan populace and catalyze a strong international reaction. Operationally, large-scale amphibious invasion is one of the most complicated military maneuvers. Success depends upon air and sea superiority, rapid buildup and sustainment of supplies on shore, and uninterrupted support. An attempt to invade Taiwan would strain China's untested armed forces and invite international intervention. These stresses, combined with China's combat force attrition and the complexity of urban warfare and counterinsurgency (assuming a successful landing and breakout), make amphibious invasion of Taiwan a significant political and military risk. Taiwan's investments to harden infrastructure and strengthen defensive capabilities could also decrease Beijing's ability to achieve its objectives.

U.S.-China Military-to-Military Contacts

Overview

Over the past two decades, the PRC has steadily transformed a poorly equipped, terrestrially focused military into a more capable force that is assuming diverse missions well beyond China's shores. Given this trajectory, the need for a robust U.S.- China military-to-military relationship that builds trust and helps manage friction continues to grow. During their January 2011 summit, U.S. President Barack Obama and PRC President Hu Jintao jointly affirmed that a —healthy, stable, and reliable military-tomilitary relationship is an essential part of [their] shared vision for a positive, cooperative, and comprehensive U.S. China relationship. Both sides have repeatedly endorsed this objective. However, placing the military relationship on a firm foundation has proven challenging.

In 2010, the PLA suspended military relations with the United States for a second time since 2008. The suspension on January 30, 2010 came just one day after the U.S. Government approved the sale of an arms package to Taiwan. In response, MG Qian Lihua, Director of the Ministry of Defense Foreign Affairs Office (MND/FAO), noted the PLA —expresses grave indignation and strongly condemns such a move to grossly interfere in China's internal affairs and harm China's national security interests. Although the United States and China maintained working level contact during the nine-month suspension that followed, routine military-tomilitary exchanges did not resume until the final quarter of 2010.

The fundamental purpose for two countries to conduct military-to-military relations is to gain a better understanding of how each side thinks about the role and use of military power in achieving political and strategic objectives. It is precisely during periods of tension when a working relationship is most important. Over the long term, a fully functioning relationship should help both parties develop a more acute awareness of the potential for cooperation and competition. Speaking at the Shangri-la Dialogue in June 2010, then-Secretary of Defense Robert Gates asserted that the Defense Department —wants what both Presidents Obama and Hu want: sustained and reliable military-to-military contacts at all levels that can help reduce mis-communication, misunderstanding, and the risks of miscalculation.

The United States bases its contacts and exchanges with China's military on the principles of mutual respect, mutual trust, reciprocity, mutual interest, continuous dialogue, and mutual risk reduction. The Department of Defense conducts them in a manner consistent with the provisions of Section 1201 of the National Defense Authorization Act for Fiscal Year 2000 [Public Law 106-65 (1999)], which provide the Secretary of Defense sufficient latitude to develop a program of exchanges with China that supports U.S. national interests.

Military Relations in 2010

In September 2010, after Beijing expressed a desire to resume military-to-military relations, Deputy Assistant Secretary of Defense (DASD) Michael Schiffer met with MG Qian Lihua to lay the groundwork a series of bilateral military engagements for late 2010 and early 2011.

As a starting point, in mid-October 2010, the U.S. Pacific Command hosted a plenary session of the Military Maritime Consultative Agreement (MMCA) with China's Ministry of National Defense in Honolulu, HI. During the MMCA session, the two sides discussed issues of maritime safety, including a series of increasingly close PLA intercepts of U.S. aircraft operating in international airspace. On October 17, 2010, Secretary Gates and PRC Minister of National Defense, General Liang Guanglie, met on the sidelines of the ASEAN Defense Ministerial Meeting in Hanoi. General Liang invited Secretary Gates to visit China in early 2011 and agreed to a Chairman of the Joint Chiefs of Staff counterpart visit with PLA Chief of the General Staff, General Chen Bingde.

On December 10, 2010, Under Secretary of Defense for Policy Michèle Flournoy hosted the 11th Defense Consultative Talks (DCT) in Washington, D.C. with Deputy Chief of the PLA General Staff, General Ma Xiaotian. During these talks, the two sides addressed the importance of moving beyond the on-again-off-again cycle that has characterized the relationship. They also discussed potential opportunities to build trust and expand cooperation, including a shared interest in stability on the Korean Peninsula.

Under Secretary Flournoy and General Ma agreed to develop a framework for militaryto-military relations based on the seven-point consensus established between then-Secretary Gates and Vice Chairman of the Central Military Commission Xu Caihou in 2009. This meeting also set the stage for Secretary Gates' visit to China and President Hu Jintao's subsequent visit to the United States in January 2011.

The resumption of dialogue in late 2010 enabled the U.S. and PRC militaries to candidly discuss a range of important topics, including North Korea's provocations; concerns related to Iran, Afghanistan, and Pakistan; and transnational and strategic security issues. Continuous dialogue, particularly at high levels, is an important platform for developing common approaches to challenges in the international security environment.

U.S. Strategy for Military Engagement

The complexity of the security environment both in the Asia-pacific region and globally, calls for a continuous dialogue between the armed forces of the United States and China. The U.S. position is that our engagement with China should expand cooperation in areas of mutual interest, provide a forum to candidly address areas of disagreement and improve mutual understanding. The United States sees value in sustained and reliable military ties and regards the military relationship as an integral component of a comprehensive U.S.-China relationship.

The U.S. Defense Department's plan for military-to-military engagement with the PRC supports the vision of a —positive, cooperative, and comprehensive U.S.-China relationship for the 21st century, that the U.S. and PRC presidents jointly endorsed. Sustained military engagement underpins U.S. policy objectives of promoting China's development in a manner consistent with international rules and norms and that contributes to regional and global problem-solving. The U.S. National Defense Strategy emphasizes that U.S. defense interaction with China will be long-term and multidimensional. The objective of this effort is to mitigate near term challenges while pursuing and enhancing U.S. national advantage over time.

Our military-to-military engagement with China serves three general purposes in support of the broader relationship. First, it allows the U.S. and PRC militaries to build cooperative capacity. This is achieved through activities that enhance or facilitate our ability to interact at a tactical or operational level. Second, our engagement fosters understanding of each others' military institutions in ways that dispel misconceptions and encourage common ground for dialogue. Third, military engagement allows our senior-most leaders to address the global security environment and relevant challenges. This interaction can facilitate common approaches to challenges and serves as a bridge to build more productive working relationships.

Opportunities and Challenges in U.S.-China Military-to-Military Relations

President Obama reiterated in January 2011 that the United States welcomes a —strong, prosperous, and successful China that plays a greater role in world affairs. China's military modernization has created new opportunities for cooperation with the United States, including peacekeeping efforts, humanitarian and disaster relief, and counter-piracy operations. At the same time, the PLA's development remains a potential source of friction.

The Asia-Pacific region is contending with an array of challenges including rising powers, failing states, proliferation of nuclear and ballistic missiles, extremist violence, and new technologies capable of disrupting critical arteries of global commerce. Secretary Gates has noted that —confronting these tasks is not the task of any one nation acting alone. China's growing economic and military capability makes it a natural partner in efforts to promote regional stability. It is the U.S. position that inevitable differences on certain issues should not prevent our cooperation in those areas where we share common interests.

In early January 2011, Secretary Gates traveled to China at the invitation of PRC Minister of National Defense, General Liang Guanglie. Speaking at a joint press event with General Liang, Secretary Gates noted that even though we face obstacles to genuine —strategic understanding, our two nations have many opportunities to build and improve on areas of bilateral cooperation.

China's growing capacity in areas of counter-piracy, UN peace missions, and humanitarian aid and disaster relief opens new doors for cooperation with the United States and the international community. As the Chinese military develops the capability to deliver medical and humanitarian assistance beyond its immediate region, there will be opportunities for the United States and China to collaborate and share —lessons learned from these endeavors.

The Department of Defense and China's Ministry of National Defense signed an archival arrangement in 2008 that, for the first time, gave the United States access to PLA archives containing information regarding U.S. servicemen missing in China from World War II, the Korean War and the Cold War. As a result of this agreement, the Defense POW/Missing Personnel Office has made slow but steady progress in accounting for Americans missing in China. Archival research led to the discovery of a U.S. Navy crash site from the Korean War, and consequently, in February 2011, a U.S. recovery operation supported by representatives from the PLA Archives.

The United States and China have opportunities to enhance tactical cooperation, communication, and trust through bilateral and multilateral exercises. Additionally, reciprocal exchanges between mid-grade and junior officers and institutions of professional military education cultivate a generation of rising leaders on both sides who are adept at handling this increasingly complex and vital relationship. ADM Mullen noted in the U.S. Maritime Strategy, —A Cooperative Strategy for 21st Century Seapower, that —trust and cooperation cannot be surged. The skills acquired through our peacetime interactions foster habits of cooperation and safe communication practices that mitigate risk and diffuse tensions.

The pace and scope of China's military development, combined with a relative lack of transparency, remains a point of concern in the United States and among our regional allies and partners. In recent years China has demonstrated occasional signs of assertiveness in Asia, particularly in the maritime domain. This trend has contributed to friction between China and some of its neighbors over disputed maritime territory in the East and South China Seas.

Additionally, the United States and China continue to hold differing views over the rights of coastal states in the waters and airspace beyond their territorial seas. In 2010 several PLA fighter aircraft conducted unusually close intercepts of U.S. military aircraft operating in international airspace. In recent years Chinese ships have also harassed U.S. military survey vessels operating beyond China's territorial seas.

A sustained and reliable military relationship is vital to managing these challenges and ensuring that they do not come to define the relationship or escalate into a crisis. Our military-to-military contacts should support deterrence of conflict and lower the risk of miscalculation by encouraging continuous dialogue based on open and substantive discussion of strategic issues. Although PRC leaders have repeatedly affirmed a commitment to a sustained and reliable military-to-military relationship, they have also linked continuation of engagement to —respect for China's —core interests.

SPECIAL TOPIC: CHINA'S EVOLVING MARITIME STRATEGY

The Rise of China's Maritime Security Interests

Historically a continental power, China increasingly looks to the maritime domain as a source of economic prosperity and national security. China's evolving —maritime consciousness, as reflected in senior-level rhetoric and resource allocation, has potentially far reaching consequences in the Asia Pacific region and beyond. Many PRC officials and citizens view maritime power as a prerequisite to becoming a —great power.This chapter addresses China's attention to the maritime domain, with a particular focus on the security dimension. It identifies the catalysts influencing PRC thinking on maritime interests and the steps China has taken to address these challenges, including naval development, legislation, improving civilian maritime enforcement, and diplomatic initiatives. Finally, it addresses China's specific maritime interests and addresses how China's posture could evolve in the future.

In its 2010 —China Ocean's Development Report, China's State Oceanic Administration (SOA) proclaimed, —building maritime power is China's historic task for the 21st century, and the decade from 2010- 2020 is the key historic stage for realizing this task. Although China appears to lack an official maritime strategy, PRC officials, military strategists, and academics are focused on the growing relevance of maritime power to China's interests.

The Evolution in "Maritime Consciousness"

Since the early 1980s, two important factors catalyzed a transformation in Beijing's maritime outlook. First, China's geostrategic environment fundamentally shifted after the Cold War ended. As PRC concerns over a major continental conflict, including the possibility of nuclear war with Russia, subsided, Beijing turned its attention towards a range of other challenges, particularly Taiwan, which it feared was drifting steadily toward a state of de jure independence.

The U.S. response in the 1995-96 Taiwan Strait crisis underscored to Beijing the potential challenge of U.S. military intervention and highlighted the importance of developing a modern navy, capable of conducting A2AD operations, or —counterintervention operations in the PLA's lexicon.

Second, China's expanding economic interests, including both maritime commerce and the exploitation of marine resources, have affected Beijing's perception of maritime power as it relates to national interests. Speaking in 2007, President Hu asserted that, —to develop maritime issues is one of the strategic tasks to boost our national economic development. China looks to the oceans as a critical resource, providing fish and potentially large oil and gas reserves.

The oceans also serve as a vital artery for trade and support China's economic health, with approximately ninety percent of China's imports and exports transiting by sea. A net oil exporter until 1993, China now imports over half of the oil it consumes, over 80 percent of which transits the Malacca Strait and South China Sea. Additionally, China's economic engine is concentrated in dense population centers along the country's East coast. Conflicts affecting these coastal regions would have far reaching consequences for China.

Evolving Naval Strategy

PLA General Liu Huaqing, who commanded a poorly equipped and trained PLA Navy through most of the 1980s, and later served on the CCP Politburo Standing Committee and as CMC Vice Chairman, advanced the cause of naval modernization amid a strategic culture overwhelmingly dominated by the PLA ground force. Until Liu instituted the PLA Navy's —Offshore Defense strategy in 1986, the PLA Navy was focused mainly on —resisting invasions and defending the homeland.

Often referred to as the —father of the modern Chinese Navy, Liu, who died in January 2011, called for naval operations beyond the PRC littoral and appealed for the eventual development of aircraft carriers. Years would pass before many of Liu's proposals gained political support; however, his ideas fundamentally affected the way PRC strategists conceptualize maritime power and approach maritime strategy.

Although not defined by specific boundaries, Offshore Defense is generally characterized by the maritime space within China's Exclusive Economic Zone (EEZ) or sometimes by the —first island chain, including the Yellow Sea, East China Sea, and South China Sea. In recent years, the PLA Navy has begun emphasizing missions in the so-called —far seas, an area loosely defined by the —second island chain, which stretches from Northern Japan, through the Northern Mariana Islands, through Guam.

Consideration of more distant contingencies has been accompanied by limited peacetime operations outside of this region, including counter-piracy patrols, humanitarian and disaster relief and noncombatant evacuations. These peacetime operations have provided the PLA with valuable operational experience.

New Security Interests Driving Requirements

In the early 1990s, the PRC watched with concern as more modern militaries adopted high technology weapons and platforms that were changing the nature of modern warfare, including in the maritime domain. From the perspective of many PRC strategists and military officials, military developments in developed nations made the PLA's coastal-oriented Navy appear antiquated, inadequate, and vulnerable. PRC leaders subsequently directed the PLA to prepare to fight and win —local wars under modern, high-tech conditions. The term —high-tech was later replaced with —informatized‖ to reflect the importance of network-centric warfare and information technology.

In his 1992 address to the 14th Party Congress, former President Jiang Zemin articulated the need to protect China's evolving —maritime interests. During the nearly two decades that followed, the PRC has pursued its maritime objectives through naval development, legislation, civilian enforcement, and diplomacy. Ambitious naval acquisition closed many of the capability gaps that defined China's Navy prior to and through the 1990s. China today possesses a limited ability to respond to maritime threats beyond the range of land-based aviation. This includes limited power projection capability in the farther regions of the South China Sea and western Pacific. This progress has been slow, but has begun to accelerate as new systems come on line, and China's naval forces gain additional experience in operations beyond the littoral.

Civilianand military officials have underscored the economic impetus for advancing China's maritime interests, reflecting a perception that economic welfare and national security are increasingly linked. PLA Navy Commander Wu Shengli asserted in 2006 that China requires a —powerful navy to protect fishing, resource development and strategic passageways for energy. This dimension is particularly important to the CCP, which has built its legitimacy on the promise of sustained development.

China's maritime interests, including territorial and sovereignty disputes, resource interests, and critical SLOC dependencies remain heavily concentrated in Asia.

Consequently, China's naval orientation retains a decidedly regional focus. However, the PLA is assuming more —global missions.

This reflects the recognition that Chinese economic interests, including commercial shipping and investment projects, along with PRC citizens, are now located across the globe. It also reflects a desire to cast China as a —great power. China's leaders have offered unambiguous guidance that the PLA Navy will play a growing role in protecting China's far-flung interests.

In 2004, not long after assuming Chairmanship of the CMC, Hu Jintao promulgated the —Historic Missions of the Armed Forces in the New Period of the New Century (*Xin Shiji Xin Jieduan Wojun Lishi Shiming*), commonly referred to as the —New Historic Missions. In addition to reiterating the Armed Forces' role in sustaining CCP rule, and protecting China's sovereignty and territorial integrity, the New Historic Missions highlight the PLA's role in safeguarding China's expanding —national interests and in —ensuring world peace. In drawing a clear link between China's economic interests and national security, the New Historic Missions established a justification for missions beyond China's maritime periphery. Although the PLA remains focused on regional contingencies, the New Historic Missions imply that the pursuit of China's interests would not be constrained by geographic boundaries and would evolve to meet a diverse array of challenges. China's 2006 National Defense White Paper expanded upon the New Historic Missions, when it introduced the concept of —diversified military tasks (*duoyanghua junshi renwu*—多样化军事任务). This emphasized the need for the PLA to prepare not only for traditional military missions, but also military operations other than war (MOOTW). The PLA Navy has since focused greater attention on counter-piracy, HA/DR, and noncombatant evacuation operations (NEO).

New "Firsts" for the PLA Navy

The PLA Navy's counter-piracy deployment to the Gulf of Aden, which it has sustained since 2009, remains the most visible manifestation of this policy shift under Hu Jintao. Not including naval diplomacy, the Gulf of Aden mission marked China's first operational deployment of naval forces outside of regional waters. In September 2010, the PLA Navy's hospital ship, —PEACE ARK conducted its first overseas humanitarian mission by visiting five countries in Asia and Africa.

Most recently, the PLA Navy participated in its first noncombatant evacuation operation (NEO). In February 2011, the PLA Navy deployed a JIANGKAI-II class frigate, which had been operating in the Gulf of Aden, to support its evacuation of PRC citizens from Libya. Although largely symbolic, this deployment enabled the PLA Navy to demonstrate a commitment to the protection of PRC citizens living and working overseas.

China's Maritime Interests

These increasingly —diverse missions have not supplanted regional priorities. The Taiwan challenge remains the —main strategic direction (*zhuyao zhanlue fangxiang*—主要战略方向) for China's armed forces, particularly the Navy. Aside from Taiwan, China faces several high priority maritime challenges. First is strengthening and gradually expanding China's maritime buffer zone as a means to prevent foreign attack or —interference. A second priority remains advancing China's maritime territorial claims, particularly the East and South China Seas. Third, China is focused on the protection of regional sea lines of communication (SLOCs).

Fourth, the PRC hopes to advance China's image as a —great power, and finally, China intends to deploy a survivable, sea-based nuclear deterrent in the foreseeable future.

Expanding the Maritime Periphery

China has long regarded the Yellow Sea, East China Sea, and South China Sea as areas of unique strategic importance. From the perspective of Beijing, these so called —near seas constitute a security buffer and hold potentially significant oil and gas resources. The PRC has attempted to use legal pronouncements, civilian enforcement, and naval assets to advance PRC interests within this buffer zone.

In 1992, China's National People's Congress passed the Law of Territorial Sea and Contiguous Zones, which proclaimed the South China Sea as PRC —historic waters.

Beijing has crafted a series of laws that codify PRC claims to regional territory and proscribe special restrictions on foreign activities in China's EEZ.

As the name implies, the Exclusive Economic Zone affords states exclusive access to the economic resources within a defined maritime space, not exceeding 200 nautical miles from the coastal baseline. China has attempted to apply security restrictions to the EEZ, which are inconsistent with customary international law as reflected in UNCLOS. Attempts to impede or harass sovereign U.S. vessels and aircraft operating legally in China's EEZ (beyond China's 12nm territorial seas) have repeatedly created friction in the U.S.-China relationship.

Regional Territorial Disputes

During the 1930s and 1940s, the Republic of China (ROC) began delineating essentially all of the South China Sea, including the Spratly and Paracel Islands, within a nine-dashed line. Although preserving ambiguity on the nature of this claim, the PRC maintains that the territories within the dashed line and their adjacent waters belong to China. Different portions of China's expansive claim are disputed in whole or in part by Taiwan, Vietnam, the Philippines, Malaysia, and Brunei. China's ability to employ coercion in these disputes has grown steadily in recent years. China's naval modernization, in particular, is affecting security perceptions among rival South China Sea claimants.

China is leveraging both civilian enforcement and naval assets in pursuit of its territorial objectives. In recent years, PRC naval ships and civilian law enforcement agencies have shown signs of greater assertiveness in the region, occasionally triggering friction with rival claimants. In the East China Sea, China faces a contentious dispute with Japan over maritime boundaries. Where this line is drawn has implications for disputed territory and subsea energy resources. In 2010, tensions between Tokyo and Beijing rose after a PRC fishing boat rammed a Japanese Coast Guard vessel near the disputed Senkaku Islands.

The PRC has increasingly sought to enforce its broad maritime claims with civilian assets including the maritime police, the Border Control Department (BCD), Maritime Safety Administration (MSA), State

Oceanographic Administration (SOA), Fisheries Law Enforcement Command (FLEC), and Coast Guard. Beijing wishes to present the issue of regional maritime territory as one of law enforcement rather than military rivalry. Beijing likely calculates that the employment of naval assets in these matters raises the risk of escalation, generates regional animosity, and unnecessarily burdens the PLA Navy with non-military tasks. Compared to developed countries, particularly Japan and the United States, China's civilian maritime agencies are poorly equipped and operated.

Debating China's Role in "Distant Seas"

Around the time President Hu Jinto articulated the —New Historic Missions in 2004, Chinese officials and scholars began openly discussing the extent to which China should expand its maritime power. The term —yuanhai fangwei (远海防卫) which translates to —distant/far sea defense, began appearing with increasing frequency in Chinese publications. Authors associated with the Naval Research Institute (NRI) called the —shift from offshore to open ocean naval operations an —inevitable historic choice for China noting that naval power must —match the expansion of China's maritime interests.

Navy deployment trends in recent years underscore China's interests in a limited —far seas capability. Some PRC commentators advocate a sustained shift from an —Offshore Defense strategy to —Far Seas Defense. Many others characterize Far Seas Defense as simply an extension or adjustment of the existing strategy, rather than a fundamental change. China's 2010 Defense White Paper reiterated the PLA Navy's commitment to its Offshore Defense strategy while acknowledging efforts to improve operational capabilities in far seas.

Recently, several Navy officials and commentators have broached the once-taboo topic of overseas military basing. In late 2009, Rear Admiral Yin Zhuo (retired), attracted extensive international media attention when he suggested in an interview, that China requires a —stable and permanent supply and repair base to support its overseas counter-piracy activities. With an aircraft carrier program being realized over the next decade, the Navy may face even greater incentive to improve its support options.

It is not clear if China will pursue traditional military —bases, suited for supporting distant combat operations, or a more limited set of logistical supply —places, that are better suited to peacetime deployments, such as counter-piracy and HA/DR.

However, they are improving steadily and will play an increasingly critical function in China's maritime enforcement efforts.

Sea Lane Protection

Since China's emergence as a global economic actor, it has relied nearly exclusively on the United States as the guarantor of a safe and unrestricted maritime domain. Approximately 90 percent of China's trade volume is conducted via maritime transport and approximately 50 percent of global merchant traffic passes through regional waters.

This dependency has prompted greater attention to SLOC protection missions. PRC officials have expressed particular concern over the Strait of Malacca. Even with its recent advances in naval power, would face great difficulty responding to threats to shipping in the far reaches of the South China Sea, including the Strait of Malacca.

The PLA Navy's ongoing effort in the Gulf of Aden underscores China's strong interest in protecting maritime commerce, from both traditional and non-traditional threats. The United States welcomes China's contribution to maintaining the safety and security of the global maritime domain. This deployment underscores an area where mutual interest can foster cooperation.

Great Power Status

China's ambitious naval modernization remains a great source of pride for the PRC public and leadership. China has deployed its most modern ships to engage in naval diplomacy and counter-piracy in a coalition environment. Many in China see naval power as a prerequisite for great power status.

PRC officials and commentators occasionally lament the fact that China is the only permanent member of the U.S. Security Council without an aircraft carrier. The PLA Navy's anticipated deployment of aircraft carriers over the coming decade will likely serve as a great source of national pride, regardless of actual combat capability.

China's leaders have tapped into this nationalistic sentiment, contrasting China's current naval power with the late Qing Dynasty, which was easily overwhelmed by more modern Japanese and Western naval forces. On December 27, 2006, President Hu Jintao expressed confidence in China's naval development, asserting to a group of PLA Navy officers that China was now —a great maritime power (*haiyang daguo*), adding that the PRC must continue strengthening and modernizing its Navy.

Sea-Based Nuclear Forces

China continues efforts to deploy a sea-based nuclear deterrent. Although the PLA Navy has received the JIN-class SSBN, it has faced repeated challenges with the JL-2 weapons system. The system did not reach an initial operational capability (IOC) by 2010 as DoD had anticipated. Once China overcomes remaining technical hurdles, the PLA Navy will be charged with protection of a nuclear asset.

Overcoming Key Challenges

Although areas of PLA progress frequently attract attention, lesser understood capability gaps remain. For example, the Gulf of Aden deployment has underscored the complexity of distant operations to China's military and civilian leadership. According to Rear Admiral Yin Zhuo, the Gulf of Aden mission has —shown the Navy's equipment is not particularly suited to blue water operations... [and] our equipment, our technology, especially our level of information infrastructure and communication means, as well as our blue water deployment capabilities… still have a relatively long way to go to catch up with that of the Western countries.

China's regional capabilities have improved significantly over the past two decades. However, in the near term, China would face great difficulty projecting military power beyond regional waters during a sustained conflict. China lacks overseas bases and supply infrastructure, and despite some recent progress, remains reliant on shore-based defenses. Over time, China's growing involvement in international peacekeeping efforts, military diplomacy, counter-piracy operations, humanitarian assistance and disaster relief, evacuation of Chinese citizens from overseas trouble spots, and exercise activity, will improve the PLA's capability to operate at greater distances from the mainland. This operational experience could eventually facilitate a —global military presence, should China's leadership pursue that course.

Assessing the Future

The evolution of China's economic and geostrategic interests has fundamentally altered Beijing's view of maritime power. Today, the PLA Navy and China's civilian maritime agencies are addressing gaps in regional capabilities while engaging in a small number of peacetime operations beyond the region, where their capabilities remain more limited. The expansion of missions reflects the availability of resources and the PRC's increasingly diverse interests.

Beyond immediate regional interests, China's expanding capabilities might facilitate greater attention to maritime challenges further into the Pacific and Indian Oceans. In contrast to a decade ago, many of China's new naval platforms can utilize space-based communications, advanced sensors, and area air-defense, enabling combat capability at great distances from land. Current peacetime deployments are providing PLA Navy operators with valuable experience outside of the region.

The establishment of overseas bases and the development of more than a few aircraft carriers might signal a trend towards more —global missions. Greater openness from China regarding the nature and scope of its maritime ambitions could help mitigate suspicions and ensure that China's maritime development becomes a source of global stability rather than a source of friction.

Special Topic: China's Military Engagement

The PLA has increasingly engaged with foreign militaries over the past decade. At the operational level, military engagement provides opportunities to share doctrine, tactics, techniques, and procedures with other militaries, both modern and developing. At the strategic level, military engagement allows Beijing to demonstrate its capabilities and emerging role in the international system.

China's military modernization has facilitated cooperation in two key respects. First, PLA modernization has removed capability-based constraints, allowing the PLA to operate with more advanced forces and at greater distances from the PRC mainland. Just a decade ago, for example, China's sustained deployment to the Gulf of Aden and the many associated foreign engagements would have proven exceedingly difficult, if not impossible for China.

Second, Beijing takes pride in —showing the flag with an increasingly modern array of platforms, both imported and indigenously designed. The international fanfare surrounding the PLA Navy's 60th Anniversary celebration in 2009 underscored the growing confidence in China's military development and desire to showcase these achievements.

Traditional Military Diplomacy

Senior level visits and exchanges provide the PRC with opportunities to increase military officers' international exposure, communicate China's positions to foreign audiences, better understand alternative world views, and advance foreign relations through interpersonal contacts and military assistance programs.

PLA engagement with foreign partners has grown in tandem with China's global profile, enabling China's military officers to observe and study foreign military command structures, unit formations, and operational training. PLA Navy port calls within Asia and beyond the region have steadily increased since 2002. In 2010, the PLA maintained a regular presence in over 100 countries with at least 300 attachés posted abroad, up from 201 in 2002 and 220 in 2005. The number of countries with defense attachés in Beijing is also increasing. As of 2010, 102 countries had established military attaché offices in China, up from 79 countries in 1996.

The PLA Navy's counter-piracy role in the Gulf of Aden has provided opportunities to advance China's image as a modern military that can act alongside other major world navies. PLA Navy port calls made both in the region and in transit to and from the Gulf of Aden reinforce China's political, military, and economic ties with those countries.

China hosts foreign military officers as students in its military academies. In October 2009, foreign military students from over 70 countries observed the PLA exercise VANGUARD 2009, which included a live fire demonstration. The first PLA exercise opened to observation by foreign military students was QIANFENG 2008, which reportedly involved an armored brigade conducting an offensive maneuver in a mountainous area.

The PLA's first instance of a mixed training class with both Chinese and foreign officers culminated with a June 2009 graduation ceremony at the Air Force Command College (AFCC), which included 56 officers from the air forces of 29 foreign countries and 12 officers from the PLA Air Force.

Combined Exercises

The PLA participates in a growing number of bilateral and multilateral military exercises in areas such as counter-terrorism, mobility operations, and logistics. The PLA gains operational insight by observing tactics, command decision making, and equipment used by more advanced militaries.

China is eager to present these activities as constructive, peaceful, and not directed against any other country. Many of the PLA's exercises with foreign militaries are conducted under the rubric of counterterrorism. Beijing has held exercises bilaterally with Russia, India, Pakistan, Thailand, Singapore, Australia, and multilaterally with the Shanghai Cooperation Organization and the various countries that participated in the Pakistan-hosted exercise AMAN-09. In 2010, the PLA conducted five training exercises with foreign militaries, three of which were held in China.

Additionally, China has invited foreign military observers and resident military attachés to observe PLA exercises on at least six occasions since 2003, enabling China to project an overall national image of —peaceful development and increased military transparency.

The PLA Navy routinely conducts search and rescue exercises with foreign militaries, including exercises with Australia, the United Kingdom, India, Pakistan, Japan, New Zealand, Russia, Vietnam, and others. These exercises serve training purposes and build rapport with foreign countries.

Peacekeeping Operations

Prior to 2002, Beijing generally avoided participation in UN peacekeeping operations (PKO), due to lingering skepticism of the international system and a long-stated policy of —non-interference in other countries' internal affairs. China's participation from 1991-1993 in the UN Transitional Authority in Cambodia marked a notable exception to this policy. China's attitude towards UN PKOs has changed dramatically over the past decade, particularly since Hu Jintao promulgated the New Historic Missions in 2004.

In January 2004, China had just 359 peacekeepers deployed to eight UN peacekeeping missions, with no single contingent containing more than 70 troops. Six years later, in January 2010, China had 2,131 peacekeepers (all non-combat) supporting 10 UN missions, with five separate contingents containing more than 200 troops. China is now the leading contributor of peacekeeping personnel among the five permanent members of the UN

Security Council. PRC contributions have consisted of civilian police; military observers; and engineering, logistics, and medical troops. China provided several rotations of over 100 police officers to the United Nations Stabilization Mission in Haiti (MINUSTAH). In 2010, China will shoulder approximately $300 million of the UN peacekeeping budget.

China regards participation in UN peacekeeping operations as serving multiple objectives, including improving China's international standing and image, demonstrating support for international stability in troubled regions, providing opportunities to initiate and expand intelligence collection, and enhancing relationships in the affected areas. Beijing has also demonstrated a growing willingness to deploy personnel on missions where conditions are more hazardous. After the 2006 death of a PRC peacekeeper in Lebanon, for example, the PLA increased its troop contributions to the UN Interim Force in Lebanon (UNIFIL). As of July 2010, Beijing will be deploying over 400 members of the 7th Chinese Peacekeeping Troops to support the African Union-UN Mission in Sudan.

Highlighting PRC interest in PKO's, China opened the Ministry of National Defense (MND) Peacekeeping Center in July 2009, the first PLA peacekeeping facility dedicated to professional training and international exchange. Later in September 2010, the MND co-hosted with the UN the first senior commanders' training course on peacekeeping. Although China has yet to deploy combat troops for peacekeeping duty, Beijing has openly discussed this as a future possibility.

Humanitarian Assistance/Disaster Relief

Over the past decade the PLA steadily increased its participation in international HA/DR missions. Investment in large amphibious ships, a new hospital ship, long-range transport aircraft, and improved logistics has made this mission a practical reality. Since 2002, the PLA has contributed to at least thirteen emergency relief operations in fourteen countries in China's immediate region as well as in Haiti during the aftermath of the earthquake in January 2010. Like PKOs, involvement in international HA/DR enables China to present a positive face to its military development while simultaneously advancing China's image as a responsible global power.

In late 2010, PLA Navy's new hospital ship PEACE ARK conducted the 88-day —MISSION HARMONY-2010 deployment to the Gulf of Aden to provide medical care to the PLA Navy counter-piracy flotilla and to treat needy residents in Djibouti, Kenya, Tanzania, Seychelles, and Bangladesh. This mission marked the PLA Navy's first foreign deployment of a hospital ship.

The PLA's humanitarian relief capability and capacity remains limited, but China is seeking to collaborate with regional partners to improve these capabilities. China and Indonesia drafted the —Association of Southeast Asian Nations (ASEAN) Regional Forum General Guidelines on Disaster Relief Cooperation to steer the development of Standard Operating Procedures for future HA/DR operations, which were adopted in July 2007.

China has also learned that growing capability and capacity can heighten foreign expectations for support. For example, in August 2010, critics suggested that many nations, including China, had reacted too slowly and inadequately to Pakistan's massive flooding. Despite the close political relationship between Beijing and Islamabad, China's early contributions to the 2010 disaster response were small compared to those of other nations.

Arms Sales

Beijing conducts arms sales to enhance foreign relationships and generate revenue. Although weighted more towards small arms and ammunition, PRC arms sales also include the joint development or transfer of advanced weapons systems. Chinese companies sell primarily to developing countries where China's lower-cost weapons and fewer political constraints provide a competitive advantage. Arms sales also play a role in advancing trade relationships, particularly where energy or valuable raw materials are concerned. For example, arms sales and other forms of security assistance to Iran and Sudan have deepened ties and helped to offset the cost of PRC energy imports. Arms sales play an important role in China's efforts to influence cash-strapped countries, many of which do not have access to other sources of arms for either political or economic reasons. As the quality and range of PRC-produced arms improves, Beijing will be increasingly able to wield arms sales as an instrument of influence.

From 2005-2010, China sold approximately $11 billion worth of conventional weapons systems worldwide. Pakistan remains China's primary customer for conventional weapons. Beijing engages in both arms sales and defense industrial cooperation with Islamabad. Sales to Islamabad have included the JF-17 fighter aircraft and associated production facilities; F-22P frigates with helicopters; K-8 jet trainers; F-7 fighter aircraft; early warning and control aircraft; tanks; air-to-air missiles; anti-ship cruise missiles; missile technologies; and small arms and ammunition. Sales to other countries include fighter, transport, and jet trainer aircraft; helicopters; tanks; air defense equipment, including radar, rockets, military vehicles, patrol boats, missiles and missile technology; and small arms and ammunition.

PRC Arms Sales

From 2005 to 2010, China sold approximately $11 billion worth of conventional weapons systems worldwide, ranging from general purpose materiel to major end items. PRC arms exports will likely increase in the coming years as China's domestic defense industry improves. Although China's defense industry is primarily oriented toward supplying the PLA, foreign arms sales are also important. Arms sales provide a means to cultivate relationships with important strategic partners, such as Pakistan, while generating revenue for its defense industry. PRC defense firms are marketing and selling arms throughout the world, with the bulk of their sales to Asia and the Middle East/North Africa. China is able to make gains in these markets because of modest improvements in quality of its equipment coupled with relatively low costs and favorable conditions for payment.

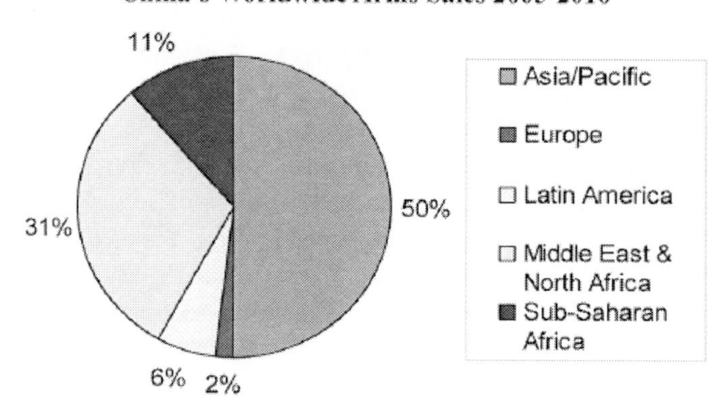

PRC Worldwide Arms Sales. Arms sales for 2005-2010, by region.

China is targeting niche markets, introducing weapons systems not offered by Russian or Western suppliers. These systems include GPS and GLOSNASS-equipped multiple rocket launcher systems and short-range ballistic missiles that have been marketed and sold to Middle East and African partners.

The volume of PRC defense sales is still modest compared to the world's leading arms sellers. However, interest in PRC arms will likely increase in the future as China's defense firms market and sell increasingly sophisticated yet affordable arms. China offers generous repayment options and technology transfer to persuade other countries to purchase from PRC firms.

Sales to Areas of Instability

Several PRC entities continue to provide arms to customers in unstable regions.

Iran: China supported UN Security Council Resolutions 1737, 1747, 1803, 1835, and 1929. China has stated that it is committed to implementing resolution 1929 and the other resolutions on Iran fully and faithfully, but China has also stated that it does not support sanctions beyond those contained in the UN resolutions. China has stated that it agrees with the United States that a nuclear-armed Iran would pose a grave regional and international threat. The United States is continuing to work closely with China on this issue. A number of PRC transfers to Iran resulted in U.S. trade penalties and sanctions against entities in China. Some weapons that PRC entities supplied to Iran were found to have been transferred to terrorist organizations in Iraq and Afghanistan. This is a serious issue that the United States continues to monitor.

Sudan: The PRC has at times used its influence with the Sudanese government to address in a positive way international concerns over Darfur and to support the implementation of the Comprehensive Peace Agreement between North and South Sudan. However, China has sided with Khartoum at the UN Security Council, including blocking targeted sanctions against Sudanese officials accused of atrocities. China continues to sell arms to Sudan despite the passage of UN Security Council Resolutions 1556 (2004) and 1591 (2005), both of which ban the transfer of arms to Darfur. Between 2004 and 2006, when the violence in Darfur was at its peak, 90 percent of small arms sales to Sudan were of PRC origin. The PRC argues that arms sales constitute part of normal commercial relations, and that the arms supplied by Chinese companies were not meant for use in Darfur. However, UN Group of Experts and NGO reports have demonstrated that Chinese arms have been used by the Sudanese government in combat operations in Darfur.

Conclusion

Beijing's approach to international engagement has evolved with its perception of its own interests in a dynamic security environment. As China's regional and international interests expand, so too will China's impetus for additional engagement, especially in the areas of peacekeeping operations, HA/DR, and joint exercises. In addition to furthering PLA modernization, these engagements will likely be geared toward building China's political ties, assuaging fears about China's rise, and expanding China's international influence, particularly in Asia.

Appendix I. China and Taiwan Forces Data

Taiwan Strait Military Balance, Ground Forces			
	China		Taiwan
	Total	Taiwan Strait Area	Total
Personnel (Active)	1.25 million	400,000	130,000
Group Armies	18	8	3
Infantry Divisions	17	5	0
Infantry Brigades	22	9	8
Mechanized Infantry Divisions	6	2	0
Mechanized Infantry Brigades	6	1	3
Armor Divisions	9	4	0
Armor Brigades	8	3	4
Artillery Divisions	2	2	0
Artillery Brigades	17	6	5
Airborne Divisions	3	3	0
Amphibious Divisions	2	2	0
Amphibious Brigades	3	3	3
Tanks	7,000	3,100	1,100
Artillery Pieces	8,000	3,400	1,600

Note: PLA active ground forces are organized into Group Armies. Infantry, armor, and artillery units are organized into a combination of divisions and brigades deployed throughout the PLA's seven MRs. A significant portion of these assets are deployed in the Taiwan Strait area, specifically the Nanjing, Guangzhou, and Jinan MRs. Taiwan has seven Defense Commands, three of which have Field Armies. Each Army contains an Artillery Command roughly equivalent to a brigade plus.

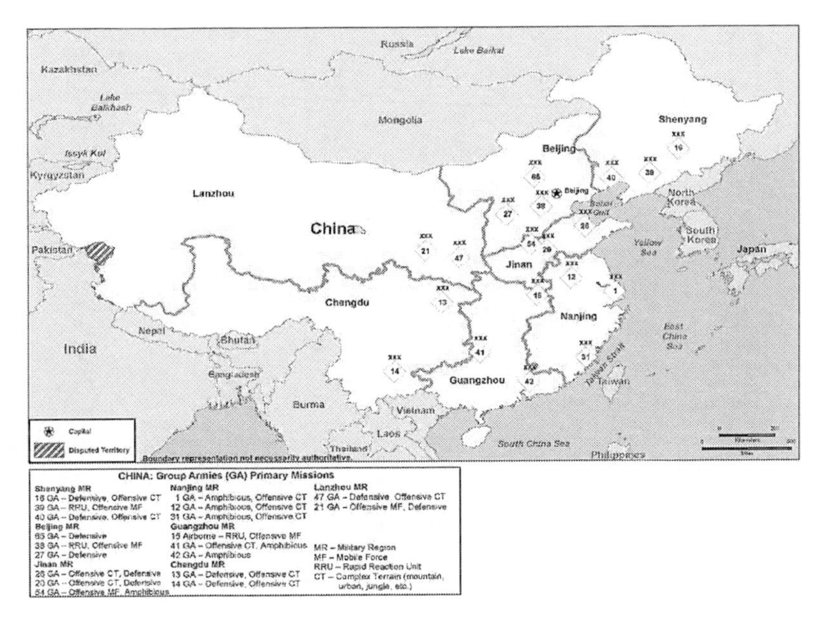

Major Ground Units.

Taiwan Strait Military Balance, Naval Forces			
	China		Taiwan
	Total	East and South Sea Fleets	Total
Destroyers	26	16	4
Frigates	53	44	22
Tank Landing Ships/ Amphibious Transport Dock	27	25	12
Medium Landing Ships	28	21	4
Diesel Attack Submarines	49	33	4
Nuclear Attack Submarines	5	2	0
Coastal Patrol (Missile)	86	68	61

Note: The PLA Navy has the largest force of principal combatants, submarines, and amphibious warfare ships in Asia. After years of neglect, the force of missile-armed patrol craft is also growing. In the event of a major Taiwan conflict, the East and South Sea Fleets would be expected to participate in direct action against the Taiwan Navy. The North Sea Fleet would be responsible primarily for protecting Beijing and the northern coast, but could provide mission-critical assets to support other fleets.

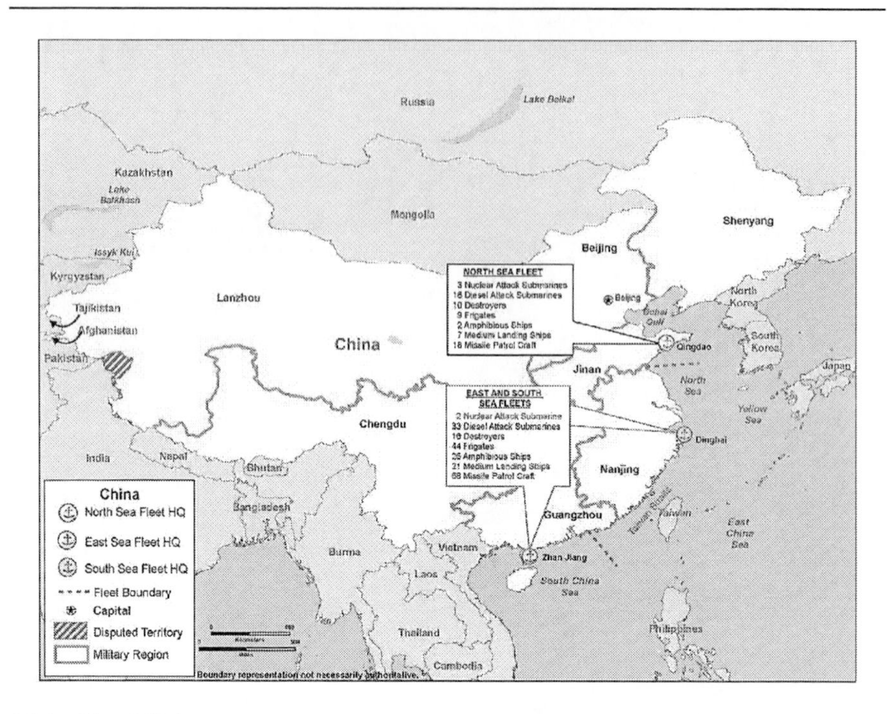

Major Naval Units.

Taiwan Strait Military Balance, Air Forces			
	China		Taiwan
Aircraft	Total	Within range of Taiwan	Total
Fighters	1,680	330	388
Bombers/Attack	620	160	22
Transport	450	40	21

Note: The PLAAF and the PLA Navy have approximately 2,300 operational combat aircraft. These consist of air defense and multi-role fighters, ground attack aircraft, fighter-bombers, and bombers. An additional 1,450 older fighters, bombers and trainers are employed for training and R&D. The two air arms also possess approximately 450 transports and over 100 surveillance and reconnaissance aircraft with intelligence, surface search, and airborne early warning capabilities. The majority of PLAAF and PLA Navy aircraft are based in the eastern half of the country. Currently, 490 aircraft could conduct combat operations against Taiwan without refueling. However, this number could be significantly increased through any combination of aircraft forward deployment, decreased ordnance loads, or altered mission profiles.

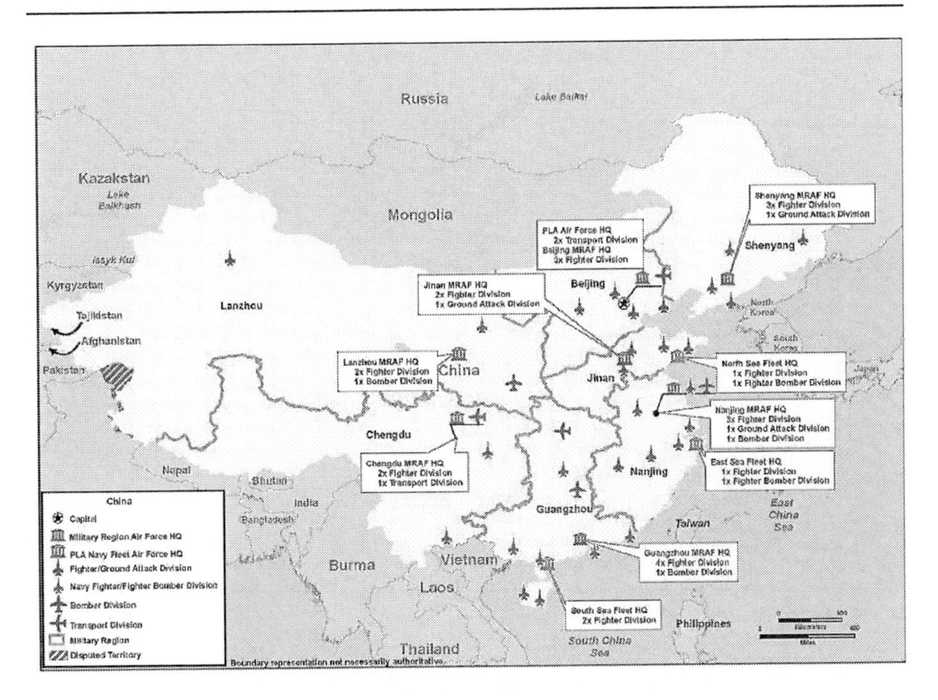

Major Air Units.

China's Missile Force			
System	Missiles	Launchers	Estimated Range
ICBM	50-75	50-75	5,400-13,000+ km
IRBM	5-20	5-20	3,000+ km
MRBM	75-100	75-100	1,750+ km
SRBM	1,000-1,200	200-250	300-600 km
GLCM	200-500	40-55	1,500+ km

APPENDIX II. MILITARY-TO-MILITARY EXCHANGES

Bilateral and Multilateral Exercises Since 2005

Year	Exercise Name	Type of Exercise	Participants
2005	China-India Friendship 2005	Search and Rescue	India
	China-Pakistan Friendship 2005	Search and Rescue	Pakistan
	China-Thailand Friendship 2005	Search and Rescue	Thailand
	Peace Mission 2005	Counter-terrorism	Russia
2006	Cooperation 2006	Counter-terrorism	Tajikistan
	Friendship 2006	Counter-terrorism	Pakistan
	Unnamed	Search and Rescue	United States

Appendix II. (Continued)

Year	Exercise Name	Type of Exercise	Participants
2007	Aman (Peace) 2007	Search and Rescue	Pakistan
	China-France Friendship 2007	Maritime	France
	China-Spain Friendship 2007	Maritime	Spain
	Cooperation 2007	Counter-terrorism	Russia
	Hand-in-Hand 2007	Counter-terrorism	India
	Peace Mission 2007	Counter-terrorism	Russia, Kazakhstan, Kyrgyzstan, Tajikistan, Uzbekistan
	Strike 2007	Counter-terrorism	Thailand
	Western Pacific Naval Symposium	Search and Rescue	United States, France, Japan, Australia, New Zealand, India, Pakistan, ROK, Singapore
	Unnamed	Maritime	India
	Unnamed	Search and Rescue	Australia, New Zealand
2008	Hand-in-Hand 2008	Counter-terrorism	India
	Strike 2008	Counter-terrorism	Thailand
2009	Aman (Peace) 2009	Maritime	Hosted by Pakistan (38 countries participated)
	Cooperation 2009	Counter-terrorism	Singapore
2009	Country-Gate Sharp Sword 2009	Counter-terrorism	Russia
	Peace Angel 2009	Medical	Gabon
	Peace Keeping Mission 2009	Peacekeeping Operations	Mongolia
	Peace Mission 2009	Counter-terrorism	Russia
	Peace Shield 2009	Counter-piracy	Russia
	Unnamed	Maritime	Singapore
2010	Blue Strike/Blue Assault 2010	Counter-terrorism	Thailand
	Cooperation 2010	Counter-terrorism	Singapore
	Friendship 2010	Counter-terrorism	Pakistan
	Friendship Action 2010	Ground (Mountain Warfare)	Romania
	Peace Angel 2010	Medical	Peru
	Peace M i ssi on 2010	Counter-terrorism	Russia, Kazakhstan, Kyrgyzstan, Tajikistan
	Strike 2010	Counter-terrorism	Thailand
	Unnamed	Search and Rescue	Australia
	Unnamed	Maritime	New Zealand
	Unnamed	Counter-Piracy	South Korea
	Unnamed	Search and Rescue	Taiwan
	Unnamed	Air	Turkey
	Unnamed	Ground	Turkey
	Unnamed	Search and Rescue	Vietnam

Chinese Involvement in bilateral and multilateral military exercises since 2005.

Countries Visited by Senior Chinese Military Leaders, 2005-2010

2005	2006	2007	2008	2009	2010
Argentina Bangladesh Cuba Denmark Egypt Germany India Kazakhstan Netherlands Philippines Russia Sudan Tajikistan Tanzania Turkey Uruguay	Australia Belarus Burma Cambodia Denmark France Hungary India Laos Malaysia New Zealand North Korea Norway Pakistan Romania Russia Singapore South Korea Tajikistan Thailand United States Vietnam	Argentina Chile Cuba Greece Japan Kuwait Kyrgyzstan Mongolia Philippines Russia South Korea Thailand United States Uzbekistan Vietnam	Bahrain Belarus Brazil Brunei Chile Germany Hungary India Indonesia Italy Japan Nepal Norway Oman Qatar Saudi Arabia Serbia- Montenegro Singapore South Korea Tajikistan Thailand United Arab Emirates Venezuela	Australia Bulgaria Burma Finland Germany Japan New Zealand North Korea Pakistan Papua New Guinea Russia Serbia- Montenegro Singapore Slovakia South Korea Thailand Turkey United States Vietnam	Angola Australia Brazil Colombia Congo Egypt Germany Indonesia Kazakhstan Kenya Macedonia Mexico Mongolia Namibia New Zealand North Korea Pakistan Romania Russia Serbia Singapore Tanzania

Senior Foreign Military Officials Visiting China in 2010

Afghanistan Algeria Angola Australia Austria Azerbaijan Belarus Bolivia Burma Cambodia Congo Cuba Ethiopia Ghana Greece	Guyana India Italy Japan Laos Lebanon Macedonia Montenegro Nepal New Zealand North Korea Norway Oman Pakistan Poland	Qatar Rwanda Serbia Singapore Switzerland Thailand Tonga Turkey Uganda United Arab Emirates United Kingdom Vietnam Zambia Zimbabwe

This list includes visits by senior defense officials and chiefs of the armed services. It excludes visits associated with multilateral military exercises.

In: Military and Security Developments in China ISBN 978-1-61942-009-0
Editors: A. Leehy and J. Wildstein

Chapter 2

DEPARTMENT OF DEFENSE PRESS BRIEFING ON THE 2011 ANNUAL REPORT TO CONGRESS: MILITARY AND SECURITY DEVELOPMENTS INVOLVING THE PEOPLE'S REPUBLIC OF CHINA

Presenter: Michael Schiffer, Deputy Assistant Secretary of Defense for East Asia[*]

August 24, 2011

MICHAEL SCHIFFER: Good afternoon, everybody. For those of you that I haven't had a chance to introduce myself yet to, I'm Michael Schiffer, the deputy assistant secretary of defense for East Asia. And I'm here this afternoon to talk to you all about the "Report to Congress on Military and Security Developments Involving the People's Republic of China" that we delivered up to Capitol Hill today.

I'll offer a few broad thoughts on the report, a couple of points about the administration's overall approach to China and then walk you through in some

* This is an edited, reformatted and augmented version of a Department of Defense Press Briefing on the 2011 Annual Report to Congress publication, dated August 24, 2011.

degree of detail - hopefully, not too painful - what's in the report this year, and then we'll have time for whatever questions you may have.

The report, as many of you know, is a report from the secretary of defense transmitted to Congress, but it is a report that we coordinate broadly across the interagency and across the entire U.S. Government, so that even though it is a DOD report, it does reflect the views and perspectives that are held broadly by the U.S. Government.

We very much intend this report to be something that is factual, objective and analytical to provide inputs and information for policymakers both in the legislative and the executive branch to consider as they contemplate the development of U.S. policy and the bilateral relationship between the United States and China.

This year's report contains new information on a number of topics, including new sections on China's evolving maritime strategy and its growing military involvement and engagement with other countries.

Let me first, as I said, offer a couple of general comments on U.S.-China relations and then the overview of the report itself.

As you know from statements that numerous senior U.S. Government officials have made, the United States welcomes a strong, prosperous and successful China that contributes to international rules and norms and enhances security and peace both in the Asia-Pacific Region and around the globe. The United States is pursuing a positive, cooperative, and comprehensive relationship with China capable of addressing common global challenges and advancing our shared interests.

China's expanding military capabilities have enabled it to contribute to the delivery of international public goods, from peacekeeping and counter-piracy to humanitarian assistance and disaster relief. However, the pace and scope of China's sustained military investments have allowed China to pursue capabilities that we believe are potentially destabilizing to regional military balances, increase the risk of misunderstanding and miscalculation, and may contribute to regional tensions and anxieties.

Such capabilities could increase Beijing's options for using military force to gain diplomatic advantage, advance its interests or resolve military disputes - resolve disputes in its favor.

And this very much speaks to the logic that we see for sustained and reliable military-to-military dialogue and military security dialogue between the United States and China so that we are able to gain the sort of transparency and strategic understanding that's necessary to forge that positive, cooperative, and comprehensive relationship.

And in fact, in many ways I might suggest that the report can best be read not simply as a piece of analysis but really as the sets of questions and issues that we would like to be able to engage in dialogue and discussion with our Chinese counterparts about. These are the questions and the issues that we think that it's important for us to be able to understand; we know our Chinese friends have questions for and about us; and that's the sort of dialogue and discussion that we welcome and that we think contributes to regional and global security and stability.

Over the next decade from 2011 to 2020, we believe that there will be a number of critical elements in play as we look at Chinese military modernization as the PLA attempts to integrate a number of new and complex platforms that they've developed and to adopt modern operational concepts, including joint operations and network-centric warfare. Indeed, as the report discusses, there are a number of new Chinese platforms and weapons systems that have reached maturity in recent years and others that we believe will soon become operational. And these are new systems that are on par with or exceed global standards.

But these efforts to integrate across systems and platforms will be a key marker in China's continued military modernization efforts going forward.

We believe that the PLA continues to be on track to achieve its goal of building a modern, regionally focused military by 2020. However, China's ability to sustain military power at a distance today remains limited.

As many of you know, as many of you reported, on August 10th of this year, China commenced sea trials with the Kuznetsov-class aircraft carrier that it purchased from the Ukraine in 1998. Our report, which was written and coordinated before this development, conveyed our expectation that sea trials would commence this year.

The aircraft carrier could become operationally available to China's navy by the end of 2012, we assess, but without aircraft. It will take a number of additional years for an air group to achieve the sort of minimal level of combat capability aboard the carrier that will be necessary for them to start to operate from the carrier itself.

China continues to invest heavily in undersea warfare with a mixture of nuclear and conventionally powered submarines. This is complemented by China's investment in new surface combatants designed to improve the PLA navy's capabilities for anti-surface and anti-air warfare. The PLA has now completed construction of a major naval base on Hainan Island. And this base, we assess, is large enough to accommodate a mix of ballistic missiles, submarines and large surface combatants, including aircraft carriers.

China also continues to invest heavily in air capabilities, including modern aircraft and long-range advanced surface-to-air missile systems. This past January - again, as many of you reported - China conducted a flight test of the next-generation fighter prototype, the J-20, which highlighted China's ambition to produce a fighter aircraft that incorporates stealth attributes, advanced avionics, and supercruise-capable engines.

China's also investing heavily in an array of space programs. China conducted a national record of 15 space launches in 2010, which includes both civilian and military systems.

Turning away from force development and to another issue that I know is of interest to you all, and that's cross-strait relations, as the report assesses, in the political, diplomatic, economic and cultural field, cross-strait relations have continued to improve over the past couple of years. But despite this political warning - warming, China's military shows no signs of slowing its effort to prepare for a cross-strait contingency. In addition to planning for Taiwan contingencies, China places a high priority on asserting and strengthening its maritime territorial claims. An increased PLA naval presence in the region, including surface, subsurface and airborne platforms and possibly one or more of China's future aircraft carriers, would provide the PLA with an enhanced extended-range power projection capability, with all the implications for regional rivalries and power dynamics that that implies.

The PLA has also in recent years demonstrated the capability to conduct limited peacetime deployments of modern forces outside Asia. This includes multiple counterpiracy deployments to the Gulf of Aden and increasing participation in international humanitarian and disaster release - relief efforts. Investments in large amphibious ships, a new hospital ship, long-range transport aircraft and improved logistics have made these sorts of missions a practical reality.

These types of peacetime operations provide the PLA with a valuable operational experience and also serve PRC diplomatic objectives.

China's comprehensive military modernization efforts are supported by robust increases in government funding. On March 4th of this year Beijing announced a 12.7 percent increase in its military budget, and that continues more than two decades of sustained budgetary growth.

The PLA has also made some modest but incremental improvements in transparency in recent years, but there are a number of uncertainties that remain. We will continue, and we do continue, to encourage China to improve transparency and openness, to act in ways that support and strengthen common political, economic and diplomatic interests of the region and of the international community.

The complexity of the global security environment as well as the advances in China's military capabilities and its expanding military operations and missions calls for continuous military-to-military dialogue between our two defense and security establishments. This is a dialogue that we believe can help us to expand practical cooperation where our national interests converge and also provide us the ability and the opportunity to discuss candidly those areas where we may have disagreements. Such dialogue, such engagements we believe is especially important during periods of friction and turbulence in the bilateral relationship.

During their January 2011 summit, President Obama and PRC President Hu Jintao jointly affirmed that a healthy, stable, and reliable military-to-military relationship is an essential part of the shared vision for a positive, cooperative, and comprehensive U.S.-China relationship. We believe - and we will continue to use military engagement with China as one of several means to demonstrate U.S. commitment to the security of the Asia-Pacific region, to encourage China to play a constructive role in the region and to press China to partner with the United States and our Asian allies and partners in addressing common security challenges.

So let me just wrap up by offering that we hope that the report, which we think has a lot of very interesting and useful - we hope has a lot of very interesting and useful information and analysis in it, will contribute in a responsible fashion to the many debates that are ongoing with respect to the military dimension of China's military modernization.

And with that, let me turn to your questions.

Q: You said at the beginning that the Chinese military buildup was destabilizing, and then you went through a whole long list of what the Chinese have done. Can you specifically say which part of that buildup is -- you consider destabilizing, which aspects that you referred to?

MR. SCHIFFER: I think I said that it was potentially destabilizing. And that speaks, again, to the importance of being able to have, not just between the United States and China but between China and the other countries of the region, deep, sustained, continuous and reliable discussions and engagement between our military and security establishments so that we can better understand China's intentions, China's thinking and approach, and so that they can better understand ours.

I think absent that, and given the lack of transparency that - even with the improvements that I cited, that still persists, that's where you have the potential to run into situations where there may be misunderstandings or miscalculations, where you would have the potential for anxiety driving a destabilizing dynamic.

Q: So just - so it's not the actual buildup of the stealth fighter or the aircraft carrier, it's the fact that the Chinese - the potentially destabilizing aspect of this is the Chinese are not transparent enough and talking enough.

(Off mic.)

MR. SCHIFFER: Well, I think it's a combination of that lack of understanding that's coming out - that has been created by the opacity of their system.

But I mean, it is also because there are very real questions, given the overall trends and trajectory in the scope and the scale of China's military modernization efforts. I wouldn't put it on any one particular platform or any one particular system. There's nothing particularly magical about any one particular item. But when you put together the entirety of what we've witnessed over the past several decades and, you know, we see these trend lines continuing off into the future, that raises questions. And as I said, again, that's why we think that it's important to be able to have the sorts of dialogues and discussions that will allow us to understand each other better and will help to contribute to regional stability.

Q: I mean, for years the report has addressed the same trend in the Taiwan Strait, that the military balance has shifted to China's favor. In this report, is there, you know, a tipping point that we are anticipating, like in 2020 Taiwan will lose its superiority or the, you know, quality advantage?

And the second question is that when General Chen Bingde is here - was here in Washington, he mentioned that there was no missile pointing at China across -- according to Taiwan, across the strait. I don't know from this report, you know, what's U.S. -- you know, estimate or evaluation.

MR. SCHIFFER: I would offer that I don't think there is a - there's not a particular tipping point, which I know may come as something of a disappointment as one thinks about how to construct the perfect newspaper headline.

But there are trends, as the report points to, that continue to be - you know, that continue to point to a very challenging military and security environment across the strait. That is a set of issues that we're committed to working with Taiwan to address, committed to meeting our commitments under the Taiwan Relations Act, in the context of the one-China policy and the three joint communiqués to assure that Taiwan has the self-defense capabilities that it needs. And that is something that obviously continues to be a concern of the Department of Defense and, indeed, the entire U.S. Government.

I will let General Chen try to clarify or characterize his own comments and what he intended and what he meant.

Please.

Q: You mentioned - from Reuters - you mentioned aircraft carriers in your spoken presentation as well. And it's touched on in the report. There have been reports since the period (of the compilation that China has indeed begun building its own indigenous carriers. Can you comment on those reports at all?

MR. SCHIFFER: We do think that China is undertaking an effort to build its own indigenous aircraft carriers. And our expectations - and again, this is addressed in the report - are that we will see Chinese indigenous aircraft carriers. I won't speculate on the number, but likely more than one being developed in the future.

Yes.

Q: Did you share this report with the Chinese government or embassy? And if so, what was your message to them?

And did the Pakistanis show the helicopter tail that was left behind during the bin Laden raid to the Chinese? Did they - were they able to obtain any information about stealth technology from that?

MR. SCHIFFER: So far the report has been briefed to Congress, and now, of course, our second-most - possibly most important audience, which is you all. We have a number of engagements with a range of people in the diplomatic community both here in the United States and overseas planned over the next several days to provide briefings on the report. You'll excuse me if I will take a pass on going into any details on any of the messages that we'll be delivering in any of those discussions.

I will also take a pass because for all the reasons that you know and not comment on the Pakistan issue and the helicopter tail.

Yeah, Tony.

Q: On the F-16s - you know, it's a hot-button issue - is there anything in this report that you feel, as a professional political-military student of Chinese capability, buttresses the case for additional non-stealthy F-16s to Taiwan?

MR. SCHIFFER: Luckily, I'm not a professional military student of Chinese capabilities, so, you know, that gives me a pass on your question.

Q: (Off mic.)

MR. SCHIFFER: (Chuckles.) Look, you know, there's no question - I don't think it's a secret to anybody - that it is a very challenging security environment across the strait. But I would point out that it is a very challenging security environment across the strait - and the report discuses this in some level of detail - across a number of different dimensions. And we are working very, very closely with Taiwan, as we have for many, many years now across administrations of both political parties, to make sure that they have the self-defense capabilities that they need. And we will continue to do so.

Q: Can I ask you one quick one? Has the Pentagon rejected a new sale of F-16s? Have they -- have you recommended rejecting a sale of new F-16s? There's been reports out of the region to that effect.

MR. SCHIFFER: I know that there have been reports out of the region to that effect, yes.

Q: Can you answer the -- whether -- the status of the issue? Have you made a recommendation to the White House saying, we don't -- we don't recommend a new sale?

MR. SCHIFFER: I will simply offer that there have been no decisions that have been made on arms sales to Taiwan. But as I said before, I mean, this is an issue that we continue to work -- in my office, we work with this question on a daily basis. And consistent with our obligations under the Taiwan Relations Act, the United States will provide to Taiwan the self-defense capabilities that it requires.

Q: Would you see a possible contradiction should the -- your department or the U.S. Government decide later on that F- 16C/Ds would not be sold to Taiwan on one hand; on the other hand, the report has -- you know, it's featured in the report that the military balance across the Taiwan Strait is, you know, continuing to move in -- to the advantage of China? Do you see a potential contradiction there? Are you concerned?

MR. SCHIFFER: As I said earlier, there -- this is a challenging security environment. It's a challenging security environment across a number of different dimensions, not just one and not just a security environment where to take the tipping point question and turn it around, where there is some, you know, silver bullet that will all of a sudden change everything. We are committed to working, consistent with the Taiwan Relations Act, with Taiwan, and consistent with the one-China policy and the three joint communiqués, to make sure that Taiwan has the self-defense capabilities that it needs across a range of a range of dimensions.

Kevin, I can –

Q: Mike, can you detail, beyond the visits by Gates and Mullen, any military exchanges going on between the U.S. and China in the interest of transparency? And in the case of the aircraft carrier sea trials, will -- was there any type of notification or action between the two -- your two sides for that, you know, first high-profile event since these big visits have, you know, made those pledges to be more transparent?

MR. SCHIFFER: We - I mean, we've engaged with the PLA in a number of working-level discussions and meetings over the course of the year, and I'd be happy to make sure that we can provide you or anybody else that's interested with the full list. But since Secretary Gates went in January of this year, we had defense policy coordination talks, which are held at my level. We've had a working group meeting of the Military Maritime Consultative Agreement. Just last week there were a number of people from my team here in the Pentagon and the Joint Staff that were in Beijing having working-level discussions about transparency and a number of other related issues. So there has been a fair amount of stuff that's been - that's been going on at the - at the working level even as we've also had these senior-level contacts.

The one other thing that I would point to is that, as many of you may know, we had established at the Strategic and Economic Dialogue this year a new joint civil-military dialogue, something that Secretary Gates had called for when he was in China in January, to allow us to discuss sensitive security issues, those things that might be most troubling for stability in the bilateral relationship in a setting that brings together both civilian and military leaders on both sides at a fairly senior level.

That's not strictly a mil-mil engagement, but that does speak to our efforts to institutionalize and regularize and deepen these sorts of dialogues and discussions with the People's Republic of China.

Yeah.

Q: Where does cyber capability fit into the matrix of China's developing capabilities that you call potentially destabilizing?

MR. SCHIFFER: We have some analysis of where we think the Chinese are going in the cyber realm and - in the report, and I guess I should do the commercial here that says that, you know, this is really a report - and I say this with all sincerity - that we really do like to allow to speak for itself, because there's a lot of very good stuff in here. And so, I'd recommend that you sort of dive into the report to pull out some of that analysis.

But you know, it's no secret, again, that, you know, cyber is a realm where deeper engagement between the United States and China, so that we can work on common rules of the road and a common way forward, is necessary. You know, we have some concerns about some of the things that we've seen, and we want to be able to work through that with China.

Yeah.

Q: (Inaudible) - this is a report that's subject to a lengthy interagency review, but it was also due in March. Could you give us any more insight as to why it took so many months to actually produce this? Were there any sticking points in the internal discussions about this?

MR. SCHIFFER: There were no - you know, I realize a good conspiracy is, you know, a lot more fun than just sort the simple banal truth of bureaucracies grinding away on a daily basis. You know, this is a very, very complex and important set of issues, as I -- as I know you all appreciate.

To turn out a good product, and to turn out a good product that we were able to coordinate across the U.S. Government, because we think that it benefits greatly from that sort of coordination, simply -- simply took time. I, you know, wish that it didn't, wish we had been able to turn it out -- to turn it out quicker, but I think the results, when you have the chance to read through the report, speak to the benefits of taking that time to really turn out a product that -- that I think -- and I don't just say this because I'm paid to say it -- but that I think really has a lot of very, very good, cogent content and analysis.

In the back.

Q: I didn't see any discussion of China's holding of American debt. And I'm curious how you see these fiscal issues play into the larger security picture between the U.S. and China.

MR. SCHIFFER: That - those sorts of issues aren't included in this report because that is, at least as our current congressional mandate -- reads a little bit outside the scope of the report and, frankly, outside the scope or the expertise of the Department of Defense. I mean, I'll simply say that this is obviously an extraordinarily complex economic relationship that -- that we have with China and an extraordinarily complex relationship that creates challenges on both sides. And I know that that's receiving a lot of extraordinarily high-level attention from both our leadership, including Vice President Biden on his -- on his trip the other week, and from China's leadership.

Q: You mentioned some of the humanitarian and disaster-relief kind of work the Chinese navy is engaged in.

How great of an emphasis do you see them placing on those sort of operations? Do you see it as a -- as almost as great of an emphasis as the U.S. has placed on it, or do you see it just kind of staying as a side mission for them?

MR. SCHIFFER: China's still, you know, in the relatively early stages of engaging fully in the region and with the international community as a provider of those sorts of goods and services. But as I said, I mean, this is something that we view as a -- as a positive development. And we want to encourage China to join with -- to join with the United States and our other allies and partners in the region and around the globe in providing those sorts of capabilities and those sorts of assets. I mean, a China that helps to respond to the threats of piracy, a China that helps to respond to humanitarian assistance and disaster relief needs, and that is playing that sort of positive and constructive role in global affairs. I mean, that's -- that's a very good thing for the United States, that's a very good thing for the region, that's a very good thing for the world.

Q: And to follow up, is -- are they interested in kind of the same regions that the U.S. are? Is there some divergence there?

MR. SCHIFFER: There -- I mean, this is a question, frankly, that, you know, you should address to -- you know, address to folks on the Chinese side to get a better sense of their current thinking. But they're -- you know, they're still, as I said, in the relatively early stages of developing their own thinking as to how they're going out into the world and conduct these operations. Although, I would point out that I think they have something like close to 18,000 folks that have participated in peacekeeping operations, you know, in recent years, which is a sizeable contribution and that's -- you know, and a number of different peacekeeping missions.

Yeah, in the very back row there.

Q: The aircraft carrier, just coming back to that: How big a deal is that? And can that development be seen in a positive light -- (inaudible)?

MR. SCHIFFER: You know, I think this is something that as I -- as I said, doesn't come as any surprise to us.

I mean, this was a development that the Chinese have been -- have been working on for -- for a number of years, and it's not at all, you know, out of character or, you know, out of -- out of the norm of the sorts of development given -- you know, given the trajectory of China's military modernization efforts over the past -- over the past couple decades.

Whether or not this proves to be a -- you know, a net plus for the region or for the globe or proves to be something that has destabilizing effects and raises blood pressure in various regional capitals I think remains to be seen; and again, not to sound like a broken record, but underscores the importance of being able to have those dialogues that allow us to reach greater strategic understanding and aim for a -- for a degree of strategic trust, not just between the United States and China, but China and its other neighbors as well.

COL LAPAN: (Off mic) We have time for one or two more.

MR. SCHIFFER: OK.

Q: You've been -- there's been a lot of discussion of the carrier, but the report also talks a great deal about the other naval capabilities the Chinese have been developing. What kind of capabilities in here do you find most noteworthy or most troubling or most of concern?

MR. SCHIFFER: Again, you know, there's no single capability that I find to be, you know, either most noteworthy or most troubling or most of concern. It is the overall trajectory of China's military modernization efforts and the fact that they are, you know, working across a number of different dimensions of power in the maritime domain that is -- that is something that I think we need to keep an eye on, need to assure that we in turn have the -- have the capabilities in place to safeguard our national security interests, need to work with our allies and partners on their -- on their capacities and their capabilities and, again, need to engage with China so that we can have a better and deeper understanding of how we're both -- how we're each approaching issues in the naval and in the maritime domain.

We can have one last question.

Q: If past years are any guide, China will generally react angrily to the release of this report. It seems like they resent the enterprise itself, let alone the contents. Is China mistaken in thinking of this report as a hostile act towards China? And in your own mil-mil dealings, have you ever received more nuanced feedback from Chinese counterparts on this report?

MR. SCHIFFER: My expectations, like yours, is that, you know, our Chinese friends will very likely have some critical comments to say about the issuance of this report. As we've tried to explain to them in our military-to-military engagements, I mean, the report can be read, and I hope that they do look at it as, an encapsulation of the sorts of questions and the sorts of issues that we have questions about, that we would like to be able to engage in discussion and dialogue with them on; and that it's our sense that if we are able to have that sort of robust, reliable, continuous military-to-military dialogue, that that will lead to a more positive relationship between the United States and China and will help contribute to regional stability and security.

So thank you all very much. I hope that was -- hope that was helpful.

INDEX

C

D

E

N

O

P

Q

R

S

T

U

V

W

Z

You're N

Xandria Williams began her career as a geochemist involved in mineral exploration but soon turned to biochemistry and the study of nutrition, naturopathy, homeopathy and botanic medicine. She then extended her studies to Neurolinguistic Programming, Time-Line Therapy, Voice Dialogue and many other methods of helping people with emotional, personal and psychological problems.

She has lectured extensively at many natural therapies colleges and conferences and holds classes and seminars on a range of aspects of physical, mental and emotional health care. She has written several hundred articles, has often been heard on radio and television and is the author of *Living with Allergies, What's in your Food, Osteoporosis, Choosing Health Intentionally, Choosing Weight Intentionally, Stress – Recognise and Resolve, Beating the Blues, Love, Health and Happiness* and *Fatigue.*

Xandria Williams has evolved her unique and highly effective approach to tackling life's problems over two decades of research into helping people at her clinics in Sydney and London, in her seminars and through her books and articles.

Xandria is now based in London and can be contacted for consultations on: Ph/Fax 0171-824-8153.

Also by Xandria Williams

Living with Allergies
What's in your Food
Osteoporosis
Choosing Health Intentionally
Choosing Weight Intentionally
Stress – Recognise and Resolve
Beating the Blues*
Love, Health and Happiness
Fatigue*

**available in Cedar*

XANDRIA WILLIAMS

You're Not Alone

A Mandarin Paperback
YOU'RE NOT ALONE

First published in Great Britain 1997
as a Cedar original
by Mandarin Paperbacks
an imprint of Reed International Books Ltd
Michelin House, 81 Fulham Road, London SW3 6RB
and Auckland, Melbourne, Singapore and Toronto

A CIP catalogue record for this title
is available from the British Library
ISBN 0 7493 2216 0

Printed and bound in Great Britain
by Cox & Wyman Ltd, Reading, Berkshire

Contents

Contents

Part III – Practicalities

Introduction

The basic idea behind this book is simple. Loneliness is a state of mind, your mind; and your state of mind results from thoughts and actions, *your* thoughts and *your* actions. Further, it is you that is in charge of your thoughts and your state of mind and it is you, and only you, that can change them. In other words, you, and only you, have the key that will free you from your loneliness. There is also no one who can interfere with your use of this key if and when you choose to use it.

If you are waiting for the magic event, the outside act, that will transform your loneliness into happiness then this may not be what you wanted to hear, but think a minute. This is actually an exciting thought, with powerful and positive consequences. It means that the key to resolving all your problems lies within yourself. Any time you choose, given tools such as those in this book, you can turn anything in your life with which you are not happy into an alternative situation that gives you the result you want.

Having said that, you may be feeling that that is all very well but you *are* lonely, that you *do not* want to be lonely, that you *have* tried to change the situation and failed, and that it is *not* your fault. So let's deal with those thoughts first, at least briefly. You may say, in answer to the suggestion that your state of mind, in this case your loneliness, is something you have created, that it isn't true, that your loneliness is not your fault. No one is saying it is a fault. There is no question here of right and wrong, good and bad, or praise and blame, and certainly not of faults or guilt. There is simply what is. It is safe to assume that no one sets out, fundamentally, to harm themselves. It is therefore also safe to assume that whatever you have done in your life that has led to your present state of loneliness was done with the best of intentions and in the anticipation of a happy outcome. However, you are now in a situation where you feel lonely. Let's now find out what you can do, from this point on, to achieve your present desired outcome, which we are assuming is the cessation of loneliness.

I stress this point because the concept of self-responsibility can immediately lead some people down the avenue of self-blame if they feel their life is not the way they want it to be. Instead, this whole concept of personal responsibility and personal power is an empowering one and one that can take you to whatever destination you desire. This is a welcome cause for celebration, since you are in control and are not dependent on someone 'out there', and you don't have to wait, hoping that they will choose to wave a magic wand over you to create the perfect life for you.

Let's take a concrete example. A man leaves his wife. She remains faithful, hoping he will come back and that this will be a point in her favour. As a result she is lonely. Friends may say her loneliness is her fault, that she has caused it by refusing to go out with other men. She may argue it is her husband's fault, that he has caused it and that she would not be lonely if he had not left her. Ultimately, however, it is *she* that has chosen the path of the single life in the hope that he will return. She has nominated her preferences. She could have chosen otherwise. Ultimately her actions may lead to the result she is after, or they may not. The point is that she has taken what, given all her underlying motives and thoughts, she thinks is the best course of action for her. If, at some point, she decides she is too lonely and wants to make a change it is up to her to do so. No one else can do it for her, no one else can stop her once she decides to make the changes, and no one can say she is right or wrong in either action.

The powerful point is that you are in control and can, if you don't like the way you feel, change your state of mind. You can do this simply by allowing your thoughts to change the way you feel, or you can do it by allowing your thoughts to change your actions, and hence the way you feel.

Your employer, for instance, may have sent you to an isolated place to work for a couple of years. You can blame the loneliness on him or accept responsibility for it yourself and change your own state of mind. After all, you could leave the job and return to the city. The fact that you haven't suggests that you feel you have more to gain by staying with the company. Alternatively, you can make the decision to leave the job and return to the city. Either way, recognise the benefits you have chosen, stop blaming your boss and decide what you can do to improve the present.

If, after considering what has been said here, you find yourself still saying such things as 'It's not my fault'. 'I can't help it', 'It's all so-and-so's fault', 'People ought to . . .' or 'There's nothing I can do', then stop and consider this. Is the way you are thinking now making you happy? Is what you are doing now making you happy? Is your current complaining making you happy? If not, how about making a change? How about considering some different ways of thinking and acting? What have you got to lose? On top of that, the changes just might make you happier than you had ever thought possible.

Other books have already been written telling you how to meet people, how to avoid being alone, how to be more involved with others. That is not the aim, here, or at least only to a small extent. Anyone who has ever complained of being lonely has almost certainly been told, by well-meaning friends and family, even by counsellors, to go out and join a club, enrol in evening classes or do voluntary work. All these things have their place, it is true, but to overcome real loneliness much more is needed. Later in the book there will be some practical suggestions. Initially, however, it is what is going on inside your head and among your emotions that is so important and upon which we will be focusing.

Loneliness is a state of mind. The ultimate solution, **the first part** dealing with loneliness, for you and every other individual is to come to a full acceptance of the sometimes unpalatable fact that each one of us is indeed a lone individual, to embrace that fact fully, to rejoice in it and to build a life based firmly on your comfortable experience of this reality.

Everyone, at the deepest level, is on their own. There is no one 'out there' who is totally involved with you. There is no one 'out there' who is primarily interested in you above all others, who puts your needs above their own, who is focused on being there when you need and want them and who will provide for and take care of all your needs, physical, mental and emotional. From time to time you may seem to have found such a person, but even then you may be in for some disappointments, some ways in which they do not exactly fulfil your needs. Everyone else is another individual, another person, also dealing with being on *their* own, with *their* own needs, desires and wants.

Perhaps you feel that for you the solution to loneliness

is to have other people caring for you, wanting to be with you, asking for your company. Perhaps you do feel that if you search hard enough, and the fates are kind, you will eventually find your soul mate and your loneliness will be solved. If the solution to your loneliness is based on the presence of the perfect partner, what will happen if that perfect partner lets you down or is no longer there? What happens if that perfect partner needs your support in such a way that it endangers your own security, happiness and personal needs? Who do you put first? Who do they put first? Which one of you will experience loneliness as a result of the needs of the other?

Ultimately the secure solution to loneliness is to be fully content with yourself. Be your own best friend, your own best companion, your own best support, be sufficient unto yourself. Once you have achieved that you have not only achieved peace, contentment, happiness and a rich emotional experience within yourself, but you also have the most to give to other people and to the many and varied relationships that will quickly fill your life. When you can give from a base of inner security and happiness you can give freely. When you can give without having to have a need of your own filled in the process you have the most to offer, both to yourself and to other people.

This does not mean that you have to prefer being on your own to having company. You may still be an outgoing extrovert, loving to have friends around you and to do things as part of the crowd. It does mean, however, that if you are on your own that is fine too. You may even come to relish the contrast and to want to have certain periods of time to yourself. It also means that if the 'right' person is not there, if the people you are with are not doing the 'right' thing, by your needs, that is fine too. You are free to enjoy what is there, knowing you are secure within yourself.

Once you can be content with yourself you no longer enter relationships as a supplicant, as someone with needs, as someone wanting to take money out of the account. You are no longer a drain on other people, demanding their time, their attention, their focus on you. You now enter relationships with something to give, something to share. You can enjoy your various relationships for what they are, sufficient unto themselves. You need no longer measure them on the scale of how much they achieve in providing for your needs, for filling the gaps in your life.

Coming to terms, fully, with the concept of yourself as an individual is a key part of overcoming loneliness.

The second part is, of course, finding the people with whom you want to share your time. For most people this means finding an ideal partner and building a loving relationship. It also means having the family you want, the friends and social life you want. It means having the work, the daily activity and the colleagues you want. It also means having people who share your interests, in the arts, in the sciences, in home and family, in politics and current affairs, in sport and hobbies, in exploration and adventure. It means people with whom you can have fun and can share and explore ideas and emotions that are important to you. It means having people around who want and value what you have to offer. If you love to give to friends and family in a social setting it means having people who like to receive what you have to give, people who like to accept your offerings and your invitations. If you love to paint, write, sing or act, to make things, it means having an audience or recipients who appreciate the results of your work. If you love to pursue certain hobbies, sports and/or interests it means having the facilities to do so, the garden to garden, the library to read, the animals to work with, the tools and resources to pursue your interests, the people you need to be there as co-participants.

Some people love to have huge crowds of people around them, they love to be part of a big family, they feel happy when endless friends drop in, when they are doing things in large groups of people. If this suits you then the second part of dealing with loneliness is to find these groups of people. The role you play within this large group can vary:

- You may want to be the centre of attention, the recipient of adulation, the actor or actress, the performer, the raconteur, or simply the one to whom others listen and whose company they enjoy and seek out knowing they too will have a good time as a result of your presence.
- You may want to be one of the leaders or the high achievers, admired and acknowledged by the people around you, the one who takes the initiative and makes the decisions.
- You may want to be one of the nurturers or carers, finding your role in giving to others, loving to help them and to provide succour and comfort. It may be you who does the cooking, provides the transport, makes the arrangements, and is there when needed for babysitting, an ear to listen, or hands to make what is needed.
- Or you may like to be part of the crowd in a more passive sense, not wanting the limelight, not wanting to set the pace, but happy to be part of the group, to maintain the traditions and routines of life and to be at ease, confident that things will continue along well-worn paths.

Other people like to be on their own, feeling more lonely

in large groups where they are lost, and much more comfortable when relating to only one or two people. You may even like to spend large amounts of time on your own, needing this time and space to 'reunite' with yourself. Consider again the four types of people above:

- You may like to 'perform' by sharing ideas and activities with just one other person. You may like to create in private, sharing of yourself through the final result, the garden, the meal on the table, the work of art, the completed project.
- You may like to lead and to achieve but to do so without a high level of involvement with the people around you. You may prefer to hold yourself apart from the crowd. You may need and want time to yourself, to escape, to be on your own. Yet you may still need the people, the knowledge that what you do is eventually appreciated by others.
- You may still like to care for others, and so need the people to care for, but to do so without being visible; you may be embarrassed if attention is drawn to your contribution, you may want time for quiet contemplation, for thought and reflection on the meaning of life, the search for the purpose behind what you are doing.
- Or you may simply want to remain part of the crowd, content to be the audience, to feel a part of the whole.

In any of these roles you may even prefer to be solitary much of the time. Yet the role, your part in the whole, whether large or small, makes you feel part of the situation, part of the life of the people around you, and stops you feeling lonely.

Whether you are an extrovert or an introvert you can be lonely. Whether you are an extrovert or an introvert it is important that, having fully come to terms with being an individual, as already discussed, you find the level of companionship you want. You need to shape the environment of your life to suit your own particular needs and desires.

The third part of dealing with loneliness is coming to terms with your own level of needs and wants and not feeling you have to conform to some standard set by society, by other people. There are people who love to be part of a crowd but feel ashamed of this need, feeling it may indicate a lack of depth and self-sufficiency within themselves. There are others who feel ashamed and uncomfortable when they live a life with very few friends, fearing that others will take this as a measure of their unpopularity or inadequacy.

It is important that you recognise that there is no 'norm', no perfect way to be. Nor are there people with the right to judge you, unless you give them this right by deciding you must live your life by conforming to their standards rather than to your own.

There will also be times in your life when you need people and times when you don't. There will be times and situations when you have to make a special effort to come to terms with a situation that, at least on the surface, is not of your choosing. Such times may include when you leave home and set up house on your own, when a partner leaves you or you leave them, when you lose people you love, lose a job, miss an opportunity or retire and wonder who you are, now your job no longer gives you a label. They also include times when you have to do things to fit in with those around you, such as entertaining for your spouse, or doing what is expected of you as a parent, as a company employee or as a member of your local community.

In some of the above situations you may feel more lonely than other people think you should, you may feel less lonely than they think you should. So what? The important thing is for you to come to terms with yourself and your own needs and to learn, not only how to deal with them, but also to feel comfortable with yourself even if your feelings do not conform with those of the people around you or what they expect.

So we have a three-part journey to take together. As we explore the concept of loneliness, what it means to different people in general and you in particular, how to deal with it and how to solve it, we will be doing so at three levels. We will be considering how to:

- Fully embrace the concept of being an individual and being your own best friend.
- Find or create the environment that suits you in regard to the people in it, the activities you do and your surroundings.
- Accept your own level of needs and wants as appropriate, and be proud of and comfortable with them, refusing to feel criticised if other people say you should be doing things differently.

We will not undertake this journey in three specific stages as we go through the book, rather the three concepts will be interwoven as we travel though all the various aspects of learning both to understand and to solve the various problems that are inherent in the experience of loneliness. As we travel, however, keep these three concepts in mind and you will learn much more than if you simply read the book at the surface and obvious level.

In general it is the first and third concepts, those relating to you yourself rather than the people around you, that will receive most, though not exclusive, attention in the earlier chapters of the book and the second concept, your environment, that will receive more attention in the later chapters.

In this book we are going to explore loneliness itself, how it can come about, what it can mean, what you can learn from it and what you can do about it. If, having read the book, you continue to feel lonely, then read it again: you have either missed the message or you will know that loneliness is of your own choosing. By the end of the book you will have all the knowledge you need in order to alter your situation, your emotions, your thoughts, your attitudes and more. You need no longer be lonely. Have fun.

PART I

The Problem

Chapter One

Alone Versus Lonely

There is a vast difference between being on your own and being lonely, although sometimes the words are used as if they were interchangeable. Let's consider the two concepts.

Being Alone

The dictionary defines being alone as 'being solitary, unaccompanied, without another, by oneself, unique, singly'.

Being alone means just that. It means being on your own, being in a room on your own, being in a house on your own, being in an office or at work alone, or being outdoors on your own. In other words it means having no one around you.

You may or you may not be or feel lonely. Many people are wonderfully, blissfully happy on their own.

They enjoy being alone, they like the time to themselves, they appreciate the peace and quiet of not having other people around, talking to them and requiring attention. They may even find having to talk to people an effort. Without periods of being alone some people feel overwhelmed, claustrophobic, tired and frustrated. They love their privacy. For them the challenge is to find sufficient time and opportunity to be on their own. These people are alone but not lonely, and they are not the people we are addressing here.

You may feel lonely and unhappy the moment you are on your own. Perhaps you simply have to have other people around you or else you feel lonely. As long as there is someone within sight, someone you can talk to, you feel all right, but if there is no one around then you feel lonely. Is being with people, any sort of people, your answer to loneliness? Do you equate being alone with immediate loneliness?

In modern usage of the word it is also possible to be or to feel alone in a crowd. You can be alone in the streets, in shopping centres, in the crowd at a theatre or sports event, in a crowd at an airport or station. In all these and other crowds you can be alone and feel alone. You can be alone at a party if you know no one and have gone on your own. You can feel alone in a pub when you have no one to talk to. You may also feel lonely, or you may not.

Being alone in a crowd can be a form of anonymity. It may give you a sense of freedom, knowing that no one who sees you will remember you or comment on what you do or say, that this moment need not, in effect, be a part of the rest of your life. You may like it or you may not. You may also be lonely, or you may not.

You can also feel as if you are alone if you are with people with whom you have nothing in common. They may not speak your language, literally or figuratively.

They may not share your interests or ideas. Their sense of values may be totally different to yours. You may feel that you and they do not relate to each other and that you are effectively alone. Again, you may enjoy this situation or you may not: you may feel lonely.

Loneliness

The dictionary defines 'lonely' as 'alone, solitary, retired, standing by itself, uncomfortably conscious of being alone'. In other words there is implied pain in being lonely whereas 'being alone' is a more objective concept that does not inherently include any implied state of emotion.

In the rest of this book we will not be concerned about people who are alone but happy. Our concern is for you if you are unhappy, whether you say you are alone or use the word lonely, and whether you are on your own or have people around you that do not provide the companionship you desire or fulfil your other emotional needs.

To feel lonely is to have unsatisfied needs. You may feel there is no one to help you when you need help, no one who cares or who has your interests at heart. You may feel the lack of a companion with whom to share activities. You may go through your days feeling that there is no one who would miss you if you weren't there.

You may live alone, come home to an empty house at night and know that if you don't arrange a social event you will be cooking a solitary meal for yourself and filling in a lonely evening. You may work on your own and feel the lack of company, of colleagues.

Lonely in a Crowd

Or you may not live alone. You may be married, you may live with your parents, or with your children as a sole parent. You may share accommodation with friends. Yet even with other people around you, you may feel lonely, feel the lack of a relationship that satisfies your needs, and this may be true both when the situation is unhappy or when it is, ostensibly, happy.

Melinda was thirty-four when she came to see me.

'I know it seems stupid,' she said, 'considering the size of the family, but I feel so lonely. Everyone around me has someone or something else, but I seem to have no one and nothing. I'm useful to them, but no one cares about me and my needs. I just feel so alone, and I'm fed up with it.'

I could see from the written details she had given me that she was married and had three children so I asked her for more details about her life.

'Oh I know, the house is always full, there are people around all the time and I never have any peace, but it's as if they don't see me. I cook the meals for them, wash and iron their clothes, I keep the house looking nice. I drive the children to school and to their various activities, but they are so involved with their friends. George, my husband, works long hours and likes to read when he gets home. His father lives with us too, but he spends all his time, when he's not out playing bowls, either on the phone to his friends or asleep. I just seem to be a general servant. They want what I provide but they don't care about me. My needs, my wants, are ignored.'

'Have you tried talking to them about it, especially your husband?'

'Oh yes. But you know what they're like. The kids just say, "Oh Mum,*" George says, "But we do things together*

at the weekends" – and we do sometimes, but usually with the children or other couples, unless he is busy with work he has brought home. Dad tries but just says soothing things, wanting to be kind. And I still feel lonely.'

Melinda is not alone in this. Christine was single, lived with her parents and worked as a legal secretary. She had several friends from her school days but felt she was losing touch with them. They were mostly headed for marriage and motherhood; she wanted to study law and build a career.

'My parents still see me as their little girl. My boss sees me as a secretary, if he sees me at all. The other students in my class are men and mostly ignore me and I can't talk to my friends about things that interest me, for they aren't interested.'

Just like Melinda, Christine is alone in a crowd.

The same situation occurs for men, of course.

Jeremy told me how lonely he felt. He spent his days working in an office where he was more involved with computers than with people, and when he got home at night, he told me, his wife was full of talk about the children, the neighbours and the other parents. At weekends she and the two girls seemed to be doing things together and he felt excluded.

'All I am to them is a provider,' he said. 'The only time they notice me is if there isn't enough money for what they want to do or if something needs fixing around the house.'

In these and many other ways it is possible to feel lonely, even intensely lonely, within a seemingly close-knit group of people.

The Fear of Being Alone

It may not be the fact of being lonely that bothers you but the fear of it. Again this is twofold: there is the fear of being alone and the fear of being lonely.

You may go to great lengths to avoid being alone. If you are single you may share your home with someone, anyone, no matter how unsuitable they are, simply to have someone else around. You may simply be afraid of being alone, knowing that if you do live on your own you will often actually be alone and fearing that then you will feel lonely and unhappy. You may not have tried it, you may not have spent much time alone, you may simply have assumed that to be alone is to be unhappy.

If you do live alone you may still, through fear of how you might feel on your own, do all you can to reduce the time you spend alone. You may fill every evening and all weekend with social events meetings, or some other activity, just so long as it involves other people. You may do this because you genuinely hate an evening spent on your own or perhaps because you're afraid you will be unhappy if you do spend the evening alone.

Tommy was a first-year engineering student. He came from a close family living in a small town and had moved to the city to study. Knowing no one, he had moved into a single-roomed flat. He worked at the weekends to pay his way and should have been studying in the evenings but, he said, the thought of being in the room on his own for the evening was so dismaying that he kept finding reasons for going out. He'd join friends in the pub, go to a disco, anything for company. He'd tried studying in the college library but quickly realised you could be just as alone in a crowd.

I suggested that he find a friend to study with. They could spend the evening in one of their digs, study and, intermittently, share the odd conversation, perhaps even helping each other with their work. Later he told me that he'd acted on that suggestion, that he'd done it with a student doing a completely different course, so they hadn't had much to talk about.

'But it didn't seem to matter,' was his comment. 'Just so long as David was there, I could study. I've thought about it too, in the light of what you'd said. Often we wouldn't talk for an hour or more. I'd be doing exactly the same as if I was on my own, but somehow on my own I was miserable and when he was there it felt OK.'

Think about your own situation. How often have you spent the evening reading a book or watching television, alone in the room and with no one talking to you, yet not felt lonely simply because there was someone somewhere else in the house? How would you feel, doing exactly the same things, if the whole house were empty?

Sometimes all that is needed to dispel the fear of loneliness is the knowledge that there is someone within calling distance, not in the house next door, since going in to see them would constitute a call for help or would need a manufactured reason or excuse, but within the house. They may be a flatmate, someone with whom you share digs or they may be part of the family. The mere presence of another human being can, for some people, dispel the feeling and the fear of loneliness.

Many people who fear being alone have never actually been alone, or done certain things on their own. In that case the problem is as much a fear of the unknown as a fear of being alone. Try this for yourself. Purposively decide to spend a day on your own, go to the cinema alone, eat a meal alone in a restaurant, stay at home alone for the weekend with the phone off the hook, or go for a drive in the country on your own. You may well find that the situation is not only less scary and unpleasant than you thought, but that you can actually find positive experiences in it. There is more time to do what *you* want to do, for instance.

There is a second part to this. There is not only the experience of being on your own, there is the question of how you treat yourself when you are on your own. People on their own often treat themselves poorly. We will be discussing this later (Treat Yourself with Respect, p. 30) but it deserves a brief mention here. Someone on their own may eat a casual snack saying, 'It's not worth cooking a proper meal, it's only for me.' In the country on their own they might eat a sandwich in the car, whereas with a friend they would pack all they needed for a pleasant picnic by the river. I have a friend who wouldn't go out and buy a bottle of wine on her own and another who will not drink a glass of wine with a meal on her own, even though she would enjoy it. This is to equate being alone with a lower level of comfort and pleasure than when you are with other people, thus compounding the problem.

So the second part of the exercise is this. When you do, voluntarily, spend this experimental time on your own, decide to do all the things you would do if you were with one or more friends. Not only will this make you feel better about yourself, it will also, in all probability, put you into situations where you will come into contact with new people and add further to your enjoyment.

In all these ways, if you do the experiments, you may find that being on your own, even if you don't talk to anyone the whole time, is nothing like as bad as you feared. You might even enjoy it. You may also find that, when you focus on giving yourself a good time, you can even make new friends.

Chapter Two

You Are an Individual

You Are Alone

Sometimes the hardest thing to come to terms with is the thought that you really *are* alone. There is indeed no one out there batting for you, putting your needs above theirs or even fully understanding what your needs are.

When the chips are down you are on your own. This planet is peopled by several billion other individuals, all trying to make sense of *their* lives, all striving to fulfil *their* needs and all, or most, trying not to be lonely. They, like you, are focused on themselves, their own wants and their own needs.

You Are an Individual

You are an individual, a wonderful individual. There is no one else like you. There is no one with your combination of attributes, with your skills, your needs, your abilities. There is no one else who will lead a path through life that is identical to yours. There is no one who thinks like you, feels like you and has desires and needs like you.

For these, and many other reasons, there is no one who can know exactly what you want, what you need, what is best for you. Anyone who gives you advice can only, at best, advise you as to what *they* think is best for you. At worst their advice will be affected by their own needs, aims and goals. This advice may not be what you (in your heart of hearts) think is best for you. You may keep searching for someone who gives you the advice you want to give yourself, and you may feel lonely until you find them, yet that may well be a hopeless quest. The mistake is to keep searching for your soul mate, for your identical twin, for perfect understanding from another individual. Search instead for your own full understanding and appreciation of yourself, plus an exploration of other people, rejoicing in the differences and taking the shared ground as a bonus.

No One Understands Me

A common cause of loneliness is this feeling that no one understands you, that no one *truly* knows how you feel and what you want, and that as a result you are lonely. Yet it's true. They don't understand you. Nor do you *truly* understand anyone else. Even when you think you do, you don't. The chances against your truly understanding the way another person thinks and feels and of their understanding you are over five billion to one against.

Think how many times a number of people have witnessed a single event and yet described it differently. Think of the times you have thought you were close to someone only to find, later, that you really weren't thinking the same thing at all.

Even single words can have different meanings for different people. Take something as simple as the word 'tree'. To a logger it is work and a challenge. To a botanist it is a multiplicity of biological forms to be studied. To a painter it is a vision to be captured on paper. To a 'Greenie' it is something to be defended by a variety of strategies. To a child it is something to climb. To a paper miller it is raw material for the next newspaper. To a carpenter it is something to build with. To a wood turner it is something to sculpt with. To a farmer it is a possible nuisance in a paddock. To a hiker it is a place to shelter in a storm. We could continue; but from this it is clear that such a simple word as 'tree' has different connotations to, and leads to different emotions in, different people. If you say the word 'tree' to a friend and think that you will immediately understand what is going through their head and that they will understand what is going through yours, there is already the possibility of multiple errors in communication and understanding.

Then put the word into a sentence. 'The tree has been struck by lightning.' You may think at once of a glorious storm. You may think of lightning or of the time as a child when you hid under the bed. You may wonder if anyone was hurt as the tree fell and conjure up images of ambulances and hospitals. You may be more concerned for power lines and communications. You may wonder if any building was damaged and think about rebuilding and repairs. You may think of cutting the tree up and picture the fires that it will produce in people's homes. You may wonder about moving it and think of chain-saws and trucks. You may worry about the possible erosion of the soil that can result.

Just that simple sentence can lead to such diverse mental pictures as storms, childhood, ambulances, hospitals, people dying, power and communications problems, telephone lines, people cut off, building, carpenters, household fires, chain-saws, trucks, soil erosion and more, much more. When you say to someone, 'The tree has been struck by lightning', you do *not* understand what is happening inside the other person's head. You cannot know what is in their mind and if you don't know what is in their mind you cannot understand how they will be feeling.

If such possible diversification of images, thoughts and feelings can result from a single word or a simple sentence, and if you are already out of touch with the way the other person is feeling, at least in detail, then it becomes clear that during the course of daily life, when you express yourself using, or omitting, thousands of words and thousands of sentences, it is impossible to fully understand another person.

In fact *everyone* sees 'reality' in a different way. This is true even if you are looking at a single object and it is infinitely more true when considering complex situations or your life as a whole. You observe and listen to the world around you, you feel it, smell it and experience it in many different ways and *immediately* pass this through a variety of filters, filters that you started setting up the moment you were born or became conscious.

If an uncle with a beard kissed you as a baby and then growled at you, you may be nervous around men with beards. Another baby may have been exposed to a bearded grandfather who played with him or her endlessly and produced lovely things to eat. If you were the baby in the first example you cannot expect the other one, as he or she becomes a friend in adult life, to understand, or even recognise, your fear of men with beards. If you associated certain foods, sights, smells or sounds with certain emotions when young then the same foods, sights, smells or sounds are likely to trigger similar emotions or to have similar connotations now. You can hardly expect them to have the same meaning for someone else. If small dogs bit you but large dogs were playful you may still feel that large dogs are safer than, or preferable to, small ones and you may not understand that someone else, who did not have your childhood experience and is working simply on the basis of size, feels that small dogs are much safer than large ones.

There are other ways in which your experience may differ from someone else's, even when you think you are doing the same things. An optimist, for instance, will notice all the good things that happen in a day. On the other hand a pessimist might delete all the good things and only notice all the bad things that happened, might then consider his friend, the optimist, unfeeling and uncaring when she doesn't sympathise with the dreadful day he has had and may then complain that she doesn't understand him.

You may be a friendly extrovert and feel hurt when your colleague, a quiet introvert, doesn't bubble over with enthusiasm when you suggest having lunch together. You have not understood that she is delighted to have been invited but is shy. Similarly she has not understood that you are lonely but are trying to put some fun in your life. In your mind you have distorted her shy acceptance and turned it into an unwilling acceptance. People distort the intentions of others in many ways. You cannot actually get inside another person's head and know what they are thinking so some element of distortion (or assumptions that may be false) is inevitable.

We have so far considered the different meanings different people can attribute to a word, a phrase or a sentence and the ways in which different people make generalisations, deletions and distortions about everyday experiences. There are also some more fundamental differences.

In a recent book,[1] I described the four temperaments or humours, the four major personality types. It is probably fair to say that there are as many types of people as there are people. However it is also possible to group them into broad personality types. In a sweeping generalisation the ancient Greeks considered that people fell into four broad categories, the dynamic leaders (Cholerics) the fun party goers (Sanguines), the reliable traditionalists (Phlegmatics) and the artistic and caring nurturers (Melancholics).

In any given situation these types will behave differently. If you interpret everyone's behaviour in the same way you will definitely make mistakes. If you can recognise their temperament it will assist you to interpret what they say and do with greater accuracy.

If, for instance, you meet someone at a party and they swear you are the love of their life and that they are thrilled that, at last, they have met you, you may be hurt and lonely when they fail to make contact afterwards and assume that the cause was something you said or did. In fact they may have been a Sanguine, for whom the moment is all; they did mean it – but only at the time. Their subsequent lack of interest has nothing to do with you; their scatterbrained mind has been caught by another situation, another person. If you show an irate boss that there is a mistake in the proposal they have asked you to type you will be hurt and surprised if they sack you unless you understand that they are a young Choleric and that Cholerics hate to be criticised. If you give someone a job to do, later ask them to stop for a minute and do something else, and later still find they have ignored you and continued with the first task, you may feel they are being obstructive and unhelpful unless you understand that they are a Phlegmatic and they put a high priority on finishing one job before starting another. If you interpret the Melancholic's soulful moods as being that of a wet blanket instead of realising you have a gentle and caring friend you could miss out on a precious relationship because you failed to understand the subtleties of their nature. Come to that, the other three temperaments almost always fail to understand the Melancholics.

All these and thousands of situations like them lead, more often than not, to confusion and misunderstanding rather than to an identical soul experience. You did not understand the other person and, in each case, they almost certainly did not understand you.

As human beings, each of us is unique. As such you cannot, reasonably, expect another person to understand you. If they understand you in broad terms you are lucky. If you expect them to understand you in detail and if you choose to feel alone when they don't you are heading for unhappiness.

When you think about it, it would even be boring if you did understand other people and they did understand you. The wonder of other people is that they *are* different, different to you and different to each other. The world would be a dull place were this not so. Instead of bemoaning the fact that other people don't understand you, why not come out of your loneliness and study other people, with as few preconceived ideas as possible? When you fully open up to receive and explore the subtleties of another person, not only will your world expand, but you will find it less and less easy to be lonely. After all, you love it when people try to understand you – otherwise you would probably not be reading this chapter – and equally, other people usually love it when you pay attention to them. In time they may even pay more attention to you.

[1] Xandria Williams, *Love, Health and Happiness*, Hodder and Stoughton, 1996.

Chapter Three

What Do You Really Want from Life?

The first thing is to work harder at understanding yourself. Find out what it is that you really want. 'That's easy,' you may say, 'all I want is people around me that care, so that I won't feel lonely.' In fact it's rarely that simple. Developing a deeper understanding, yourself, of your own real needs (which may be very different to your surface or expressed needs) may be the true answer needed to help you solve your loneliness.

Gerald came to see me saying he was unhappy with his life but he didn't know what to do about it. He was lonely; most of his friends had married, moved into the mortgage belt and become engrossed in their family and children.

'If only,' he said, 'I could find a woman to love. That would solve everything, I wouldn't be alone any more. We could do things as a couple and so could spend time with my old friends. Because, it's funny you know, they don't seem so keen on having a single chap around, yet they seem to like me as much as ever. It's just that, being single, I don't seem to fit in to their lives any more.'

We ran a process called Values Elicitation, in which you prioritize your values through comparing a series of pairs of values, in such a way that, instead of going round in circles you get to the heart of your priorities.[1] When we did this it turned out that Gerald did not want to marry. He did not want to settle down. He wasn't even all that keen on having a steady girlfriend. He would certainly feel bogged down by suburbia and other families with lives centred around home and children. What he did want was a new group of single men that he could hang around with. Once he understood this he joined a few clubs around his interests which, after sports, were politics and community affairs. As a result he made new friends, mostly men, with common interests and solved his loneliness problem. Had he continued to look for a possible wife he could either have remained single and lonely or made a potentially disastrous marriage, one in which he continued to feel lonely as it did not satisfy his underlying needs.

Learn About Yourself

So start out by getting to understand yourself better.

One way to do this is to go through the Values Elicitation process already mentioned.[1] Another is to learn about your own temperament (as well as that of other people) by reading relevant books.[2] Read books on astrology, not for the purpose of predicting the future, but rather for finding out how closely the description of your own sun sign seems to fit you.

It is very easy to take yourself for granted, to assume that you are 'normal', and that other people think and feel as you do, or that they ought to. These are automatic and unconscious assumptions that we all make, at least part of the time. It is when you read, in detail, about other types of characters and behaviours, and compare them to your own, that you can widen your perspective and also obtain a deeper understanding of your own unique nature. For this reason, learning more about other people can also be a way of learning more about yourself.

Treat Yourself with Respect

There's another aspect to being an individual, and to being able to enjoy yourself when you are on your own. It involves the way you treat yourself when you are alone. Make it a point to treat yourself the way you would like other people to treat you.

I have heard people say so many things which indicate that they need someone else present to make the occasion or to validate what they want to do. Simply because they are on their own they fail to do whatever they would have done had someone else been there, something they would have enjoyed doing.

Ruth told me that she really enjoyed an evening at home with a drink and then a leisurely and well-prepared dinner, followed by a video. For her the quiet companionship of doing this was a valuable part of being in a relationship. She bemoaned the fact that currently she rarely had the opportunity to do this as she lived alone. When I asked her why she couldn't have this on her own she told me that when she was alone, pouring herself a drink made her feel like a closet drinker, and that it was hardly worth cooking a meal 'just for one'. A video on her own seemed to her to point up her loneliness.

Why? Do you have to have someone watching you to stop the drinking being a dangerous first step to alcoholism? Are you not worth preparing a good meal for and setting it out prettily? If there is no one else there does it necessarily mean scrambled egg on toast and a mug of instant coffee? Do you talk with the other person there, all the way through the video? Of course not.

Would you pour a drink and prepare a meal for someone else? Of course you would. Would you like someone else to pour you a drink and serve you a pleasant meal? Of course you would. So treat yourself as you would like other people to treat you. Go ahead. Do not compound the problem of being on your own, if you perceive that as being a problem, by treating yourself worse than you would do if someone else were there, worse than you would treat them or worse than you would like them to treat you.

By doing what she was doing Ruth was really telling herself that she wasn't worth much, that she wasn't worth the effort when it came to preparing and presenting a good meal, that without a guest she didn't amount to much. After we had talked she made some changes and was then able to tell me that she really looked forward to her evenings alone at home now. She had her drink, prepared the meal and served it prettily on a tray. She then watched a good video she had brought home or curled up with a book and thoroughly enjoyed the evening. 'What you lose in chat you make up for in that you can do everything just the way you want to' was her conclusion.

Teresa loved the opera. As often as possible she would find a friend to go with. They would dress up, arrive in time to enjoy a light meal beforehand, share the buzz of the crowd, arrange drinks in the intervals and go out for coffee afterwards, making a wonderful night out of it. She came to see me because she was lonely and, as she said, 'All my friends have either married or moved out of town.' As a result, among many other components of her problem, she had no one with whom to go to the opera and, she claimed, it really wasn't much fun on her own. She tended to arrive just on time, to stay in her seat in the interval, feeling conspicuous on her own, then rush home afterwards.

I encouraged her to do the same as she had done with a companion and to look around and see who else was there on their own. To her surprise, as she reported back, there were always quite a few people there on their own and all very happy to talk. In time, since she went to a lot of operas, she came to make quite a few new friends this way.

Men seem to have less trouble than women when it comes to going out on their own. They are more inclined to go to a pub and to talk to whoever is standing at the bar. If a woman does that there are some obvious pitfalls. Yet none the less, many men succumb to the syndrome described above. With a friend, male or female, they may organise a good meal for themselves or go out to eat. On their own they may open a tin of beans.

Donald loved going for long walks but said he had to have a companion to share it with or it was no fun. My idle suggestion to 'take a few photos and share it with someone later' led to him investing in a video camera, filming the walk and talking a running commentary. Not only did this bring the walk alive for him, it led to a whole new hobby. Yet he could also have had that conversation with himself, inside his own head. His experience would have been none the less real simply because there was no one there with him to share it with.

You are an individual. You do not need someone else around to validate you. You can have a good time with yourself. It is all a question of your own internal attitude. Certainly you may prefer to be with people. If this is so, then make the appropriate arrangements, initiate social situations, join clubs, go places where there are people. But if you are totally dependent on other people being present as the basis for having a good time, for pampering yourself, for cooking, having a drink, dressing up, going places, and for avoiding the feelings of loneliness and unhappiness, then you are heading for trouble.

Be an individual. Get to know yourself, acknowledge and like yourself. Validate yourself, have a good time with yourself. Experiences are no less real just because someone else is not there to notice you having them. As soon as you can really come to terms with the fact that you are on your own, and enjoy it, you will notice and rejoice in all the times you *do* have other people around you, others with whom to share. You will notice and enjoy the positives (company) rather than focusing on and feeling unhappy about the times there is no one there for you.

Do You Need Other People to Validate You?

Having suggested that you should treat yourself as you would like other people to treat you, I now want to take this concept a bit further.

Do you really need to know the person on the seat beside you before you can enjoy a film, a play or a concert? Certainly, for most people most of the time, it is more fun to go with a friend than alone. Equally there are times when a friend can be a distraction. The point is that there are two aspects to the occasion; there is the play or film itself and there is the company in the intervals.

Do you like to go walking in the countryside? Do you enjoy the exercise, the scenery, the plants and flowers; do you enjoy talking to the people you meet, stopping for a cup of tea or a drink somewhere, meeting more people? Think about it. These are all things you might do with a friend. Is there really any reason why you shouldn't do them on your own?

Certainly, you may prefer to do these and other activities with one or more friends. That is not the point. The point is, if you are on your own and if you love doing these things, there really is nothing to stop you doing them on your own. You may have less fun than if you had company, but you can still have a lot of fun. If you are on your own and feeling lonely it makes no sense to rule out the possibility of doing some of the things you love just because you are on your own. That is double deprivation, being on your own and forgoing the film or the walk.

If you need to have someone with you to validate your experience then maybe you should recognise that as a major part of your problem and deal with it. After all, the flowers are just as beautiful for one person or a crowd, the music is just as moving, the play as dramatic, the art as beautiful, when you are on your own as when two or more people are present. Ultimately the enjoyment is an inner experience. If you can only enjoy it when you have company this says more about you than about the experience and the company or lack of it. It could well be time that you examined the situation and started to be an independent individual, not one who needs other people in order not to be unhappy.

You can also start to look for some of the benefits of being on your own. Since, at times, you do not have a companion you are more free to talk to other people, to get acquainted and make new friends. Start treating each new outing, whether it be for pleasure, or to do the shopping or necessary travel for some other purpose, as an opportunity to meet people. The irony is, there are thousands of other people 'out there' on their own, just as lonely as you, who would be thrilled if someone pleasant took the time to have a chat with them and get to know them. The nice thing about this is that, if you like them, you can continue the conversation, if you don't you can move off. If you are with a prearranged group of people and one of them annoys you, you are stuck with them until the end of the event for which you have gathered. If you look for the positive benefits of being on your own you may be surprised to find how many there are.

You may not be able to solve the problem of being on your own, not immediately anyway, but you can change the way you feel about it. You on your own are totally able to change this and ultimately it is only you that *can* change this. In other words, whether you choose to feel lonely, or to enjoy the situation anyway, is a matter of internal decision, within your power and up to you.

You may say, 'But that's not the sort of person I am,' or 'I could never go to a film on my own,' and that may be true. But it is only true because you have decided it is true. You can just as easily decide it is not true and make the appropriate internal changes.

Are You Only OK if Someone Else Says You Are?

Some people only feel good when they are complimented; they need approval and they need to be aware of this approval. Do you only feel you look good if someone says you do? Why? Alternatively, do you feel competent to assess someone else's looks and tell them they look good? You probably do. Then surely you can do the same for yourself. You don't *need* someone else to validate you unless you think you do, and since this is a decision you have made it is also a decision you can change.

Thomas enjoyed going to art galleries and he was secretly proud of this since most of his friends were happy-go-lucky rugby players and beer drinkers who wouldn't have been able to tell the difference between a Constable and a

Turner. This meant that for him, when he took a girlfriend to an art gallery, his enjoyment came as much from the fact that she knew he enjoyed it and was impressed at his sensitivity as from his pleasure in the pictures themselves. When he didn't have a girlfriend to go with he stayed away and spent much of his time on his own and unhappy. As we worked together he was encouraged first to go on his own and report back to me, having me there, if you like, in his mind as he walked around. Then I stopped him telling me about it and encouraged him to enjoy it for himself and for the experience. Once he'd mastered that it was, as he said, a revelation, 'I'll never be lonely again, I can always go and do these things on my own and, in fact, the inner experience is much greater when I'm not worrying what other people are thinking, or showing off to someone.'

If you need someone else present before you can fully enjoy an experience, consider what element of Thomas's style of thinking is also a component of your own.

If you can be your own best friend in these and other activities you are free to be happy when you are on your own *and* happy when you are with people. For as long as you need someone else there to validate your activity you are susceptible to feeling unhappy when there is no one there to do that.

Are You Ashamed to be Seen to be on Your Own?

For some people the problem is not being on their own but being seen to be on their own. Many people feel conspicuous when doing something on their own while surrounded by other people doing the same thing in pairs or in groups.

Donald loved going to concerts but felt ashamed when he went on his own because, when we explored why, he came to realise that he thought other people were looking down on him and feeling sorry for him because he had no one to go with him.

I asked him what he had done when he had been married, since he had already told me that his wife hadn't shared many of his interests, and she certainly hadn't enjoyed concerts.

'It didn't seem a problem then,' he said.

When we explored why, he realised that it was because he *knew he had a wife at home, whereas now* he *knew there was no one at home waiting for him, not even an unsatisfactory wife. Ultimately it really came down to what he was thinking about himself, rather than what other people were thinking. After all, you cannot know what other people are thinking, you can only attribute thoughts to them, thoughts that are actually a reflection of what you are thinking yourself.*

For Donald the answer was simple. He started to imagine that there was someone at home, or that he did have a girlfriend, and that he would be telling her all about the evening when he got home. In time he didn't even need to do this, he became comfortable enjoying the experience within himself and for himself.

Have a Preference Rather than an Addiction for Having People with You

It's now time to talk about addictions and preferences. Addictions are things, people, situations, emotions etc., that you *must* have in your life. Things that, you tell yourself, you absolutely must have or you will be sad, miserable, unhappy or, in this case, lonely. Addictions are things that you make essential and the absence of which will create a variety of negative emotions in you.

Addictions can be large or small. You may be addicted to having a loving partner or a boon companion, to the people you love being alive, well and happy, to peace rather than war. You may also be addicted to having meals on time, to your clothes being uncreased.

If your addictions are satisfied, so go the underlying thoughts and emotions, you can be happy; if they are not you will be unhappy. In fact this is not true. If you are addicted to something for your happiness, then when you don't have it you will be unhappy. Yet even when you do have it you will often find you are spending a lot of time fretting about what will happen if you lose it.

Preferences are things, people, situations and emotions that you would *like* to have in your life. Preferences, when they are fulfilled, enrich your life, add to the pleasure and joy. Preferences can be just as strong and important as addictions.

Like addictions, preferences too can be large or small. You may have a preference for having a loving partner, for your family being safe, for your own physical security. You may also have preferences for the details in your life being the way you want them to be.

Unlike addictions, however, where you just *know* you'll be miserable without them, preferences are such that you know you can cope if they are not satisfied. The difference between addictions and preferences is in no way a measure of their real value or importance in your life. The difference lies in your attitude, in the way you deal with the various situations of loss or lack as and when they arise.

If you are addicted to having people around you then you will be miserable when you are on your own. If you have a strong preference for having people around you then you can enjoy every minute of the time you are with them, without fretting about some time in the future when you are on your own, and you can also be content, you can cope, when you are on your own.

What we have said so far is not meant to suggest that

you should train yourself to prefer being on your own to being with people. By and large, we humans are a gregarious species. We like doing things in couples or in groups. Sharing is fun and can often enrich an experience. So do not tell yourself, unless it is true, that your present state, that of being on your own, is better than being with people and that you really don't want people anyway. That is a sour-grapes type of attitude and will not lead to happiness. Instead the goal is, unless you truly prefer to be on your own (in which case you would hardly be reading this book), to have a preference for having other people around you rather than being addicted to it. In this way you can enjoy yourself either on your own or with people.

[1] This process is described fully in *Beating the Blues* by Xandria Williams, Cedar, 1995. A simplified version can also be found in the Appendix on p. 265.

[2] Including the aforementioned *Love, Health and Happiness* by Xandria Williams.

Chapter Four

Be Independent

No One Can Let You Down Unless You are Leaning on Them

Many people have said they felt alone when the people they relied on let them down. What has to happen before someone can let you down? You have to be leaning on them, relying on them to perform some function or be in some place.

No one cares about you as much as you. Why should they – who do you care most about? You care most about yourself, of course, and quite rightly so. Now before you jump up and down and exclaim that this is a selfish attitude and quite wrong, think about it for a minute.

At the deepest level there is no altruism, we all do what we want to do. The problem people have is in acknowledging this. It does not make people better or worse; many of the things they do are wonderfully 'selfless' as we like to call it. It simply means that these people enjoy giving and helping others.

I am not a therapist in a self-sacrificial way, doing what I do for the good of other people in spite of what I would rather be doing. I do it because I love it. I love what I do, I love helping other people and watching them become healthier and happier, I do it because it gives me pleasure. As such I should not, and don't, expect an accolade for doing something for other people. I am doing what I enjoy. I am no better a person than the person who paints because they 'simply have to', or the clerk doing a routine job because it makes them feel safe. People who give do it either because it gives them pleasure to do it, they enjoy to see other people happy but they too are deriving pleasure from giving, or because they hope to gain something by doing it. Be honest about yourself for a minute, isn't this the truth? You give to feel good about yourself, because other people will appreciate you, because you like to see them smiling and so forth.

Years ago Ayn Rand wrote a book called *The Virtue of Selfishness*.[1] Her thesis is that enormous harm is done in the world by people who insist they are doing things for 'someone else's good' How many relationships have been bedevilled by 'Look what I did for you', or 'I did this for you, the least you can do is do that for me', or 'I'm doing this for you', the implication being that a debt of gratitude is now owed.

So let's get back to our theme. Ultimately, at the deepest level, people do what they want to do, what is important to them. Everyone is doing what gives them pleasure, and so are you. If it gives them pleasure to be with you they will be, if it doesn't they won't. If it gives them pleasure to put themselves out, come to your house, cook you a meal and cheer you up, they will do it. If it doesn't, they won't. This doesn't make them more or less self-centredly selfish. This is an honest assessment of the situation. They are none the less generous and giving for having a personality that enjoys giving, but let it be recognised that they are getting some benefit from the process, and that you are not irrevocably in their debt. Thus 'being with you' may mean that the friend spends the day with you when you need them, even if they do say or think they would rather have been doing something else. The deeper truth is that they would rather spend the time with you, invest in their relationship with you, feel good about giving, and/or avoid feeling guilty for not doing so, than go off and do whatever else they might have done, and worry about you and what you think of them for not being helpful.

If you both recognise that they are doing what they want to do and you are doing what you want to do, does it make any sense to lean on someone else, to depend on them to solve your problems? Of course it doesn't. What does make sense is to find out what you want in your life, and create it. Create it yourself. If someone else helps you that is a bonus and you can thank them. This way leads to happiness. If, on the other hand, they do not help you you can simply say 'That's a shame, but I'll just have to find another way.' This way too, in time, can lead to a happy outcome. If, on the other hand, you choose to feel let down each time someone doesn't do something for you that you want, and you then interpret this feeling of being let down as 'no one cares' and feel lonely as a result, then you will be unhappy.

Be responsible for yourself – you don't need other people to blame for wrong decisions or things that happen to you. After all they cannot know your needs as well as you do.

You may be part of the closest possible relationship. You may have a parent who adores you and is willing to put your needs first, above their own. You may have a lover or partner on whom you feel you can totally rely. But can they truly get 'inside your head'? Can they truly know what you want, what is best for you, what your real needs are? No matter how close someone in your life has seemed to be it is almost certain that you will be able to recall times when they just didn't seem to understand you, or to know what you wanted or how you felt. Simply because they are normally so close, because you do normally feel confident that you can rely totally on them for support, the sudden lack of closeness, the absence of complete understanding, or their unwillingness to adapt to your needs, when it does occur, can be all the more devastating. You suddenly have to tell yourself that you cannot rely on them, that your sense of security, based on the assumption that you could, was false, that you have been living in a fool's paradise, and that you have been let down.

'What has happened?' you cry. 'They know I rely on them. How could they have let me down? Just when I need them they aren't here, I'm alone and I can't cope.' You may then feel the loneliness and the pain on two levels. At the first level there is the pain of feeling alone. At the second level there is the yawning pit of finding that what you took to be a secure support is suddenly missing. If, on the other hand, you had not been leaning on them you would not have fallen over when they were 'not there'.

It comes back to recognising that you are an individual and it is time you became self-sufficient. Keep in mind, however, that I do not mean that you should be cold and graspingly selfish in this. I do not mean that you should act outside your nature and become self-centredly selfish and uncaring of other people's needs. I do mean that you should acknowledge the underlying emotions and processes and be at ease with them.

All this may seem terribly obvious and logical when viewed in this way. Yet so often in life and in relationships there is the assumption that things are the other way around. You hear such things as 'How could they do that, just when I needed them?', 'There's no one I can truly rely on' and 'When the chips are down I simply have to do things myself'. This latter is usually said with implied complaint or a sense of 'Why should something so dreadful happen to me?' And this in itself underlies what we are saying. Many people do seem to believe that, when the chips are down, there should be someone else there to pick up the pieces, someone else there to look after them, someone else there to make sure their needs are taken care of.

Think about the other person in this process of leaning. It is unrealistic to expect someone always to be there for you such that it is safe for you to lean on them. If their needs are in conflict with your needs what will they do, what should they do? Further, if their values are in conflict with your values what should they do? Should they drop their beliefs and ideas, their needs and their values, and fit in with what you want? Would you respect them if they bent to your every wish and idea?

Let's take it a step further. If you really are relying on someone, do you want them to be the sort of person that will bend to your needs, or do you want them to be strong and have a will and a mind of their own? Ironically it often comes down to this. If someone else is strong enough for you to lean on them they may not be sufficiently bendable or flexible to adapt to your needs!

Ask yourself the same questions. What would you do if someone you loved and truly cared for wanted to do something that was contrary to your needs and values? For instance, what would you do if you were lonely and the person you relied on said they wanted to go away for a while? Alternatively, what would you do if someone needed your company and your involvement in their life at a time when you had a vital project to complete, another person who needed you just as much, or a pressing need for solitude or support yourself? Would you unfailingly drop everything and fulfil the need of the first person? We all have our individual lives to lead. You were not born with one mentor, one companion, an assistant or a support person whose sole purpose is to make sure you are not alone, do not feel lonely, and have all your needs met.

It is wonderful when there is someone there for you, but that should be viewed as a bonus, not as a right, a wonderful benefit and gift when it occurs, not a horror about which you can complain when it doesn't.

Celebrate the Differences

Start to stand on your own two feet. Be your own best friend. Rejoice in your own individuality. Decide to be the arbiter of your own destiny. Once you stop looking for people who you can lean on, or who will be an extension of yourself, you can stop feeling disappointed and let down when you don't find them. Start to explore new relationships and move out of loneliness.

Marian had been divorced twice and was about to break up with her current partner with whom she had been living for three years.

'It's always the same,' was her opening remark. 'Each time I start a relationship I feel sure I have found my perfect mate. Then as the months and years go by they turn into a disappointment. Take Colin, for example. When we were first going out together we used to share so much. I went to motor races with him and out sailing, he came to the theatre and concerts with me. We shared each other's friends and we did things together. Now he's always too busy or too tired to go out with me in the evenings, though he's got plenty of time to meet his friends in the pub. And he's no help around the house at the weekends, the garden's a mess.'

I asked her when she last went to a race or out sailing with Colin and was told that there just wasn't time for all that, now that they had their home to look after, and especially since he expected her to do all the work.

It was obvious that, as is so often the case, they had each put themselves out, in the early days of their relationship, to learn about the other and to get involved in the other person's hobbies and friends; they had rejoiced in their differences and made the effort to explore them. As time went on, however, they had each settled down to their own wants. While initially it had been fun to explore the individual called Colin, Marian now wanted Colin to fit in with her, to be like her and to share her needs and aspirations.

Once I had discussed this and a variety of possibilities with Marian she decided to work with me and to make a project out of the relationship. As she said, 'It's probably going to end anyway, I think we're both bored with each other and neither of us is getting the companionship and support that we want. I know I'm not. So I might as well experiment, you can't spoil something that is hardly there any more so I won't be taking any risk.'

In the next week the first project I gave her was to write down as many differences as she could find between herself and Colin and then bring her list in to me. When she brought it in it was obvious that she had viewed each variation as a relative good–bad pattern. Overwhelmingly it was things such as:

Colin is not as tidy as me

Colin does not enjoy opera the way he used to

Colin has more time for his friends than for me.

When I pointed out how often she was interpreting the difference as a criticism of Colin she was quite shocked.

'I guess what I should do, next week, is list the differences in which I think he is better than me,' was her response.

On the contrary, I suggested that she remove the value judgement of better than or worse than, altogether, and simply look for differences. 'Treat the project,' I told her, 'as a chance to explore another human being not for right and wrong but simply to find out what is. Then take an interest in what you find.'

After doing this for two weeks she said that she had learnt an enormous amount. She hadn't realised before just what really mattered to Colin, what drove him, what he wanted in his life and what he was aiming for.

The next thing I suggested was an exercise in 'walking in Colin's moccasins'. For this project he would have to know what she was doing. I also suggested that it might be fun for them to reverse roles once she had done it. These were the instructions. For one hour she was to move around behind Colin exactly imitating everything he did. She was to take the same number of steps, walk at the same pace, make the same body movements, say whatever he said. She was to copy him as closely as she possibly could. Then they would swap roles.

When she came back she said it had been an amazing experience. Colin was more active, quicker moving, more impatient than her. He was also interested in so much more that was going on around him. 'I hadn't realised how much he turns his head, it's as if he simply has to see everything. I used to think he was just looking at the women, in fact I'd often get quite jealous, but when I copied his movements I found he was just interested in everything. And the funny thing is, though in a way I was quite exhausted at the end of the hour, I'd also seen things I'd never noticed before. I think I actually began to feel a bit like Colin. We talked about it afterwards, after he had copied me for an hour too, and he said much the same. He found it amazing to be so much in touch with his feelings as I am. I'd pick a leaf and really experience it whereas to Colin a leaf was just a leaf, he'd take a quick look and then pass on to other things. He said he'd never noticed the sky the way I did.'

Whether or not these exercises would save the relationship only time would tell but Marian thought they would.

She said it was truly an exciting experience to start celebrating the differences. It also made her realise that Colin was not necessarily uncaring when he didn't give her the particular emotional support she wanted at any one time. It was simply that he had different experiences, different needs, and didn't automatically know what she wanted. When he was told, then he could demonstrate his care and concern.

You are an individual. Be glad of it. Life would really be very boring if everyone else was a copy of you. Once you stop expecting other people to relate to you in exactly the way you want, you will stop being disappointed. Further, when you do get the support you want it will be a bonus.

In the long run, however, it is up to you. This is not a negative. It leaves you free to create your own life, your own destiny. Further, you, knowing yourself so well, have all the tools you need to create whatever you want for yourself.

Learn About Other People

Get to know other people better, truly know them. Do this with an open-minded curiosity as to what they are, instead of searching for ways in which they are like you or can be of benefit to you. Glory in the differences rather than bewail their lack of ('self'-centred) 'understanding' for you and your loneliness.

Read books. There are thousands of books written about different types of people. There are many books on astrology and the twelve different sun sign types. I'm willing to bet that every time you have glanced at such a book you have turned first to the section on yourself, or been inclined to do so. Don't, you've already done that. It is now time to turn instead to the section on someone you know, or think you know, and learn more about them. Turn to the sections that do not involve people you know and learn about those personality types.

Read *Love, Health and Happiness* and consider the *other* temperaments as well as your own. There is a quick-question way to elicit another person's temperament by asking four simple questions, as described towards the end of that book. If you want to be more subtle, read books about the sixteen types, the four subtypes of each of the four temperaments. These are described briefly, very briefly, in *Love, Health and Happiness.* They are described more fully in *Please Understand Me* by David Keirsey and Marilyn Bates[2] and *Type Talk* by Otto Kroeger and Janet Thuesen.[3]

Read books on introverts versus extroverts, or optimists versus pessimists. And again, study the *other* types of personality, not just your own type. The Chinese divide people into groups on a different basis; read books on this. There are many studies of people and you can learn from them all.

Read novels, read biographies, see plays and so forth. Instead of assessing each personality on the basis of your own emotions, likes and dislikes, instead of comparing their actions to the way you would behave and their ideals to your own ideals, be more open minded, set out to discover the ways in which the other person is different to you.

I once ran a Values Elicitation process on a small group of people and then listened as they each shared their results. Some people put love, happiness and people at the top of their list; others put giving, sharing and caring. Some valued possessions and financial security; others could see no relevance to this and wanted excitement, variety and freedom. One person's highest value was 'Be true to myself' and another saw that as wishy-washy and without substance; they wanted success. A third person also wanted success but used entirely different criteria to the first to define success. As each person listened to the values hierarchies of the others they came to understand the uniqueness of each individual and, as one of them said, 'The wonder is that we ever get even a partial understanding of another person, not that people fail to understand us.'

It is not that these different classifications or assessments are of prime importance for our purpose at the moment. What is important now is that you begin to get a fuller picture of what other people are like. If you are wishing other people understood you better it is almost certain that they would like you to understand them better. Further, as you read and learn in detail of the different types of characters and personalities that exist, you may find that, instead of bemoaning the fact that other people don't understand you, you will be thrilled and excited when someone else does show signs of understanding you just a little. In other words, any understanding of you by other people is a bonus each time it happens and not a source of pain when it doesn't.

A word of warning. When you discover that someone shares your view and experience in one aspect of your life (when they seem to understand you) do not assume that this automatically means they and you will feel the same way about everything and that they will automatically understand you fully. You may find that someone who is wonderfully understanding at work is at total odds with you over social matters and has completely different values, codes and behaviour patterns in this setting. They may sympathise with you when the boss is demanding and critical but not when your husband tells you to do something you don't want to do. It is not that they have suddenly let you down and failed to understand you. You made too many extrapolated assumptions.

As a result of this process, of starting to focus on other people, and the differences between them and you, on their own uniqueness, you will be free to receive the wonders of discovery (of other people) accompanied by the occasional gift of unexpected understanding (when you and they do have something in common), and your life will be the richer for it.

Take an Interest in Other People

Yvette came to see me when her loneliness was suddenly too much and unbearable. She had moved to the city following her divorce, rented a small flat and started in a new job. To start with she had been busy settling in but after a while she found she was going home each evening and watching television.

'There's nothing so lonely as a big city, it seems to be so difficult to make friends.'

'That can be true, but you say you've been lonely for a while; what made you finally decide to come and see me?'

'Well it's funny. I was finally beginning to think I was meeting a few people and making a few friends, mainly through another woman at the office. Then she had a party a couple of weeks ago and she invited me.'

'What happened?' I asked as she stopped talking and pursed her lips.

'I don't know, it was suddenly all too much, I think. And I'd been really looking forward to it too, I suppose that's what made it all worse in a way. I realised that I was in a room with a crowd of people who knew each other, that I didn't have much in common with them, I didn't know the people and situations they were talking

about, they really didn't need me and I wasn't a part of the group. Here I was with a crowd of happy people, at an event I'd been looking forward to, and I suddenly felt even more lonely than when I was alone in my flat. I just got so depressed I made an excuse and left.'

What had depressed Yvette was not only the fact of being alone, but that even the obvious answer to loneliness, being with a group of people, had not solved her problem. Yvette had gone to that party with one purpose. She wanted to stop feeling lonely, she wanted to meet people and have friends. She wanted people who would take an interest in her and become part of her life. When they continued to be interested in each other and, though friendly to her and happy to include her in their chat, not focusing their attention on her, she felt even more depressed than when she was on her own.

The problem was, Yvette wanted them to be interested in her. She had not gone along with a positive curiosity about them, nor was she particularly interested in them for their own sake. Of course they were not particularly interested in focusing on her, they were surrounded by friends they hadn't seen for a while.

When you're really honest with yourself, what are most people interested in? They're interested in themselves, of course, just as you are. Who has the most friends? The happy gregarious person who is truly interested in, and shows their interest in, other people. If you want to have lots of friends around you, lots of people wanting your company, then take an interest in them.

I suggested this to Edward. 'No way' was his response. 'I don't want to spend all my free time listening to other people's problems, I have enough of my own.'

This attitude, in the long run, will lead to loneliness and continued loneliness.

Jeremy, on the other hand, saw my point. He had recently been through a divorce and was trying to hold down a full-time job and look after his young son. On Saturday nights he had a babysitter and had his one night out. He went to 'Parents without Partners', organised by the local church, and met other people in a similar situation. He had made a few friends there but said that even those evenings were getting to be a bit boring. After we had talked he made a decision. Each time he went he would spend the first hour actively searching out someone new to talk to and then spend the full time listening to their story. After a few weeks he said, the results were amazing.

'Some of them certainly are crashing bores,' he reported, 'but a few of them I have got to know really well. And because I took such an interest in them, or at least I suppose that's the reason, they really seem to like me and want to spend time with me. What I do now is search actively for something they and their children enjoy doing that I and my son also enjoy doing, and then I suggest we meet up and do it. I've made quite a few new friends that way.'

'What else have you noticed?'

'Well. It's funny, you know, it's actually getting quite hard to keep doing this on the Saturday meetings. As soon as I go in the people I already know crowd around and I have to make an effort to break away and search out a new person.'

All this came about because he made the effort to take an active interest in other people in the crowd, not wait for someone in the crowd to take an active interest in him. Had he time to be lonely? No, of course not. Though, as he said, 'If I stop and ask myself the question, "who is interested in me?" the answer is that very few of them are. Most of them enjoy the fact that I am interested in them. But the odd thing is, although it started out as an exercise, I've found I've actually become much more interested in other people.'

It all depends on your attitude, and since your attitude is a product of your thinking and you are in control of your thinking – after all, no one else does your thinking for you – you can change your thinking, hence your attitude and hence your sense of loneliness.

I once knew a woman who had been single for many years and her one goal in life seemed to be to find a partner. Any time she went out, any time she was invited anywhere, any time she went to the pub with friends, to a meeting of her local club or to a business meeting, she had her eye out for the best-looking man and would then quickly find out whether or not he was single. If he wasn't she would leave and search elsewhere. If there was no available single man she had been known to leave the event even before it had got under way. Her phrase being, when I discussed this with her, 'Why not, there was no point in staying.' Sadly, she had earned a name for herself as being 'on the hunt'. Since people, friends and potential hosts and hostesses recognised that she was simply using them in her search for a single man and had no other interest in them, they soon stopped inviting her to be part of their social life.

She couldn't understand why a friend of hers, also in her fifties, always had a man friend around. I pointed out that the second woman was genuinely interested in other people. She wanted to make friends in general, she was quite happy to have an evening with a group of women or of other couples because she genuinely enjoyed people and took an interest in them. At the same time, of course, she was also hoping there would be an interesting single man there, but it wasn't her sole focus. When she did meet a man she continued to demonstrate her interest in other people by being interested in him, rather than being busy assessing his interest in her. No wonder she always had a partner to accompany her.

If you are lonely by all means go and find a group of people to be with, but whether you are with one or two people or with a crowd, remember that the way out of loneliness is to be interested in other people rather than waiting for them to take an interest in you. The interest should be genuine too. Find out how they think and what is important to them, do not simply spend time thinking how what they are saying could work in your favour.

When you do this it is difficult to be alone in a crowd. A crowd is no longer a group of people you are hoping (often without success) will be interested in you, but a large group of people in whom you can take an interest and for you to explore and get to know.

[1] Ayn Rand, *The Virtue of Selfishness – A new concept of egoism*, New American Library, 1965.

[2] David Keirsey and Marilyn Bates, *Please Understand Me*, Prometheus Nemesis Book Company, 1984.

[3] Otto Kroeger and Janet Thuesen, *Type Talk*, Delacorte Press, 1988.

PART II

Solutions

Chapter Five

Falling in Love . . . With Yourself

For many people the answer to being lonely is to fall in love. If you are in your teens and feeling lonely you may be thinking that if you had your own special person you no longer would be lonely. If you had someone you could share things with and who shared things with you – above all, if you had someone who loved you – you would not be lonely. This situation is not confined to your teenage years. It is just as powerful a dream in your twenties and thirties. What may surprise you, if you are under forty, is that it continues to be a dream of many, probably the majority, of single people in their forties, fifties and beyond. So let's see what falling in love is all about, how to make it happen, and how to create situations where it solves your problem of loneliness.

At a recent seminar I gave on 'Falling in Love' I asked participants to write down a list of all the things they wanted from the relationship they were seeking. If you really want to get the most out of reading this chapter then stop reading now. Find a sheet of paper and a pen and write down your own list. Then, and only then, read on.

Here is a list of some of the answers:

Someone who loves me.
Someone to love.
Someone to be there for me.
Someone to share things with.
Someone to go to social events with.
Someone who will like me no matter what I do.
Someone who cares how I feel.
Someone who shares my interests.
Someone who supports me when I need help, feel lonely or am in trouble.
Someone who will know what to do when I get stuck.
Someone who will protect me from my relatives.
Someone who defends me when I am criticised.
Someone I can relax with.
Someone who'll look after me.
Someone who's wealthy and good-looking.

Consider that list. By and large the points are all about what the individuals wanted for themselves, the requirements the people had. They wanted, as a result of falling in love, to have a partner who would build their lives round the individual concerned. They wanted the other person to focus on them. In most people's lists there were elements of sharing, of loving as well as being loved and of having a companion, but the overwhelming number of requirements revolved around the benefit the other person provided to the individual concerned by focusing on the needs of that individual.

Let's see what the opposite list would have been, the

list as it would have to be from the point of view of the person you want to fall in love with you:

Someone to love.
Someone who loves me.
Someone I can focus on.
Someone to share things with.
Someone to go to social events with.
Someone I can like no matter what they do.
Someone whose feelings I can care about.
Someone whose interests I can share.
Someone I can support when they need help, feel lonely or are in trouble.
Someone I will know how to help when they get stuck.
Someone I can protect from their relatives.
Someone I can defend when they are criticised.
Someone who can relax with me.
Someone I can look after.
Someone I can spend money on and look good for.

When you read the first list you may have thought it was a reasonable one. That if you could find someone who filled those requirements for you, you could be happy, and would stop feeling lonely. Yet when you read the list from the second perspective it becomes obvious how self-focused the original list was. Ask yourself this. Who do you know, realistically, who would write down the second list as their requirement for falling in love? The answer is almost certainly 'no one'.

If you are single, if you are lonely then ask yourself this. Assuming you did as was suggested and wrote your own list before reading this, how many self-focused requirements are there in your list of what you want in a loving partnership? If you did not write your own list now is the time to be honest with yourself. If you were to write it now how many of the items would involve the other person focusing on you?

Someone, out there, willing to focus on you will be very hard to find. If you need someone else to make you whole, someone else who can fill in the gaps, provide you with the strengths you don't have and the back-up you feel you cannot give yourself, then you may be in for a long search.

We have already talked about the desirability of looking at other people as new and interesting people to get to know in their own right, rather than in the light of what they can do for you. Yet the sad fact is, that when two lonely people get together and decide they are falling in love, they may well find that in fact they have each been feeding the other's needs in such a way that neither of them becomes whole, neither of them benefits.

Sara came to see me because she had recently 'fallen in love' and started to live with, as she put it, 'the most wonderful man'.

'I know it sounds silly, coming here I mean, when I'm madly in love. But at the same time, I'm not happy, he doesn't seem to need me. He told me that, if ever I want to leave, to end the relationship, to simply say the word and he would go. I couldn't bear it if he left, not only do I love him, but I was so lonely on my own.'

'Why do you think he said what he did?' I asked.

'I don't really know. It's true that we come from different social spheres, I went to university and he didn't, and my family is pretty well off whereas he had to make his own way. But he's successful now. So I don't really think it can be that. But I'm starting to feel so insecure. Perhaps he doesn't really love me. After all, how could he say that, if he did?'

'Did you ask him why he said it?'

'Yes, of course, and he said he hated seeing relationships where one person really wasn't happy and wanted to separate but the other person was hanging on.'

'Does he love you?'

'Yes, I'm sure he does, in fact I've never felt so loved.'

'So what's the problem?'

'I don't know, I guess it's sort of as if I'm not needed. As if he can manage on his own without me, even though he does love me . . .' And her voice trailed off.

Obviously here was the crux of the matter. They both loved each other, but she had a need *for him (an addiction) and felt that if he left her she would be bereft and lost, whereas he knew he had a centre within himself and that the relationship he experienced with her was a wonderful bonus, but not an absolute necessity for his well-being (a preference). We worked together on this and then I didn't see her for a few years. When I eventually did see her again I asked her how it was going and her response was immediate.*

'It's wonderful, I followed up on what you said and what we did together and as a result I've learnt to be emotionally independent, at peace within myself, just like he is. As a result we love each other, but we don't lean on each other, and we each have so much more to give to the relationship and neither of us feels trapped or restricted by it. We are independent people yet offering so much to each other.'

'And looking back on it, what do you think was the crucial step in getting to that state?' I asked.

'Oh without doubt, as you said it would be, when I learnt to love, respect and honour myself.'

Loving yourself is so important, yet, for many people, it is so difficult both to do and to acknowledge. Why is this? We are taught from birth to put other people first. Our parents and teachers see this as teaching us manners, consideration for others and social graces. To the toddler and young child, however, who live, inevitably and appropriately, in a self-oriented world, this simply tells them that other people are more important than they are themselves. This in turn tells them that they are not as good as other people. If little Jamie, the friend who comes in from next door, must have first choice and be able to pick the biggest and the nicest biscuit, then he must be better than I am, so goes the internal and often unconscious reasoning. If Jennifer, also rushing to join the queue, must be allowed to go first, when you are told not to push or shove, it tells you she is better or more important than you are.

It doesn't matter that, when you go next door to visit, Jamie's mother makes sure you get the first choice and can pick the biggest biscuit, it is what *your* parent tells you that sets the tone. In addition there will inevitably be more situations in which you are told to defer to others, both of your own, young, age group and older, than when they are told to defer to you.

The next step concerns what you say about yourself. As a toddler you are excited when you can do something. At first it's a case of 'Look Mummy, see what I can do' which is met with encouragement and praise. Soon, however, for some reason you are unable to fathom, things start to go wrong and saying, 'I came top, I did better than David, I'm cleverer than he is' is met with 'Yes dear, very good, but don't boast.' The knife really falls when you announce, 'I'm good at singing,' and you're told not to be so conceited and that you must learn to be more modest – definite disapproval for the behaviour you have displayed.

All this is done with the best intent. It is done in the interest, as we have seen, of teaching manners, but it does nothing to build a person's often fragile self-confidence. Eventually you learn that if you want praise and approval it must come from other people, on no account must you voice it yourself. Furthermore, even then, when you do receive it, you are supposed to downplay it and look self-effacing. Over the years all this leads to a pattern of poor self-image and dependency on the approval of other people. Of course you're lonely and unhappy if you don't have someone else to love you; you can't, so goes the conventional wisdom, love and approve of yourself so you need someone else to do it for you. Nonsense. The sooner you start to love, admire, respect, acknowledge and feel good about yourself, the better.

This does not mean you run around grandstanding, that you spend all your time talking about yourself and the wonderful things you can do. Of course there are social and appropriate limits. It does, however, mean that you become very comfortable with yourself, that you start focusing on your good points and stop criticising yourself, that you become content with who you are, confident that it is your own opinion of yourself that matters and that you can look in the mirror in the morning and say to the image you see, in full confidence, 'I love you and recognise you as a wonderful person.' None of this means that you are perfect, or that you don't want to develop and change. That can be happening at the same time. After all, you love and approve of other people if they aren't perfect. You want someone to love and approve of you, warts and all. Why not do it for yourself as well?

It is time for you to take out pen and paper again. Make two lists, one of everything you normally say to yourself that is critical, the other of all your good points, the ones you frequently acknowledge to yourself. Which list is the longer? You might also want to make a list of the character traits you have that you are trying to change and improve. This will give you something to work on, but that is part of another story, another project. You can learn a lot about yourself this way. Notice how you felt while you were writing each list, which one made you the more uncomfortable, and in what way. Did you find it easier to criticise yourself than to praise yourself? Did you criticise yourself for doing things that you condone in other people? Did you find you expected yourself to have everyone else's best attributes, all rolled into one? Do you refuse to forgive yourself for any or all past transgressions or omissions? Did you, on the other hand, make a much longer list on the praise side than on the criticism side? Do you refuse to recognise things that could be changed? It is great to feel proud of yourself and to love yourself but if, at the moment, you are lonely, it may be worth looking for a few possible changes that could alter this situation. Remember to do it all in a positive frame of mind though, without blame, but with a positive intent to change for the better, if that is appropriate.

Theresa looked dubious when I asked her to do this, saying, 'OK, I'll do it, but I don't see how it is going to help, I already know myself, it won't change anything.' When she came in the following week she had a long list of criticisms and negative comments she had made about herself and a short list of positive comments. As I read aloud her first list she remained silent, but as I started on the positive list she made several comments to downplay what she had written.

'Which list was the easier to write?' I asked.

'Oh, the long one of course, the one full of criticisms. When I tried to write positive things, I kept feeling I had to make other comments on the side.'

'Such as?'

'Well, when I said I have a good figure, I felt I should add that I still ought to lose a few pounds, and when I said I was good at my job I found I wanted to list the mistakes I had made and that shouldn't have happened. I know I can be good company, but I'm shy and have to

force myself so I didn't really feel that was a positive. I had to keep the list hidden too, I didn't want anyone to see it.'

'Which part of it?'

'Well, all the boasting of course.'

She hadn't minded letting people see a list of her faults in her own handwriting, feeling, in part, that by writing down and acknowledging her sins and omissions she would be forgiven them. She had minded other people seeing her own positive opinions of herself, feeling that other people might argue with her and she would then have to defend them. In other words, not only was her list of criticisms much longer than her list of personal praise or acknowledgement, she was also a lot more sure of it.

She was then asked to relax, close her eyes and slow down the mental chatter going on in her head, as I gave her the following instructions:

'Feel yourself, sitting in the chair, arms supported, feet relaxed and on the ground, focusing on my voice. Now start to float up, leaving your body behind, let your mind take you up until you are on the ceiling, looking down. Look down on Theresa, there below you. Can you see her?'

'Yes.'

'Good, now float up higher still. You can see Xandria and Theresa, both in the room together?'

'Yes.'

'Good, now notice that you can see other people too, people in Theresa's life. Notice them, but bring your focus back on Theresa. Watch her as she gets on with her life, mentally look down at her as she goes to work, goes home, meets her friends, does the shopping. Now start to list the positive things you say about her.'

Theresa continued to do this for some time, then I told

her to be back down in her body, feeling the chair, becoming aware of the room again, and her body.

'Wow, that was interesting,' was her first comment. 'It was much easier to be positive about myself when I felt I was describing someone else. From up there I really did seem to have a lot more to offer.'

I suggested that she should practise doing this.

You can do the same. Each day, take some time to float up and look down on yourself, from second position. Recognise all the wonderful things you did in the day, the achievements, large and small. Grow to feel more positive about yourself and then learn to love yourself. Because you have been taught to see the best in other people, when you are looking down on yourself as another person, it is often much easier to recognise your good points. You are less likely to be unnecessarily hard on yourself.

As I said before, you may still want to develop and improve. Seeing yourself in this objective light you may still decide there are changes you want to make. However, there is a difference. Instead of saying, 'Idiot, I should *not* have done that,' and then blaming yourself, you are more likely to think, 'Mmm, next time I must do it differently.'

Several things are achieved by this exercise. You will find it is much easier to be objective about yourself when you are out of your body, looking down on yourself. It is much easier to recognise and acknowledge the good things and be able to articulate them. You are less likely to be self-critical. You can begin to see yourself as others see you. When you look down on yourself in relation to other people it is easier to see how they could come to love you and want to spend time with you. As a result it is also easier to feel positive about yourself and start the process of learning to love yourself.

There are other ways in which you can continue this process of learning to love yourself – and you can do this, as you hope someone else will, without having to be perfect first. So now is the time to do some more exercises.

Think of someone you know and love dearly. Ideally you could use a photo of them. If you don't have one then call their image to mind as vividly as you can. Focus on them totally and as you look at them, bring up all the warm and loving feelings you have about them. Then instantly put a photo of yourself, or your image of yourself, in its place and *keep the same feelings going*. As soon as the loving fades put the other person's picture back up and renew the feelings, then replace it with yours again. Do this over and over again until you can feel as loving about yourself as you can about them. You can strengthen the process by using pictures or images of different people you love. This is a two-way process and if you find, every time you look at your own image, that your feelings are negative, there could be a risk of transferring this negativity to the person in the photo. By using a variety of different people you love you can avoid this risk and strengthen the positive effect on yourself.

Notice that the people you love are not all perfect. They do not have to be perfect for you to love them. Similarly you do not have to be perfect to love yourself. Having warm and loving feelings about yourself is not dependent on you being perfect, it does not have to wait until such time as you stop criticising yourself or recognising there are things about yourself that you want to change.

As one patient said to me, with wonder in his eyes, 'Goodness, I'm prepared to love a lot of people, faults and all, but I've been refusing to love myself until I'm perfect.

No wonder it's taking me so long.' Once he got over that hurdle his self-confidence grew and he was able to make friends much more easily.

Some people feel they have to be good-looking to be popular. They look in the mirror and say something like, 'With a face like that, who is going to like you?' If that is your thought, think about people you know who are not considered to be particularly attractive physically, they may even be ugly, yet who are fun to be with and popular. Looks vary with the fashion. Two hundred years ago curves were beautiful, now slim is beautiful. There are no absolutes. An attractive face can look ugly if the owner has a negative self-image and a plain person can look stunning when love, interest, humour and affection shine out of their eyes.

Some people feel they must be outgoing and positive before they can like themselves or be popular, but think about this. What would happen if everyone was a talkative extrovert? There would be no listeners. If you feel shy, practise focusing on listening to others, being interested in them, and letting them know it. You don't have to be brilliant, witty and highly intelligent to be popular and lovable. Yet many people castigate themselves for their lack of these attributes and dislike themselves as a result.

There are no rights and wrongs. There is no way that you should be or should not be. Whatever you are is whatever you are. There is no absolute authority with the right to judge how you, or anyone else, should be. Everyone has attributes they want to build on and others they would like to drop. The point is to focus on your positive aspects, love yourself as you are and, in time, make the changes you want to make.

Here is another exercise using a mirror. Talk to the image you see. Find a time when no one can hear you if you are afraid of feeling embarrassed. Talk out loud and say, 'I love you, you are a warm and wonderful person' to the image you see. Magic of magic, the image will, of course be saying it back to you. Do this as often as you can until you come to feel that the image is your best friend, someone who is always there for you – they are, aren't they – and who loves you just as frequently as you love them. Become comfortable with yourself.

A interesting psychological study of successful people produced some results that are of value to us here. It was shown that as soon as these successful people started to have a peak experience, be that one of being successful in something they had accomplished, of saying something witty and being applauded, of doing something caring and being praised, or of giving and being hugged in return, they immediately built on that experience. They started to create, unconsciously and involuntarily, more such experiences for themselves. If they experienced being loved as a pleasurable experience they, in many subtle and unconscious ways, did things that brought that experience into their life with increasing frequency. If they enjoyed praise they started to do more things that brought praise. In this way they built on their successes and became more successful.

In the same way, if you become used to experiencing love from yourself, if you start to create the warm and comfortable feeling that that can generate, you will almost certainly, in many small but significant ways, do things that bring the same experience into your life from other sources as well. This process may be conscious, but it will also be happening unconsciously. Without thinking about it, but as a result of your positive feelings for yourself, you will gradually start to do things that make other people feel warm and positive about you. If you keep repeating the exercise the whole process will continue to grow until you find you are much happier and certainly not lonely.

Ian didn't believe this. 'How can loving myself in the mirror every morning make some woman fall in love with me?' This was his immediate question when I discussed the above ideas with him.

Rather than talk any more I suggested that he be willing to take the idea on trust and practise it. After all, since he lived alone, no one would know what he was doing. After a slow start he got the hang of it and came to see me a few months later in great excitement.

'I did what you suggested,' he said, 'and it seemed pretty stupid at first. But after a while it got easier and easier, and then a funny thing happened. I'd see a pretty woman looking at me, in the pub for instance, with a group of friends, or in the office, and I'd find myself automatically assuming that she liked me. It was almost as if I was saying to her in my mind, "See, I'm really a nice guy." Before I did this exercise I would have thought that she was just being polite, because I knew I was a pretty dull sort of a chap. When I assumed she liked me I then found I would smile back at her much more warmly, I'd take it for granted she wanted to be friendly and we'd strike up a conversation. All the time now, I find I feel pretty good about such situations, relaxed, you know, not wondering what it is the other person sees in me.'

'And have you fallen in love?' I asked.

'Not yet, but I'm certainly not lonely any more, I seem to be able to make friends so much more easily, and I'm much more relaxed about myself and my life. In fact I'm having such a good time I'm not sure I want to settle down any more!'

The process works. So does the opposite one. If you look in the mirror each morning and grimace at it, accompanied by some negative comments, you can lower your self-image and your self-esteem, behave accordingly, and drive people away just as easily as you can attract them. It's up to you. Look at your image and choose whether or not you want to feel positive or negative about it and, in turn, whether you want to convey to other people a positive or a negative message. The great thing about all this is that you are in control, you can choose, and you can create your life the way you want it to be. No one can stop you, it's up to you.

There is another facet to loving yourself, and another benefit that comes from it. You know yourself better than anyone else does. If you, by your actions and deeds, as well as by your speech and displays of emotion, let the world know that you don't think much of yourself, that you don't particularly like yourself, that you don't think you are a warm and loving person, an interesting person and someone whose company is desirable, then people will, however subconsciously, take their cue from you. If you judge yourself to be dull and boring you will inevitably demonstrate this in many subtle ways and as a result others will almost certainly start to think so too. If you think you are unlovable they may also get that message. When you start to display a behaviour that lets people know, however subtly and circumspectly, that you are wonderful, interesting and fun to be with, that you have much to offer in a relationship, of whatever sort, then other people get this message and you will find, as Ian did, that you become much more popular. The interest is genuine, and the way out of loneliness is at hand.

Chapter Six

Making Yourself Lonely

It is all too easy to make yourself lonely, to do things that contribute, either directly or indirectly, to your own isolation and lack of obvious popularity.

Few people have a full quota of self-confidence and self-assurance. Even those who appear confident frequently have their inner doubts. The nature of most people's upbringing militates against complete confidence. From soon after birth, and certainly from as soon as you could understand what was being said, you were criticised far more often than you were praised. A much-quoted American study showed that children were told off, or made wrong, on average ten times as often as they were complimented or praised.

As a result of this, and other factors in early childhood and programming, the majority of people have a healthy slice of self-doubt and self-criticism. Many people focus on their faults, or their perceived faults. They feel they are too selfish and demanding, too irritable and impatient, too dull and uninteresting, too silly and stupid. They may consider themselves thoughtless, boring, horrid, deceitful, aggressive and more. This is not always true, yet at the same time, people tend to live up to their own image of themselves and so, to all intents and purposes, it often either becomes true or seems to become true.

One client said she declined invitations to small dinner parties as she felt she was stupid and had nothing clever to say. As such she preferred to stay away from situations in which she would have to contribute to the conversation and be listened to by several people, rather than go along, make a fool of herself, and not be invited again, or to other events. After several refusals on her part people soon stopped asking her out at all and she became even more lonely, the very thing she had, ostensibly, sought to avoid.

Another client was frequently cross and bad-tempered. When this happened, when he got irritated or lost his temper with someone, he would stalk off, saying he didn't want to see that person again. He didn't mean it, but when his temper got the better of him he found it hard to bite his words and, once said, he found it nearly impossible to back down, to apologise or to mend the bridges that had been broken.

Freida liked to be popular and in demand. One way to achieve this, she felt, was to show the people she was with that other people liked her, trusted her and shared confidences with her. To demonstrate this she then had to pass on the information that she had received. Thus she became known as a gossip. Not only that, but since bad news is generally thought to be more exciting and interesting than good news she was always searching out and sharing the bad news. Much as this might, initially, interest her listeners, they inevitably began to wonder what she was passing on about them and they became cautious when around her. In time her friends found it easier to avoid her altogether, for the harm she could do them.

Arnold wanted to get on to the committee of his local club. He was unsure of his own abilities, afraid other people had more chance than he did, so he found ways to criticise the competition. He would tell the chairman that so-and-so had made a mess of this project and that someone else had not fulfilled his commitment on another project. Not only did this not get him on to the committee, but it was the cause of him losing a lot of the support that he had had.

Margaret had moved to a new town and lived alone. Since she hated to be alone she was always looking for things to do, where she could be with people. Not only that, but she went in search of the most interesting social situation, the place or event at which she would meet the most interesting people. Because she was lonely she would accept any invitation that came along, however uninterested she was in it. Then, if a better invitation came along she would accept that in turn, and then cancel the previous one. The friends she did have soon came to feel they were being used. Not only did her friends have the inconvenience of cancelled invitations, they also experienced the rejection of being found wanting when measured against an alternative invitation. Inevitably the few friends she started with, and any new ones she made, recognised the pattern and they soon stopped inviting her, so Margaret became even more lonely.

Do you do any of these things, or anything that could make you similarly unpopular? Are you critical, do you get jealous, are you a gossip, are you inconsiderate? You don't have to admit or acknowledge any of this to anybody else, but this is the time to be honest, totally honest, with yourself. Remember, this is not about blame and self-castigation. You still *are* lovable, within yourself. However, this is also a time for honest self-appraisal. It is a time to recognise the characteristics, the behaviours, that you might decide are worth changing. If you are lonely, if you are not invited to things to which you would like to be invited, if people do not rush to accept your invitations, if groups you are in seem to disintegrate, then consider in what way your behaviour causes the people involved not to be especially keen to spend time with you.

You may have some particularly nasty social habits (and remember, it is the habit that is the problem, not you as a person; habits are not you, they are behaviours that can be changed). You may have only moderately unwelcome habits, such as those mentioned earlier. You may even have only very minor habits that are interfering with your desired social life. You may be so introverted and shy that people don't notice you in the crowd since you add little or nothing to the occasion; you may be so protective of yourself that you share little and people feel you are cold and unfeeling. You may simply prefer to listen rather than chatter, yet social interactions are all about sharing and, if you want to be invited again, it behoves you to contribute something, however small. Alternatively, you may hog the limelight. You may simply talk too much and show too little interest in other people. After all, they too want other people, including you, to pay attention to them.

Keep in mind too, as indicated above, that it is not you that is inherently bad or unwanted, it is only your current behaviour. Behaviour is something you can change. There is too little distinction made, in our use of language, between the person and the behaviour. You frequently hear someone saying, 'You are bad,' or 'You are wrong,' when what they really mean is, 'You are wonderful but what you just did is bad,' or 'You are terrific, but I think in this instance your assessment is incorrect.' No one is inherently bad, stupid, unwanted, unlovable etc. It is what they are currently doing, saying or thinking that is under consideration, and what you are doing, saying or thinking are all things you can change, voluntarily, and any time you like.

Remember too, it is not a question of whether you are right or wrong, or whether your behaviour is right or wrong. You may indeed have behaved, by your standards, better than the other person or people did. That is not the point. If you want to be with people, if you want them to want to be with you, then you must have something to offer them. If someone is demanding and selfish but you want to be with them and want them to want you then, up to a point, you must fit in with them. You must give them something, be it your patience, your tolerance or your willingness to put up with their moods. You cannot make a friend of them by insisting they change their behaviour to suite you and your needs and demands. If this does not seem like a fair exchange to you then look elsewhere for friends.

As many people have quoted and requoted, 'The meaning of your communication is the response you get.' You may mean to tell someone you like them and want to help them but if they feel criticised by your comment then, no matter what you actually meant, criticism is what you have communicated. Similarly, 'The result that you get is the consequence of your strategy.' If you gossip as a means of trying to show that you are friends with lots of people but, as a result, the people at work avoid you, then your strategy has led to loneliness, no matter what you intended.

Having come this far let us assume that you really do want to do whatever it takes to eradicate the loneliness. Since it is very much easier to make changes in yourself than to demand that other people make them, that is the strategy we are adopting and it is now time to see what changes you could make to become someone who is more in demand, who has more friends and who has less chance of being lonely. Now is the time to 'become a(n even) nicer person' and the next few chapters will give you a lot of clues as to how to do it.

As a final thought, consider this. If the strategy you are presently adopting is not achieving the goal you are after then change your strategy. If you decide the effort isn't worth it then recognise that it is you that have chosen to stay lonely. It is not the fault of other people. Faced with this thought, few people who are lonely will not change what they are doing unless they are getting some benefit from being lonely. The benefit may only be that of not having to make the effort to change, or it may be more, as we have already discussed, but there is indeed some benefit or you *would* change.

Chapter Seven

Stop Being a Victim

Many people do get a benefit out of being the victim, of being unhappy, of being lonely or of being treated poorly. Unsure whether people will like them for themselves perhaps, or want to be around and listen to them, they may feel, at some unconscious level at least, that people will feel constrained to spend more time with them when they say they are lonely; they will be with them to cheer them up when things go wrong, to make them happy if they are sad, ill or lonely.

Although the word 'victim' is commonly used in this context, the implication is not that you are being seriously victimised. This concept applies to anyone who feels that they are being badly done by, that things are happening in their life that they don't like, and over which, they complain, they have no control.

Some people recognise this trait in themselves relatively easily. Others will insist that there is no positive benefit to being the victim, to having things go wrong, yet underneath, there is often an element of enjoying victim status in even the most positive person. So before you brush this off as rubbish think about the times you have told a story about yourself in which you are the one who is suffering. Have you told someone about the dreadful flight you had, the parking problem you had, the health problem or the time when someone cheated on you? Have you complained about poor service or your rotten luck? What is the point of these stories? Are you really proud to tell your listener(s) how other people were able to take advantage of you, how you made poor choices of airline or going by car? No, you were the victim, you were the loser, the person who was suffering. Subconsciously you are after a different gain. As a result of telling the story your listeners are going to be sympathetic and their attention will be focused on you. As the result of telling a bigger negative story than the last person you get a bigger slice of the attention and sympathy.

Next time you are with a group of people, make a conscious decision not to tell a story in which something negative happens to you. The extent to which you have to make an effort to hold your tongue is a measure of the amount of time you spend being a victim.

Some people even remain lonely because, at some deep level, they are fearful of forgoing the sympathy that their loneliness elicits from others. To the extent that this is true they either don't try to solve the problem, they don't do the things that would take them out and among people, or they sabotage the efforts which they, or other people, do make.

Before going further into this section keep the following in mind. No one, ultimately, does things to harm themselves. Everyone thinks there will be some positive gain out of what they are doing. Do not blame yourself, if you come to recognise that you have been choosing victim status, even if only occasionally, as a way out of your problems, as a strategy for getting attention. You undoubtedly did, in the past, whatever you did with the best possible intent. You saw it, consciously or unconsciously, as a useful strategy for dealing with a situation you didn't like. What you should now consider is whether or not this is the best possible strategy. Since victim status rarely is the best possible strategy, if for no other reason than that it keeps you in an unresourceful state, now may be the time to consider making appropriate changes.

Donald was a computer programmer whose job involved fixing the problems of the company's clients. He and his colleagues worked a roster system, twenty-four hours a day, so that in theory, once he had done his shift he was free to go home. Home, however, was a bachelor flat and, since he was shy and had found it difficult to make friends, his social life was limited. He bought computer magazines and spent much of his spare time on his own, reading.

After a few treatment sessions he was beginning to make an effort to meet people and to change some of his attitudes as we've already discussed, and all seemed to be going well. Then he told me that it was really rather difficult and that, because of his shift work, he had to keep refusing the few invitations he had begun to get. I was surprised at this since I knew he was given his roster in advance and could plan ahead.

When I asked for specific details it soon became obvious that on many occasions he could have made it, he could have gone to the dinner party, could have met up with the people who had invited him; instead he had stayed on at work after *his shift. He always had a good reason; he was in the middle of working with a client's problem and it would have been difficult for someone else to take over without having to start again, or he'd dealt with the client before so it made sense for him to do this job.*

When I worked a bit further with him I began to suspect that he was using work as an excuse to turn down invitations, so I used the technique of 'Running a Phrase'[1] to help him identify the root cause. To use this technique you start with a phrase, a half-sentence.

This keeps your conscious mind busy. It also implies that you know how to complete the phrase, so your subconscious mind, instead of blocking the information as it might do if confronted with a direct question, works hard to come up with a completion. The first completions, as the following work with Donald shows, may reveal little, but if you persist, refusing to enter into dialogue and, robot-like, keep repeating the initial phrase, or one that logically and constructively suggests itself to you as an alternative, you will eventually get completions that give you the information you are after. This is how it went with Donald.

'A reason you turn down social invitations in preference to work is . . .' I prompted.

' . . . the work seems important.'

' . . . I can't let my clients down.'

' . . . I find their problems interesting.'

Clearly this was getting us nowhere so I switched to 'A benefit I get from turning down the social invitations is . . .' and waited.

'I don't get one, there is no benefit,' was his initial response, but I encouraged him to continue by repeating the phrase with a slight modification, 'A result I get from turning down the social invitations when I do extra work is . . .' and waited again.

' . . . I feel proud that I have put work first and the client is happy.'

' . . . I stay at home more.'

' . . . I don't get asked out so much.'

'And the result of that is . . .'

' . . . I get lonely again.'

'And a benefit you derive from that is . . .'

' . . . I don't know, there isn't one.'

'A benefit you derive from that is . . .' I prompted again.

' . . . I suppose I feel that people will be more sym-

pathetic to me. And I guess, in some funny way, I feel I'll be invited out more. I guess I feel that they only invite me out because I am lonely. Isn't that weird?'

He laughed slightly at that. 'Silly isn't it. It seems that if I keep accepting invitations and start mixing with people and stop being lonely I feel they'll have no more reason to invite me out.'

The answer in Donald's case was for him to work on his self-esteem so that he came to realise that people actually could like him for himself. He didn't have to be a victim to loneliness before people would include him in what they were doing.

Now it's time for you to do a similar exercise. Run the phrase for yourself, 'A benefit I get from staying lonely is . . .' and repeat it over and over, writing down as many completions as you get. If your conscious mind is too busy chattering and denying that there is any benefit from being lonely, do as I did with Donald and change the phrase to 'A result I get from being lonely is . . .'

No matter how lonely you are, how on your own you seem to be, there is always something you could do to change the situation. You always have choices. You may not like the other alternatives much, but you do have choices.

Jennifer was the mother of three small children under five. Her husband worked long hours and often came home late having gone down to the pub on the way home. They had no money and Jennifer couldn't get out except to go shopping and take the kids to school. There was no money for a social life and she felt isolated at home. After we worked together she realised she had been using her lonely state as a factor to throw at her husband in their frequent arguments. Once she was willing to let go of that she got together with some other women in a similar situation and organised a babysitting roster so they could do things together socially in groups and each have some time on their own.

In her case the solution was a practical one, one she could apply as soon as she was willing to let go of the need to blame her husband for her situation. To achieve this she had had to do some soul searching. Since an argument takes a minimum of two people, and since she recognised that the easiest thing to change was herself, she was willing to sort her own ideas out. In another situation it might have been important to sit down with her husband and discuss and resolve their differences. As she started spending more time with her women friends she found, to her surprise, that her husband also wanted to do more things with her, utilising the same babysitting roster, and her life changed even further.

Howard was lonely after his wife died. His arthritis was bad and the pension didn't stretch to assistance. He stayed lonely because it was too much effort to go out and meet new people and, as he repeated several times, it was up to his children to come and cheer him up and invite him out. Since they didn't, or not often enough to please him, he chose to remain lonely and complain to the neighbours. After our discussion he finally acknowledged that what he was doing wasn't working, it wasn't leading to more visits from his children, in fact it was driving them even further away. He recognised that he couldn't force them to come and visit him so he agreed to look for company from elsewhere. His solution was to arrange for a social worker to drive him to a nursing home nearby where he read to people each afternoon. As so often happens, he found that when he made these changes himself, he became livelier and happier, his family began to think of him as being more fun, and so they brought the grandchildren to visit him more often. When they did come, instead of complaining, as in the old days, he started playing games with them.

Stan complained that he was lonely and miserable now that he had retired – early through a company take-over. His had been a job that kept his mind fully alert and occupied. Now he said that the crossword was about the most intelligent thing he did and he was bored and lonely, lonely because he got fed up with the gossip and chatter that passed for conversation among the few people he did meet.

'It's no good at my age. After you're fifty people think your brain has addled and no one wants the knowledge you've built up.' He preferred to sit around on his own rather than get involved in the social activities that were easily available to him. After three years of loneliness and bellyaching about the unfairness of being retrenched and of the idiots that surrounded him he finally came to realise that if he wasn't to vegetate for the rest of his life it was up to him to make a change. He started doing studies at the Open University. Since he couldn't get about much physically he taught himself to use a computer and the internet and in that way 'talked' to the other students in the classes he was doing.

'And it's wonderful.' he said with a grin. 'They don't know my age and I don't know theirs, it really is mind talking to mind. It almost makes me glad I don't have to go to work any more and do have the time for it.'

In these and a million other situations people could be lonely if they chose. You can be a victim if you so choose, but in the long run it rarely pays off or gets you the benefits you want. Running a Phrase is one of the best methods of finding the hidden agenda, the hidden benefits. However, some straightforward self-assessment may also do it. Decide to monitor your thoughts and words for the next week or more. Every time you find yourself saying something negative, complaining about something or telling a story of something negative that has happened in your life, stop, write it down, at least enough to remember it later on. Then give yourself a quiet time each day and in that time review what you have written. Ask yourself what you derived from it, what the result was of saying what you did.

Sometimes you will find that your goal was to make someone else wrong, to show them up as being to blame or at fault. At other times there may have been a slightly more positive outcome, such as getting attention, sympathy etc. Whatever the goal was, write it down. If the goal really seemed negative, like making someone else wrong, search a little deeper. Even a criticism of someone else may have a positive goal, such as to show your own discernment (see Chapter Ten). Whatever the benefit of what you have been doing by choosing to be a victim, the next step is to find ways to get the same positive outcome by a method that leaves you in control of your own life, as the people described above did.

Then, having recognised what you are doing, stop yourself every time you are about to say anything that would involve you being a victim, one of the sufferers. As we said earlier, if this means you suddenly have very little to say you will realise just how entrenched the pattern was.

If you truly don't want to be lonely there is certainly something you can do, you just have to be sufficiently determined. It may not lead you to your heart's desire. You may not find the knight in shining armour, win the lottery, have all your old friends flock around you, get your old job back or convert the children into your image of what they should be, but there are things you can do that can make a difference to your life; and the results may well surprise you, as they certainly did in Stan's case.

Stop Complaining

A friend of mine was complaining that she wished she could afford to live in a fashionable part of London when another guest, living in Clapham, turned to her and said, 'At least you live north of the river.' Suddenly my friend realised that she took for granted living in a part of London that other people would love to live in and for which they envied her. 'All at once,' she said, 'I realised that while I was busy envying other people and complaining about where I lived and what I had, there were other people, a lot worse off, who would have given their eye-teeth to have what I have and live where I live. It made me stop and fully appreciate, for the first time, just what I do have. I promised myself then I'd never complain again – or that if I did I'd stop and remind myself of what I've got.'

It's all too easy to say such things as 'Other people are worse off, I should be grateful for what I've got,' but it sometimes takes more, as my friend found, to drive the point home.

People who are lonely may be complainers. You may be one. You may not see yourself as such, you may not hear what you are saying to people, how you are complaining about the way you feel about this and about that, even if it's only about feeling lonely. Yet it is possible that you are, and there is nothing like complaining to drive other people away. None of us is so poor or so badly off that there are not other people who envy us. Even if there were, complaining would do little good.

For a start, listen to yourself. Make it a project to discover any single comment you make that could be construed as a complaint, as discontent. Make a list, write them all down. Then make a second list. Write down one hundred things that you have in your life that you like and appreciate. They need not be big things, they could include individual aspects of your health, aspects of your home down to the smallest detail, your work, your clothes, your friends, your family. When you have listed one hundred things start again and list another hundred, then a third. By the time you have listed a thousand things that you do have, the ones that you don't have will seem less important. And there will be a thousand positive things you can list. You almost certainly have at least a thousand things in your life that other people would value, you only have to think of some of the worst problem areas in the world to realise that.

Margaret had psoriasis. She was thirty-seven, single and living alone. Because of her skin condition she refused to go out and meet people when it was bad. When she did go out she complained. She insisted it was because of her health that she was lonely and that unless she got rid of the psoriasis she would continue to be lonely. I encouraged her to list all the health assets she had and told her I wanted at least a hundred. Eventually she listed many more than that. She didn't have cancer, she didn't have Aids, she didn't have arthritis, high blood pressure or diabetes, she wasn't in pain, and so it went, as she listed all the other diseases and problems she didn't have. She had good eyesight, she could hear, she had control of all her bodily functions (and she listed them) her teeth were good.

'That's all very well, though, but other people don't have those problems either.'

I simply looked at her in obvious disbelief.

'Well, you know what I mean, most people don't.'

'Maybe not, but think of the hundreds of thousands of people that do. If you sat in my seat you would see, daily, thoroughly normal and generally happy-looking people describing incredible health and emotional problems.'

Her attitude had changed by her next visit.

'I've been thinking about those lists that I made. And I've watched people this week. There's a woman at work with arthritis and there are lots of things she can't do. Even getting up and down steps is difficult, yet she never complains and she's very popular.'

Is the glass half full or half empty? Think positively rather than in double negatives. If you think, 'I mustn't complain,' your subconscious will focus on complaining. Furthermore, such habits are ingrained and not easily altered. The better way is to make the internal shift so that you truly stop feeling you have anything to complain about. Focus instead on what you do have, on the 'half full' aspects of your life.

Peter, a quiet bachelor in his early thirties, complained that he was poor. If he had more money, he insisted, he could afford a better lifestyle. He would then be able to do more socially, would have more fun and be less lonely. As it was he made barely enough to make ends meet. He turned down invitations to the pub, saying he couldn't afford the cost of a beer, and he turned down suggestions of outings for the same reason. He also blamed his lack of a girlfriend on lack of funds.

I told him to make a list of a hundred ways in which he was wealthy, financially, of a hundred things he could afford. He looked dubious initially but then got into the swing of it as I suggested that he could afford clothes:

'But I haven't bought anything new for months.'

'List all the clothes you do have.'

Food:

'But I can't eat out – I never do, it's too expensive. And I have to be careful in the supermarkets too.'

'List all the types of food you can afford to buy.'

Travel:

'Hah, that's a laugh. I'm never likely to own a car. I get a monthly travel pass, I need that to go to work each day and that's it, I can't afford anything more.'

'So write down every station you can travel to with that pass and every bus you can go on. Then plan excursions with some friends.'

Entertainment:

'Now you're really off track. Even the cinema is expensive.'

'So list all the programmes you can see on television and listen to on the radio, the films you can watch free, the concerts, the sports etc.'

'That's all very well, but watching a movie on television won't stop me being lonely.'

'It would if you asked a few friends round and told each of them to bring an offering of food.'

Bills:

'Stop thinking of bills as punishments. List all the bills you do *manage to pay each month, the electricity, the phone, the gas and so forth. As you pay each one tell yourself you are wealthy since you* can *pay them.'*

Possessions:

'List all the possessions you do *have.'*

And so it went on. By the end Peter was feeling a lot more comfortable – not happy, but at least he was beginning to recognise all the things he did have that other people might be wishing for.

We also worked on the concept that complaining was not improving the situation. It was not getting more money for him and it certainly wasn't making him popular. I suggested that since his present strategy wasn't *achieving the result he wanted he might be prepared to consider changing his strategy.*

Finally I suggested that he sit down quietly at home one evening and devise ideas for having a low-cost social life, ways in which he could make things happen within the limit of his resources. The next step too, I suggested, was that if he really wanted more money he should think about ways of achieving this; however, I was pretty sure that in his case the money aspect was an excuse for his loneliness rather than the real reason, and indeed that is how it turned out.

Once he realised how much he did have he stopped complaining. When he stopped complaining and became more positive he found there were more people who wanted to talk with him. When he talked with people and suggested low-cost social activities he found there were others, like himself, who had limited funds. In Peter's case he started to invite friends round for musical evenings in which they each brought a favourite record, he organised outings (free pass travel) to art galleries (free) and invited friends home for games evenings to which he added a variety of twists such as a green evening when everyone had to wear green, or a 'tin' night when everyone had to bring a tin of food and they then, together, concocted an outrageous meal of many courses.

Some people have no major problem, they simply complain about everything. We spoke earlier of people choosing to be victims, as if by having things to complain about people will have sympathy for you and take pity on you. Put yourself in their shoes. How do you feel about someone who complains all the time? You may feel sympathy initially but isn't it true that you soon become bored with them or irritated by them when they don't change and the complaining goes on month after month?

Think of it another way. You have created your life. You have made the decisions that got you to where you are today. No matter what assets you feel you have or don't have there are other people with similar or fewer assets that have created a different or better lifestyle for themselves. It is never the outward circumstances that dictate the details of your life, it is what is going on inside your head and your heart, it is how you deal with things, how you respond and what you choose to do. This being so, do you really want to keep telling people, by your frequent complaints, that you have created such a poor life for yourself? Surely not.

People won't like you the less because things are going right for you and they no longer need to feel sorry for you. It is highly unlikely that they will avoid you because you are too happy. Moths are drawn round a bright light, not to a dark corner. Be willing to focus on what you do have and to share it with others.

Stop Blaming Others

Obviously you can only be a victim if there is a victimiser. This victimiser need not even be a person, it may be circumstances, yet at the end of the day, these are also created by people. If you are feeling like a victim there is inevitably someone or a group of people, somewhere, that you are blaming for your situation.

It's very easy to blame other people for your problems, for your loneliness. You can blame friends for being so involved with their own families, you can blame people who no longer keep in touch with you or societies that don't keep chasing you up for involvement. You can blame your partner for having left you, your children for being so involved with their own lives, the people at work for being unsociable, city people for being unfriendly and reserved, country people for being conservative, your partner for being disinclined to socialise or for being too popular, other people for not returning invitations, the neighbours for being thoughtless, other people for being so wrapped up in themselves. You can say that if only all or even some of these things were different you wouldn't be so lonely.

It's also easy to blame circumstances and outside events for your loneliness. It's because of the long hours you work, or because you're stuck at home with a child; it's because the public transport is so bad or because you only have the one car and your partner uses it; it's because you're single or because you're tied to a relationship; it's because you have children or it's because you don't; it's because you're wealthier than the people around you or because you're poor; it's because you're too old or because you're too young; it's because you're isolated in the country or stuck in the middle of a big city; it's because of the government, the taxes, the crime rate, modern technology, the break-up of family life in our society, etc.

The problem with these scenarios is manifold. Firstly, they do exist, yet you still want to be happy. Secondly, other people in a similar situation are happy, so it can be done. Thirdly, blaming other people simply drives them away and leaves you feeling even more lonely.

The various people and circumstances that you blame for your loneliness doubtless do exist and, by and large, they are outside your immediate control. You may not want to change some of the circumstances that you are blaming and you may not be able to change others. You can't force your friends, for instance, to be less involved with their own families, you can't *make* people keep in touch with you or societies chase you up for your involvement. You can't force your partner to remain in the relationship, the children to spend more time with you, the people at work to be more sociable, city people to be more friendly or country people to be less conservative, your partner, if he or she is a stay-at-home, stick-in-the-mud, to socialise and be more popular, people to return invitations, the neighbours to be more thoughtful, or people to be less wrapped up in themselves. You cannot change the world. You cannot change the people around you and make them behave differently by blaming them for your circumstances and demanding that they change for your convenience and happiness.

You cannot force other people to change their lives, to do things with the aim of reducing your loneliness. If it was indeed true that your loneliness was the direct result of these outside factors and that the solution was dependent on changes they had to make, you really would have a problem. In other words, if you are indeed lonely because of these factors then you may be stuck with being lonely. Fortunately, however, they are not the real cause, and the sooner you recognise that and act accordingly the sooner you can stop feeling lonely. You can make the changes and it is up to you to do so if you want to change your present situation.

Any time you hear yourself saying, 'I wouldn't be so lonely if only . . .' or 'I'm lonely because . . .' or 'If it wasn't for . . . I wouldn't be so lonely', stop and listen. What is it you're blaming for your loneliness? Write it down. Make a list, just as you did with regard to complaining. Then make it a project not to blame your feelings on any outside event. After a while it will become second nature. Look back to the suggestions made for dealing with those times when you choose to be a victim, after all, blaming others is simply the reverse side of this coin.

Stop blaming other people and circumstances for your loneliness. Become responsible for yourself. The only thing you *can* change is yourself and the way you behave. The only thing you *have* to change is yourself and the way you behave. Thus you have the power to stop being lonely and you can use it any time you choose to. Indeed, it is only by changing your own attitudes and behaviour in a positive way that you have any real chance of altering the people and circumstances that do not suit you.

[1] See p. 208 for a more detailed exploration.

Chapter Eight

Dealing with Other People's Negative Comments

Now let's take a look at ways of dealing with remarks, made either directly to you or in your hearing, that are intended to be negative and to make the listener feel less happy.

Mary was living with and looking after an elderly and somewhat querulous relative. On the day Mary was going out and the nurse was coming Mary bustled around early doing a few extra things which would make her aunt more comfortable. As she was leaving she asked if there was anything else she could do, to which her aunt replied, 'No, the nurse will manage. Stop fussing. I suppose offering to do all those extra things just makes you feel better.' Clearly this was a loaded statement, with all sorts of undercurrent meanings.

Her aunt's comment could have been interpreted by Mary as a criticism and she could have replied that she was entitled to a day off. She could have acted negatively and protested that she was genuinely trying to help. She could have muttered about her bad-tempered aunt, got into a bad mood herself and complained to her companion for the day. She could have had an argument on the spot. These and countless responses like them could, and with some justification, have seemed reasonable to Mary, but they would have benefited nobody and they would certainly have spoilt Mary's day.

At a more neutral level she could have rationalised to herself that her aunt was ill and in pain, she could have decided to make allowances for her and to ignore the comment. Yet it would still have had an effect on her, either festering inside her or requiring the energy involved in endeavouring to ignore it.

The third alternative, and the one she had learnt to choose, was the most positive. She simply said, 'Yes,' and 'if the nurse can do everything you need, that's great. Have a good day.'

Mary chose not to be a victim. She chose to take her aunt's statement at face value and to assume no implied criticism or complaint. She also chose to acknowledge that her giving was not self-sacrificingly unselfish (after all, as we've already said, it rarely is – most givers enjoy giving, for a variety of reasons, but that is another story), that she liked to give and do things for other people, her aunt in particular, and that she felt good when she did. She chose not to criticise her aunt for being grumpy. Instead she left, happily, for her day off and her aunt learnt she could not manipulate Mary by her 'poor me' attitude. In this way it is likely that, in time, her aunt will come round to simply wishing her a good day when she goes off and their time together will be happier.

There is almost no comment or criticism that cannot be received by you, the listener, in such a way as to neutralise any possible negative intention or deflect any harmful intent on the part of the speaker and leave you feeling good, certainly a lot better than if you engaged in victim-based self-defence or in arguments. The alternative, defending yourself, is usually done by attacking the other person ['I'm right, you're wrong'] and leads to argument, alienation and possible loneliness.

Remember, the meaning you read into someone else's statement is simply that – the meaning *you* read into it. You cannot know *for sure* that their intention was to criticise, however likely it may seem. It's your choice. You can certainly choose to assume there was no critical intent, as Mary did. If the criticism is implied rather than direct, this method works well. If the criticism is overt then agreeing with the speaker is a simple way of defusing the situation.

'You're a hopeless navigator,' exploded David as his girlfriend directed him into a street clearly going in the wrong direction. What could she do? She could argue that it wasn't her fault, that the map was an old one, that he was driving too fast and not giving her enough time, or that the streets weren't where she expected them to be. They could have had endless arguments and aggravations every time they went out together. As a result they could both have been bad-tempered, with each other and with other people, when they arrived at their destination, and it could have ruined their own relationship, possibly leading to loneliness.

Instead she chose to say, 'That's right.' The next time it happened she said the same thing, adding, ' . . . and you know that.' This then left him to recognise that he could either ask her to drive and navigate himself or he could plan a trip as he would had he been on his own and again, do his own navigating. Further, since she chose to respond in a neutral, rather than a defensive tone, David got the quiet message that she didn't feel diminished by this, that being a poor navigator did not lead to her feeling criticised. It was a simple statement of fact, rather like saying, 'You have blond hair.'

There are many times when a quiet agreement, such as

this, is effective and in no way self-diminishing. At other times a slight variation is all that is needed to neutralise the situation. Much depends on your own attitude and the tone in which you respond.

Roger was a quiet, thoughtful chap who, when given a new piece of equipment to work with, would spend time going through the instructions carefully before even touching it. This would exasperate his colleague, friend, relative or whoever was with him at the time, who would usually grab it from him saying something like, 'Give it to me, you're too slow.' To this Roger's inevitable reply was, 'For you.' In this way he made it clear to the other person that he didn't feel threatened or criticised by the comment, that he was perfectly happy with the speed at which he did things, and there were no more negative vibes as a result.

Angela had a different strategy. Whenever anyone criticised either her or someone else she would say, 'That's an interesting point of view,' thereby letting the speaker know that she had heard what they had to say, that she wasn't arguing against them, but at the same time other points of view existed and that, in all probability, her own was different. Sometimes she would extend it by saying, 'That's an interesting point of view, now would you like to hear mine?' If they said 'No' she immediately shut up and said nothing more, which had the same effect as before. If they said 'Yes', then she would say what she had in mind and, if interrupted, she would gently ask that they remain quiet and listen to her, since they had said they wanted to know what she thought, otherwise she would move on. This still had the effect of conveying the unspoken message that she had a different point of view. In this way, she felt, she avoided taking on a negative comment or criticism, and avoided getting involved in a controversy.

Part of the key to turning these negative statements into positives is in the words you use. Another aspect is the way you say them. If Angela had said, 'That's an interesting point of view, now do you want to hear mine?' in an angry and aggressive tone, she would have created a different scenario to the one in which she said the same words in a mild and questioning way.

Yet another part, and the part that ensures its effectiveness, is having a positive feeling about yourself and a positive attitude towards yourself. Once you have developed a quiet self-assurance you will no longer feel the need to argue back when someone criticises you or offers a negative comment. You won't have to prove the other person wrong, and thus alienate them; you can be content to let what they say rest as their opinion without the need to defend yourself and contribute to the disharmony.

Ultimately, if you let negative comments induce further negative comments from you, arguments and separation from people can result, and this is, of course, what you want to avoid if you are already feeling lonely.

There's another way to change any negative response you may have to what is being said. Go through the following steps:

1 Be aware of exactly what was said.
2 Ask yourself what interpretation you were putting on the statement.
3 Check out how you feel, inside, as a result.
4 Ask yourself what alternative interpretation you could put.
5 Apply that and check out how you feel as a result.
6 Decide which way you prefer to feel and apply that interpretation.

After all, you cannot know exactly what the other person

meant to convey. One-hundred-per-cent perfect communication simply does not occur. All you can do is interpret the statement in your own way. You may *think* you know what they meant, but do you? No, of course not, you can't. So why not apply the *most useful* interpretation, the one that makes you happiest and reduces your chances of being lonely?

Malcolm was relatively new at his job in a large warehouse. He came to me because he didn't want to give up the job but his boss was forever criticising him and he had started to dread going to work each day.

'What exactly does your boss say?' I asked.

'Well, it's hard to pin him down exactly, he doesn't say things in such a way that I can defend myself, I just know that by the end of the day I feel wretched. He says things like, "Look at this mess, people who can't keep the place tidy shouldn't be working here," or "If people arrived in good time then we wouldn't be behind with our work," and I just know he's talking about me.'

'How do you know that?'

'Well, if he didn't mean me, he'd say so wouldn't he? He's making the remarks to me so of course he means me.'

I suggested he apply the above criteria and, as I explained the idea, he did agree that much of his mood was due to the interpretation he placed on what his boss was saying. He also agreed that he could interpret the situation by assuming that the boss was talking to him about other *workers and treating him as a colleague.*

'But that's silly,' said Malcolm, 'I'm too new, and I know I do make mistakes and get behind.'

However, Malcolm agreed that he had nothing to lose by applying the second, more positive, interpretation and that it would certainly be a more useful way of looking at things, so he would do so and act accordingly. His response was immediate. Within a week he was back, saying, 'You know, that was amazing. I simply agreed with the boss that what he said was true, that, for instance, untidy and disorganised people shouldn't be working here. I got a few funny looks, but you know, he seems to have stopped doing it now. And I'm doing my best to put right the things that I know I do wrong. I think I'll make out in the end.'

Many times it does not take a negative statement from someone to cause conflict or unhappiness. The statement or comment may have been neutral, but you may have interpreted it differently. A simple question such as, 'Where is the book I was reading?' can be interpreted as an accusation as, 'Where did you put my book?' If you resent this and argue back or make such comments as, 'I don't know, I didn't put it anywhere, don't blame me,' you can turn someone's perfectly normal question into a reason for dissension and disharmony.

You may respond in that way if you feel unsure of yourself, if you think other people don't like you, don't respect you or think you are inadequate. Your response is then an uncalled-for defence. If you hear yourself being defensive then check out your own inner assessment of yourself. It's a bit like, 'Don't look now, but your slip is showing' – the more you protest and defend the more you tell the world you are unsure of your own worth. Is that what you want to say? Because the sad truth is that they will accept the view of yourself that you convey in this way. More importantly, it leads to estrangement rather than friendship and that, if you are lonely, is not what you want.

Make it a practice to check your comments for a few days and, if any are defensive or involve a negative interpretation of what has been said, stop yourself or, if the words are already out, voice an alternative comment based on a positive assessment. If you do this a few times it will soon become a habit.

Your Own Statements

Just as you may feel some people are constantly making negative statements – never mind that this assessment is essentially in the ear of the listener – other people may feel that you yourself are constantly making negative statements. Again, you can argue that this too is in the ear of the listener and that if they think that way they should change their interpretation, just as I have, in this chapter, been suggesting that you should change yours. However, since it is also true that the meaning of your communication is the response that you get and since it is you that is lonely and wants to have more friends, it would be a good idea to consider in what ways you could change your remarks and, if necessary, the intention behind them, so that the response you get is positive and friendly.

Chapter N

Give What You Would L
Receive

I know you think you are unique – and in many ways, of course, you are. Yet you are not the only lonely person, there are lots of other people out there who are just as lonely as you, possibly even more so. They would love to be made a fuss of, they would love to be invited out, to a dinner, the theatre, a day in the country. They would love to be wanted and needed by other people, you included. They would love it if they were paid compliments, thanked for their input, sought out for their ideas. They would love to be liked and cared for. Most of all they would love to stop being lonely.

A wonderful way to get what you want is to give to other people what they want. If you would like to be made a fuss of then make a fuss of someone else, or of several people. If you would like to be invited to the theatre then invite someone to the theatre. If you would like to be included on a picnic then hold a picnic and invite people. If you want people to care about you then start caring about them.

Make other people feel good and it will surely rebound on you. However, a word of warning is appropriate. You must, of course, be sincere. If you invite someone out and then sit back and wait for them to

ing else your
pay them a
you one there
ne to realise
ey are nice
give some-

r, particu-
t because
se if you
he other
e to be
omeone else
that you could have fun
when you both go out together. If you
like someone to listen to you then there is a good chance **(a)** that someone else has a similar need and **(b)** that when you have listened to them they may well feel inclined to listen to you. All the same, for it to be effective the giving should be done without strings attached. Give unconditionally and be sincere. Certainly, at the beginning, your words and actions may have a component of 'Fake it till you make it', but get beyond this as fast as you can. This applies particularly to the emotional content of what you do. However, there are also a lot of practical things you can do and you may find it easier to get started with these.

Jill lived in a small country town. She was single and taught in the local school. She maintained that there was nothing to do, the place was dead. 'There is only one cinema and the programme is the same for a whole week, the few restaurants there are are more like cafés and are hardly exciting, and there is nothing much else to do,' she insisted. 'I love theatre and ballet but getting to the city is impossible. The other teachers are married and I don't seem to be able to get to know anyone else.'

In the end the plan we came up with for Jill was simple. She started with a film group. She did this by inviting a friend to go with her to the cinema one Friday evening, they discussed the film afterwards and then started on the plan. Each of them was to invite one other person along to the film the following week, no matter what it was, and they would go out afterwards and discuss it. Again, each of these people were to invite someone new, and so it went. In the end they had a large group of people, couples and singles, who went to the cinema on a Wednesday night every week and then out to dinner on the Friday to discuss the film. Not everyone turned up for both occasions each week but enough did so that there was a regular group. As a surprising spin-off the two somewhat reasonable restaurants in the village began to vie with each other for their patronage, as there were commonly about twenty diners, and the quality of the food improved.

If you would like to be invited to a dinner party then have a dinner party and invite people to it. Don't do this just once and then sit back and wait for return invitations. Do it again. Have a dinner party once a week and invite all and sundry, people you know well but also people that are only acquaintances, after all they could be lonely too. I suggested this to one of my clients and her response was, 'I'd be too ashamed to do that. If I keep inviting people and they don't ask me back people will think I'm unpopular.' Not at all. The old-fashioned 'At Home' days had a lot going for them.

One client took up the idea and gave a dinner party every Friday evening, no matter what. In the end it became known as 'Marjorie's dinner party night' and people did all they could to get invited, including inviting Marjorie to events of their own. She had just one rule. Everyone she invited had to bring a partner of the opposite sex and someone that she didn't know, even including couples. In this way she met a lot of interesting people.

Marjorie could afford the cost of this. If you can't there are still possibilities. You can reduce the cost by creating wonderful and economical dishes with pasta, or curries. You can also ask people to bring a 'plate' – full of food of course. This may be a peculiarly Australian tradition and not much practised in England but give it a try. Or tell them to bring the wine in, as a friend put it, industrial quantities. You can also get together with a few friends and share the occasion.

Keith and Betty had newly arrived in the city and they developed a slightly interesting variation on this idea. They picked a theme for the evening, designed the banquet and then asked each person to provide a specific dish, for which they gave them a recipe. The first evening it was a Turkish night and they invited the three colleagues from Keith's office and their wives. Keith and Betty found a book on Turkish cooking, planned the menu and gave each couple detailed instructions. It was such a success they repeated the idea with different nationalities until just before Christmas when they decided on a seven-course feast in the English style of a couple of a hundred years ago. They also expanded the numbers by telling people to bring another couple.

If you would like to be invited out to dinner and like dining in restaurants then get together with a group of people and suggest a night out. One couple I know did this, but with a difference. They decided to go out once a month and to start at the end of one street, famous for the number of restaurants in it, and move progressively along the street, month by month.

If eating is not your bent then start a games night. Invite people round to play Monopoly or whatever game or games appeal to you. There are lots of people sitting at home, alone, watching television, just like you. Invite them round, and use the snowball technique of asking each of them to bring a friend.

Do you sometimes feel like a wallflower among a group of people? Would you like people to come up and talk to you? Then look around next time you are in a group. Search out the quiet person, the least interesting-looking person, make the effort to talk to them. You never know who you might meet behind the seemingly unlikely exterior and even if you don't make a new friend you will have made someone feel wanted.

Make the effort. Create the events that you would like to participate in. Phone people up for a chat when you think they are lonely. Pay the compliments we spoke of earlier. Be the person who initiates things rather than waiting for other people to do it.

Is shopping a bore? Other people may think so too so offer to get things for them, especially if they are elderly or unwell. Or invite someone to go with you and make an outing of it.

These are just a few ideas. This is the way for you to get started. Write down every 'I wish' you have that involves someone else doing something for or to you. Don't censor the list. Write down everything you can think of, every 'I wish' or 'If only'. Then make a point of going out and doing or saying these same things for or to other people.

Your list might include: if only people were more understanding, would invite me out, would include me in what they do, would share their ideas with me; if only I had more friends, people who would be there when I need them. Your job would then be to focus on being more understanding with other people, inviting people out, including them in what you do, sharing your ideas with people, being friendly to more people and being willing to make the effort to help someone when they are in need even if it isn't convenient for you at the time.

Give what you would like to receive. You may be unique, but the chances are high that if you are lonely and have certain wants there will be a lot of other people like you and in a similar situation who will appreciate your fulfilling their need. As a result of doing that you will meet more people and people will want to have you around. At the start, as mentioned earlier, it may mean a bit of faking, but as soon as you can, make it as genuine a caring and a giving as you can. And remember, the rewards are just as likely to be indirect as direct. The person to whom you give may not give back to you, but someone else will. It's the way of the world.

Chapter Ten

Stop Being Critical

There is nothing like being critical to drive people away. Do you like being criticised? Or do you prefer compliments? The average person is all too aware of their faults. They list them to themselves all the time, as you have probably already discovered. 'Dumb, dumb, how could you have been so stupid?' 'Why ever did you say that?' 'Idiot.' 'I look a mess.' 'Why did I do that?' 'You're going to be late.' 'No one will talk to you when you get there.' 'You're going to know no one.' 'I won't know what to say.' 'I'm a failure.' 'I look awful.' 'Please God, would someone please tell me what is good about me. Would someone please reassure me that I am worthwhile, that I have attributes that other people do value, that I am wanted, that I am not a hopeless case.' These and a million other such comments are part of the internal dialogue that most people create for themselves and listen to each day. You and this internal voice can have the most amazing conversations in which a limitless number of faults, real and imaginary, can be dreamed up and made plausible. You don't need to hear it from other people too. Do you?

Join the club. There are millions of other people out there just like you, fully aware of their own deficiencies, who would love to be reassured that they are indeed worthwhile people, that they do have some positive traits, that they are liked and admired, that they are desirable and wanted. You can either pick on their faults or comment positively on something you like about them.

Remember the parable of Jesus, when he was walking with his disciples, who saw the carcass of a dog on the road. It was dead and rotting and the disciples crossed the road to avoid it but Jesus commented on the beautiful teeth it had. There is always something good you can find to say about everyone and everything. If you doubt this then it is time to reread (or read) *How to Win Friends and Influence People* by Dale Carnegie. First written in 1936 it is still totally applicable today. People will not like you if you criticise them. They will love you if you compliment them. The compliment, however, must be real. Do not tell them they look stunningly smart when they are in some daggy old clothes, but do tell them you admire them for their ability to relax when they get the chance.

Little kids know their mothers love them, yet the American study discussed earlier showed that over four hundred times a day they heard a critical comment – 'Be quiet,' Keep still,' 'Not now, can't you see I'm busy,' 'Don't do that,' 'Be careful,' 'Don't shout,' 'Do behave' . . . and so forth. Less than forty times a day they heard a positive comment – 'Well done,' 'Mummy loves you,' 'Thank you darling'. With a ten-to-one score against you how can you feel positive about yourself? How can other people feel positive about themselves? They need all the help they can get.

If you want people to like you, to want to be with you, to enjoy and seek out your company, then give them pleasure. Give them the compliments you would like to receive yourself. Do you do this now? I doubt it, few people do. If you think you do now, then do it more.

Listen to conversations as they go on around you in a

crowded room, at a dinner party, in a gathering of people, even in one-to-one conversations. It is just as easy to say something nice or complimentary as something nasty or critical. Yet many people seem to focus on what they can criticise. They would rather say that someone is fat than that they have pretty hair, that the vegetables were soggy than that the flavouring in the sauce was excellent, that one of the actors was poor than that the directing was good or that one man was difficult rather than that they eventually completed the project well.

It's almost as if they feel that, by criticising other people, they show their discernment. They show that they recognise the inadequacy of whatever it is that they criticise and that they feel they're giving a subliminal message that says, 'I wouldn't do that, wear that, look like that or say that.' Criticism may sometimes be a way in which people try to show their superiority. Yet the converse is generally true, so it is time to reconsider your tendency to criticise and what it says about you. It might well be a better thing to tell the world that you notice the good points, the finer features, the positive attributes. Do you always praise people? Do you, in conversations with others, comment on various people's good points, on the advantages of various situations, on positive aspects of what is happening?

John was a strong and dynamic Choleric.[1] He knew he was destined to be a leader. He had a quick brain and he could see the problems, he recognised the weaknesses in other people. He knew what had to be corrected in them. Yet he could not see the problems within himself, the growing and developing he still had to do. At the same time he was not fully confident, he knew he still had to prove himself. His automatic way of doing this was to show others that he saw what had to be done, what they had to do; that he recognised the faults, their faults. Only when he had pointed out what was wrong with the hotel in which they were staying, how the restaurant could (and should) have improved its service, what was needed to build a successful business, did he feel free to enjoy himself.

This tendency to criticise is unfortunate because, more often than not, being critical, making negative comments, can rebound on you.

Gordan was twenty-eight, intelligent, self-contained and worked as a computer engineer, dealing with and training the sales people. He lived alone, had only a few friends and hadn't had a serious girlfriend for over two years.

'I wish,' he had said at the first interview, 'that my friends would drop in on me as they seem to do on each other. I do do things with them but I'm beginning to notice that I only get invited if I'm with them when they are planning it. Otherwise they don't make the effort to phone and include me. And so I'm often left on my own.'

By the second interview he had come to realise that he was frequently critical of others.

'Most of the discussion at work, in my section, is either about the computers and programs themselves or about the salesmen who go out and sell them. I guess I really am pretty critical of them. I mean they're so stupid, they know so little about the machines it's embarrassing. And they have to sell them. No wonder our sales are not as high as they could be. There was this one the other day . . .' And he launched into a lengthy story of how one man had been demonstrating to a potential customer and hadn't been able to answer their, in Gordan's view, really simple question, and had had to phone in for the answer and then go back to the customer.

Later in the day, during a tea break, he had regaled his colleagues, from various departments, with the story.

'You know David, he was with this customer and he couldn't tell him . . .'

I asked him, 'Should all your salesmen have known the answer to that particular question, is that part of their basic training?'

'Well, no, I guess not, but it is such a fundamental thing when you are working with computers.'

'Is it David's job to work with computers or to sell them?'

'Well, to sell them of course.'

'OK. So how about you doing some homework for me?'

I purposely chose not to pursue the conversation any further. I didn't want to push him to the point of defending his actions. I wanted Gordan to think about what he had just said. Instead I asked him, before the next interview, to make a number of lists and bring them in to me.

a) *He was to make a list of all the things David was good at.*

b) *He was to list all the things David did in his work that Gordan would not like to have to do.*

I specifically didn't ask Gordan to make a comparison between David and himself, I didn't want to make Gordan seem wrong, inadequate or less good than David, only to recognise the differences.

c) *He was to list the benefits he got from criticising David to others.*

For this one I suggested he ran the phrase, 'A benefit I got out of criticising David was . . .' and that he do this to the limit and still kept going, that he kept doing it long after he felt there was nothing else his subconscious could come up with, and see what happened.

d) *Finally he was to list his responses to running the phrase, 'A possible consequence of my criticising David to others is . . .'*

On this third interview it was clear as soon as Gordan walked into the office that he was a changed man.

'That was a really interesting process you started for me,' was his opening comment. 'I realised that David is very different to me. He is an extrovert, he's outgoing, and friendly, he likes people, likes talking to them and cracking jokes with them. And people like him. He's also quite a good salesman too. When I asked at the office I found he actually accomplishes a lot of sales. I thought he didn't work hard but when I did that homework you set me and thought about it I realised that although he often goes off early at the end of the day, it's to socialise with clients. They just seem to like him and I suppose, when I think of it, that really is still part of his work.

'I also realised that I would hate his job. I'm more introverted, I get annoyed at talking with people who are not intelligent and who want to simply chatter and banter. I prefer to work with ideas rather than with people. I also like to settle down and work on one thing at a time whereas in David's job I'd have to work with several different customers at a time and take calls from others in between.'

The response to his third task had been even more enlightening. 'I was quite staggered when I did your third task,' he said, acknowledging the insights that had come about. 'I realised that I am jealous of David, he's so popular, he's always included in things. If he's not around when we plan to do something someone will say something like, "We must get hold of David and see if he's free, he's always good for a laugh," whereas I know they wouldn't say that about me.'

Finally, Gordan had learnt that by criticising David, endeavouring to pull him down to size, he was, subconsciously, trying to let other people know that he was as good as David, that he was smarter than David, that he too had attributes. He was making a silent plea to people to understand that he was as good as David and that they should appreciate, value and want him as much as they did David.

'It's as if I thought that, by criticising David, or anyone else for that matter, I demonstrated that I was better than them and that people, the listeners, should like me more for it. It sounds dreadful when I say it as baldly as that . . .'

'Not at all, we all have underlying agendas that dictate our actions. After all, deep down, everyone looks after number one, and quite right too; if you don't, who will? There is a strong streak of self-preservation in all of us. You were simply getting your needs met in the safest way you knew how. What would have happened if you had gone to your colleagues and said, "I'm lonely, I want to be as popular as David, please like me as much as you like him and include me in your activities as enthusiastically as you include him?" Would that have worked?'

It was obvious from Gordan's face that it wouldn't, that that would have been an impossible request to have made and that, in any case, it wouldn't have achieved his desired outcome. As he said, 'If I'd said that my mates would have laughed at me and thought me pretty stupid.'

The fourth task had really crystallised things for Gordan. On his own he had come to realise that by criticising David and others like him he was not proving himself to be the better person and the one more deserving of their regard. Rather, he was the loser. Some of the responses he had come up with to 'A possible consequence of my criticising David to others is . . .' were 'They will think I'm negative', 'They will think I'm mean', 'They will find me depressing to be around', 'They may be afraid that I criticise them behind their backs', 'I could lose friends', 'I could become unpopular'.

After we had discussed this Gordan made a personal commitment to watch what he said and to do two things

– to avoid making any critical comment, and to take every opportunity he could find for making a complimentary remark. Later he told me that it had become an interesting game for him. Even if he was asked for his opinion on something that did deserve a criticism he began to take a delight in circumventing it.

'I was asked what I thought of our new stores manager and how he was fitting in with the rest of the staff. I was able to say I thought he was good at the paperwork side of things. And you know it was interesting, the silence that followed told the manager that the stores manager wasn't popular with the rest of the staff, I didn't have to say a thing. And this way I came out as being a nicer person than if I had criticised him directly in words.'

This wasn't the end of the matter for Gordan. At this point it was a game, a mental exercise, and an experiment he was enjoying. When he stopped making the conscious effort to compliment rather than criticise there was the danger he would slip back into his old ways. He also had to work on his own self-esteem so that his compliments could come from a base of security, of confidence in his own worth and the sense that he could afford to say how nice other people were because he too was a nice person. In his case this was fairly easy to do once he focused on his own strengths.

Gordan came to realise that his temperament was that of a Phlegmatic.[2] He understood that his strengths were his loyalty and steadiness, his persistence when working with a given task and his determination to see it through, with or without supervision. It was not in his nature to be the life and soul of the party, as it was David's, but if he refrained from criticising people, to their face or behind their back, was more willing to comment on the good in people, he would always have friends and would always be included in social situations.

Listen to yourself with honesty. Do you criticise other people or things more often than you praise them? If so, ask yourself why. Do you criticise to make yourself feel good? Do you criticise other people to show you have discernment? Do you criticise for lack of anything else to say? Do you feel you have to comment on anything you don't like or that otherwise you will, by omission, be deemed to have either liked it or not noticed how awful it was? If so it is time you developed more confidence in yourself. Consider again the first chapter of this section.

Gossips are Rarely Popular

Who likes a gossip? You might do, when you want to know something. You might think that other people do when they listen avidly to something you have to say and make you feel important, at least temporarily. In general, however, people are loath to share their secrets, their confidences, their inner feelings, with someone when they know that that information will then be spread around to all and sundry.

Do you gossip, and if so why? Do you feel this makes you more important? Some people will tell all they know about a third person as a means of boosting their own importance. 'I know such-and-such, so-and-so told me' can be another way of trying to say, 'I am in so-and-so's confidence, they are my friend, if they like me you should do too.'

We have already covered the importance of taking an interest in people. When you do that, and when you show genuine concern and interest, you may learn a lot more about people than they would normally share. They will have shared because they detected your sincere interest in them. They will have shared because you made them feel good. As a result they may be inclined to make a friend of you. Don't spoil it all by passing this information on to others. It will inevitably get back to the first person who may well then feel betrayed. As a result all your efforts to build a friendship will have gone for naught. Not only that but you have shown that you weren't really interested in them for their own sake, only for what you could get out of it for yourself.

People who are only out for what they can get for themselves are likely to have few friends and to be lonely. This does not conflict with what was said earlier about the fact that we are all fundamentally selfish in the sense of doing things for some personal benefit, including the benefit of feeling good when you give etc. That is a 'selfishness' that does no harm to others, in fact it avoids doing harm to others since it includes honesty and a refusal to manipulate other people and their emotions (as in, 'Look what I've done for you, now you should do something for me to show your gratitude'). The unhelpful type of selfishness, what we might call graspingness or self-aggrandizement, the boasting, the bandstanding, that is to be avoided if you truly do want to be a nicer person.

There are many reasons for gossiping. As we have seen some people feel it makes them important since they have information to impart. Others feel that it will make them popular as people will want to be with them to hear the latest news. Other people have little else to say, they are not interested in the broader horizons of what is happening in the world, of arts or sport, of concepts and ideas, and so they fall back on gossip to fill in the silences. Some people take the ability to gossip as a sign of intelligence, of worldly knowledge. Some people simply like to be the centre of attention and feel they can achieve this through gossip. Some are trying to prove they are better than other people and endeavour to do this by passing on negative information, for most gossip is negative. Think about the people you know who gossip. Think about the times you have passed on titbits of information you have gleaned. I'm sure you'll find, if you are honest with yourself, that most of the time the titillating bits are the bits that show other people up in a bad light. For gossips and for newspapers it is the bad news that sells, not the good.

Would you like people to discuss negative things about you? Of course not. Would you mind if they discussed positive things about you? Probably not. Yet even if you had achieved a success or a plan was working out, if you had shared it with a friend in confidence, one you trusted, you might still be dismayed to find that it had become common knowledge.

There are far greater chances for developing friendships if you are known as someone people can trust with their confidences than if you are known as the local source of information, the local gossip. Eventually gossip isn't even interesting. I have had to struggle to stay awake through many social occasions where the discussion was all gossip about other people. There are many more interesting things to talk about, common interests to explore that can bring people together, new ideas and areas of interest to discover that can lead you to new friends. You haven't time to gossip, there is so much more to do and learn.

Make the decision now to stop gossiping. Everyone does it, at least to some extent. To the extent that you can stop, to that extent you are increasing your chances of becoming a trusted friend. So monitor what you say. Make a conscious effort for the next seven days not to pass on a single piece of gossip, not to mention a single negative thing that is happening in the lives of other people.

Obviously there is a distinction to be made between

gossip and passing on good news you know that the people concerned would like to share. There is also a distinction to be made between gossip and current affairs. These are distinctions that I will leave up to you. If you are not sure, then keep in mind the saying, 'First, do no harm.'

Criticisms are Revealing

Let's move back, now, to more specific criticisms. Criticisms that you make about other people, situations or events can be very revealing. I frequently recall one of the homilies I heard as a child, 'What Peter tells me about Paul tells me more about Peter than about Paul.' When you criticise someone or something you are, in effect, telling the listener more about yourself than about the person or thing you are criticising.

Imagine a family picnic on a beach. Some of the comments you might hear could include, 'It was a steamy hot day, the sand got into the food and it was all a great waste of time. I don't see why we can't eat in a restaurant when we go out.' 'How lovely, to be able to sit down and relax, no jobs staring at you demanding attention.' 'It would have been a pleasant afternoon but all the children running around spoilt it.' 'It was a glorious day, wonderful to see the sun again.' 'What a lot of squabbling, all about which beach we should go to.' 'It was nice to have all the family together for a change.' 'I get so bored at picnics, I'd rather be doing something active.' 'What a worry all the preparation was, I was quite exhausted by the time I got there.' What have you learnt? You have almost certainly built up a quick cameo picture of the people who made each of the remarks, but have you learnt much about the picnic? No, of course you haven't, nothing that you didn't already know when told it was a family picnic.

Think of a piece of pop music and the comments you might hear about it. 'What a loud and raucous noise.' 'What a wonderful rhythm.' 'All that emphasis on sex.' 'What an honest piece.' Clearly one speaker likes pop music and the other doesn't, but you haven't learnt much about the music itself.

Think about someone's work and what they might say about it. 'It's a dull and boring job, the monotony gets on my nerves.' Or 'It's a steady routine job and there's no stress.' 'The boss keeps breathing down my neck, it's as if he's waiting to find fault.' Or 'The boss keeps an eye on what I'm doing so I don't have to worry that I might have missed something.' 'I like the open-plan, there's plenty of company and you know what's going on.' Or 'The open-plan is ghastly, there's no privacy and so many distractions, it's hard to concentrate.' When you hear these comments you know a lot more about the people making them than about their work environment, other than the superficial. You don't know how routine it is, simply that it is sufficiently routine to irritate one person and that someone else is not stressed. You don't know whether or not the open-plan layout works well, only that it is somewhere between open, warm and friendly on the one hand and rowdy and distracting on the other. You certainly don't know how you would have responded to each situation; whether it was too routine for you, there was too much or too little supervision for you or the noise and distraction level was appealing or annoying.

In all these situations outlined above you have learnt more about the speakers than about the situation and this is a useful thought to keep in mind when you are making criticisms. When you complain that people are too noisy and exuberant you are saying that you like peace and quiet. When you say you are stressed by the uncertainties at work you are saying that you like a steady, even a monotonous, routine. You may also be saying that you cannot cope with what is expected of you. If you object to supervision you may be saying that you fear you are making mistakes. If you complain that people ignore you at parties or don't invite you out you may be saying that you think people don't like you or want you.

In addition to the obvious (unspoken) messages there is a further one. People that spend a lot of time being critical are commonly unhappy, discontented, not pleased with themselves, not confident, not, in short, people that you like to hang around with; as a result they are often lonely. Do you want to be like them?

A further factor steps in here. The listener will filter your comments through their interpretation of them. When you criticise people for being too noisy and exuberant the listener may decide that you must be dull and boring not to enjoy a crowd. When you say no one invites you out they may decide to do the same since they trust other people's knowledge of you above their own.

Learn to Pay Compliments

There is always something positive you could find to say, even though you may have to work hard to find it. If you really can find nothing good to say about someone then don't make any comment at all. However, since it is often easier to find a new behaviour pattern than to simply stop following an old one, you may find that rather than simply refraining from criticising people it is actually easier to focus on paying compliments. Make a positive decision to look for something complimentary to say about everyone who comes up for discussion or to whom you are talking.

In this you do not have to go against your values. You

do not have to say that you like someone when you find them offensive, that you trust or respect someone when you know they tell lies. Instead there is almost always *something* positive you can find to say about everyone and everything. You never know, you might even find that, by focusing on people's good points instead of the aspects of them that you dislike, you could come to like more people and so have more friends, which is just what you want if you have been lonely.

I said this to Rowena during one consultation and she laughed. She said, 'That's exactly what happened to me recently. My husband and I were having dinner with a colleague and his wife a couple of evenings ago. It was the first time I had met his wife and I took an instant dislike to her, she was so pushy and full of herself and her work. I knew it was important to my husband that I get on with her so I put into practice what you have said over the last few sessions. I found myself telling her how much I admired her for having the initiative to have her own career. You know, in no time she told me that she would really have loved to have had children and had been devastated when told she couldn't. I then came to understand that her comments about her success were a cover for the pain and inadequacy she felt at being childless and after that we did become friends.'

Remember the American study in which it was found that children up to the age of four or five heard about four hundred criticisms a day, comments such as 'Be quiet,' 'Not now, Mummy's busy,' 'Don't do that,' 'Put that down,' and only forty (actually thirty-six) compliments such as 'That's a good girl,' 'Well done,' and 'Thank you.' This has an adverse effect on the confidence of the young child. However, it also causes another problem. As you grow up you tend to copy this pattern yourself since most people tend to follow and copy the behaviour patterns they observe in their early and formative years. So it is hardly surprising that many people have a greater tendency to criticise than to pay compliments. It is a learned behaviour. Equally, this does not mean that this learned behaviour cannot be unlearned and a new behaviour adopted, so go ahead and do it. Learn the behaviour of paying compliments and unlearn the behaviour of frequent criticising and you may be surprised by the warmth of the response you get and the joy this will bring to you.

The Three-Step Sandwich

You may well be thinking that at times you do have to criticise people, you do have to tell them they are doing something wrong, you do have to tell them that what they are doing is not working and that they must change. Perhaps you want to suggest someone wears different colours, or stops shouting at their children, arguing with the staff or driving so fast. There are ways and ways of doing it.

Firstly ask yourself what your motive is. If your real motive is to make the other person wrong, to show that you were right, or to show them that they have behaved badly, have no colour sense or are inadequate in some way, then you will certainly lose friends and become lonely. This is destructive criticism and will get you nowhere except on your own.

If, however, you really do have to criticise someone else and if you truly want the criticism to be constructive, then here is a sure-fire way of doing it with minimum pain and maximum benefit. My patients know it as the 'Three-Step Sandwich' and it goes like this:

1 Find something positive to say about the other person.

2 Cover the problem, or the situation that needs to be changed and make the comments you feel you have to make.
3 Pay them another compliment or find something else that is positive that you can say to them.

If you think a friend is wearing an outfit that clashes with her hair and makes her skin look sallow you will cause pain and may well lose a friend if you say, 'Gosh you look awful in that outfit, it makes you look sick and ten years older.'

Try the 'Sandwich' instead. It could go something like this:

1 'You normally dress really well, and I love the way you combine colours.'
2 'But I'm not sure this is one of your best choices, it doesn't do you justice.'
3 'I love the pink outfit you wore the other day, it shows off your hair beautifully.'

Most people are vulnerable to criticism. Generally it hurts, though often the hurt is buried as people put on a brave face. Rarely do people like or thank the criticiser.

My publisher does a wonderful job with the sandwich, possibly quite unconsciously. I have a letter from her that says, 'We're delighted with the manuscript, it looks excellent (Sandwich Step 1). I would however suggest a few minor changes here and there, and a couple of big ones in Chapter Seven (Sandwich Step 2), but overall it looks good and we are confident that it will be a success (Sandwich Step 3).' After that followed a long list of minor suggestions and some major suggestions for Chapter Seven, all of which I tackled with a will because of the first and third parts of the Sandwich. My reaction would have been very different if she had simply thanked me for the manuscript and listed all the changes she wanted made.

As another example, from a husband who is tired of the arguments his wife has with the children, the following would work: 'You do such a wonderful job with the children, making sure they have all they need each day (Step 1). Do you think you could shout at them a little less in the evening; it doesn't really do you credit (Step 2) and in all other ways you are such a patient person (Step 3).' Do you think she would respond better to that than a terse comment such as, 'For goodness sake, stop shouting at the children'? Of course she would.

Your Action Plan

1 If you find yourself making critical comments . . . STOP.
2 Go through the processes that Gordan followed. Take whatever remedial steps seem appropriate.
3 Commit to going a month without making a single critical comment except . . .
4 If you absolutely have to make a constructive critical comment, use the Three-Step Sandwich. You could be surprised at the results.
5 Make a point of paying compliments at every opportunity.

[1] and [2] *Love, Health and Happiness, understanding yourself through an understanding of the four temperaments.* By Xandria Williams, Hodder and Stoughton, 1995.

Chapter Eleven

Do You Judge Others – And Find Them Wanting?

This chapter is a logical extension to the previous one on criticism. It may seem similar, yet in important details it is different. To criticise someone you obviously have to have made a judgement and found them wanting. Yet the issues behind judging go far beyond this.

What Judging Does

When you judge someone you almost inevitably alienate them. How do you feel when someone judges you and finds you wanting? How do you feel when they tell you what you ought to be doing? How do you feel when they tell you how to run your life, what to buy, with whom to be friends, or what you should do about the problems you face? Unless their opinion coincides with yours you are likely to feel that they are interfering. If you follow their advice or instructions and things go wrong you will probably hold them to blame. If things go right you may resent them for being wiser than you and showing you up for being about to make a stupid decision. If, on the other hand, you don't follow their advice you may feel guilty, that you have shown you don't respect their judgement or that you don't trust them. These and a myriad other emotions can get in the way of a friendship when someone judges you. The same can happen, of course, when you judge other people.

Setting yourself up as a judge and jury for other people is a sure way to lose friends even if you think you are simply trying to be helpful and if your intentions are of the very best. This applies if you are judging what they have done in the past or what they should do in the future. No one can know what is right for another person. No one can know what another person should do. And certainly, no one can carry the consequence if the advice they give is taken and the outcome is not what the person concerned wanted.

To judge another person, their situation and their relationships, and to let the other person know that you do, is not friendship; it is intrusion into their life, and an intrusion that is often unwelcome, that can, in the long run, lose you friends and leave you lonely. Can you help another person? Of course you can. If you truly want to help them to achieve what *they* want, and don't simply want to impose your decision, your judgement and your view of the world on them, make the effort to find out what they really want to do and then assist them in that process. They know what their values are. They know what is important to them. They know what they are willing to put up with to achieve their goals, you don't.

Margaret was lonely and wanted to make a friend of her neighbour, Sarah. Unfortunately, instead of creating a friendship she drove Sarah away, simply because she judged her and found her wanting. Margaret knew that Sarah rarely had any money of her own. There were many times when she had suggested she and Sarah go out to lunch or to a film together but had been turned down. She soon realised that finances were a major part of the problem and that, although Sarah worked part-time, her wages went into the family's joint account and she didn't like to ask her husband for money other than what he decided was an appropriate amount for the household expenditure. Margaret, who also worked part-time and who managed her own part of the family budget, kept telling her she should demand some independence, that she should talk to her husband, that she should keep back part of her wages. She pointed out that he went out with his friends and had the money for his share of drinks and so forth. Sarah, however, felt that it would be selfish of her to demand money of her own, that it would suggest she didn't trust her husband's judgement and that he had the right to say how the family budget was spent. The more Margaret tried to push her into standing up for herself the more upset Sarah got. It was more important to her to live by the standards she thought were right, and not to upset her husband, than to have the money and do things with Margaret, and in the end she took to avoiding Margaret, even though she realised she had the best of intentions. By the standards of this century Sarah was possibly out of step, yet Margaret, who thought she was both trying to help and to create a friendship, lost her as a friend because of the judgements she applied. Had Margaret stopped judging and been willing to recognise the value Sarah placed on her family relationships things could have been very different.

Know What's Best for You

Do you want to be friends with your children when they grow up? Of course you do. Do you want to be friends with other young people, over whom you may have some control or authority? You probably do. Yet do you, in your position of authority, judge them, assume that you know what is best for them and then endeavour to exert your influence to dictate what they should do? If you do, this can be another cause of loneliness.

What happens when parents tell children what sort of career they should have, when they make a judgement as to what is best for the child's future? Frequently the parent is sure, based on their years of maturity, that they know what is best for their child. They *know* that leaving school early will be a disaster, that the child *must* have an education. Often this is true. Yet it can also happen that this child prefers to be a carpenter, to farm, to work with their hands, to go on the stage, or to do some job for which schooling is unnecessary.

In other words the parent may 'know what's best' in the majority of cases, but they cannot know what's best in the case of the particular individual that is the child in question. They may think they do, future events may even show them to have been right, but if they push the issue to the limit they may do more harm than good.

The child may, overwhelmed by parental determination, stay at school, rather than following the course they would like to pursue; but what about the relationship between parent and child? If the child turns into a young adult who is forced into a job they dislike there will almost certainly be some ongoing resentment against the parent. There may also be other, unforeseen, negative consequences.

I recall a young man, forced to stay at school by a father who said, 'I didn't have a chance at an education, I had to leave school when I was fifteen and go straight into the factory. I've worked hard all my life to give you a decent education so you can have a better start than I did, and you're bloody well going to go to university.' We recognise this as the classic case of the father living vicariously, living the life he couldn't have, through his son. Yet in this case, the son, bored and restless at university, pursuing a degree in accountancy that didn't interest him, turned to social excesses to relieve the tedium and eventually accepted drugs when they were offered. He never forgave his father and maintained a resentment against him for not letting him go out to work when he wanted to. The father, in his old age, was saddened by the absence of his son and lonely as a result.

If you have, in the past, judged your children and are estranged from them as a result, this might be the time to rebuild the relationship. Recognise that they are free individuals, that they had the right to choose their path in life without unwanted instruction from you. Be willing to acknowledge them, without judgement. Then talk with them, communicate with them and let them know how your attitude has changed.

When you judge someone else, be they your child or another person, you set yourself up as being wiser than them. If you judge that what they are doing is wrong there is the inherent assumption that you know right from wrong better than they do. If you tell them they should be doing something other than they are, you are assuming you know what is best for them. If you judge the way they are treating other people, or another person, you are assuming you know what is best, not only for the person you are judging but for the other person or people involved. This is a great way to drive people away and become lonely. The irony is that, however well-meaning you are, you simply cannot know what is best for the other person, what it is that they really want.

I recall a patient who, during her first visit, was telling me about her life and her worries. She and her husband had only limited funds with which to bring up two small children, partly because he was frequently out of work.

He was rude to her and abusive. He got drunk on a nightly basis. He was also physically violent and had beaten her up on numerous occasions. Clearly, as she had said when she arrived, she was stressed, and equally clearly she was nearly at the end of her tether. Although I had long since learned not to prejudge situations I was mentally reviewing ways she could cope as a single parent, once she left this husband. I was in for a surprise.

As she finished her story, and thinking I knew the answer, that she wanted advice on how to get out of her situation, I asked, 'And how can I help, what is it you want?'

'The awful thing is . . . I think he's seeing another woman, and if he is . . . I don't think I could bear it.' And she dissolved in tears as I digested this unexpected reply.

You can never tell what is best for someone else. You can never be sure that what you want for them is what they want for themselves. People love to give advice, but if you do, ask yourself what your motive is. Are you doing it because you truly want to help the other person? Or are you doing it to show how wise you are, how competent, how knowledgeable, how strong? Are you doing it to assert your power over the other person?

If you hold back your own judgements and truly and actively listen to what other people are saying, observe what they are doing, and try to get in touch with what is important to them, you may find yourself moving from judging to learning, from passing comments that are ultimately destructive to beginning to get a glimpse of the wonderful tapestry and variety that makes up another person. As you do this you will find that instead of losing friends and feeling lonely, you will develop greater empathy for other people and closer friendships.

Chapter Twelve

Intolerance – Fear

Intolerance can take many forms, and be the basis for a lot of loneliness. Most of us now live in multicultural societies. There are very few towns or cities where you do not see people of different races, different nationalities, different religions. There are always obvious differences of income, manners, social style and so forth. To a considerable extent racial intolerance has diminished, yet it still exists. We are all more aware than ever before of the many and different religions that exist. For many people and families religion has played a diminishing role in their lives over the past few decades. Yet religious intolerance is still the basis for wars, hatred and fear. The old structures of society, the class system and the hierarchies that existed within it are diminishing, yet they still exist. In the past people have fought wars and been killed for their political beliefs, and differences of political opinion can still range from the violent to that which makes or breaks friendships.

There are many types of intolerance. These are only some of the major ones. This is not the place to discuss any particular form of intolerance or the rights and wrongs of the various situations. The issue here is whether or not your behaviour in this regard is contributing to your loneliness.

If you refuse to speak to or make friends with people

of other races or nationalities, with people of a different religion, a different political persuasion or of a different social class to your own, you are seriously limiting the number of people you can know.

Nancy and Colin had moved. Colin's company had transferred him and as a result they now lived surrounded largely by people of different races to themselves. Nancy came to see me with a minor health problem but it soon became obvious that she was really lonely and bored, with little or nothing to do all day and no one to talk to. I asked her about the neighbours and was told she had none. When pressed, she said, 'Well, of course there are people living close by, but they're all Indian or Pakistani.'

'So?'

'Well, I can't talk to them.'

'Why not?'

Fortunately, by the end of the session, she was willing to agree that yes, they were people, yes, they did speak English, yes, she was lonely and yes, if she did speak to them and get to know them she might make some new friends. Later I discovered that she had been pleasantly surprised by the friendships she had made.

'In fact, it's been a remarkably interesting experience, learning about different cultures and ways of doing things, and also sharing my own ideas with them,' she told me next time I saw her. She had the grace to look somewhat shamefaced at her previous intolerance.

Many forms of intolerance or prejudice go largely unnoticed. 'I couldn't be friends with them, they have such dull interests', or 'Culturally we have so little in common, I really can't be bothered with them', or 'They're all so old and boring', or 'They're all young and silly', or 'They're just a bunch of women' (i.e. no eligible men in sight), or 'They're too stupid', or 'They look so (scruffy/overdressed/etc.), I couldn't be seen with them' or 'You could tell by looking that they and I would have little in common.'

I recall a woman in her early seventies who lived alone in a tiny flat. She was unable to get about much and often didn't see anyone for several days at a time. She was lonely and miserable. Yet she refused to move into a retirement village where she could easily have mixed with people. Her response to the suggestion that she might benefit from doing so was, 'What's the point, they're just a bunch of old people waiting to die?' Yet we can all think of many warm friendships made in such circumstances.

If you are willing to withhold judgement, to talk to people, no matter which prejudice of yours they represent, you may well be surprised at the result. By this I do not mean that you should necessarily go and look for people who are totally different to you. What I do mean is that whenever you have the opportunity to get to know someone, be it socially, at work, in buses or shops, at meetings and so forth, don't rule out eighty per cent of the people because of a variety of prejudices. Be willing to meet them with an open mind, find out about them, *be interested in them*. We have already discussed the importance of being interested in other people rather than expecting them to be interested in you. They may or may not become friends but you will almost certainly be in for some pleasant surprises. If nothing else you will learn a lot.

Consider also the basis of your intolerance. Often it is fear, either fear of the unknown (person, people, way of thinking and behaving) or fear of your own inadequacies. You may be afraid of people you cannot understand, of people of other nationalities, insofar as you feel you cannot interpret the actions of the other person or know what they mean. That's fine, spend time asking questions and learning. Once behaviours become known and understood there is less reason to fear. You may be afraid of people because you feel they know more than you do, are more intelligent or better educated. So ask questions. Don't pretend. Few people like poseurs but many people are delighted to explain what they know; they will interpret this, rightly, as an expression of your interest in them and what they have to say. Most people like compliments and asking for their information, their knowledge, their teaching is, after all, a form of a compliment.

The mistake many lonely people make is to go out looking for a bosom friend. *You don't find close friends, you grow them,* and the only way to start doing that is to make general friendships with a lot of people. Among them you can then find the seeds of close friendships, often quite unexpected friendships, that can grow into very close ones.

Examine your prejudices, are they really worth keeping? Prejudices never do you any credit and they may be exposing your fears and uncertainties.

None of this is to say that you should go looking for friends among people you couldn't possibly like. There is a difference between having sets of fundamental values to which you hold and prejudices or blind spots. You may be honest and not want to associate with crooks, fair enough. But if one of your values is 'intelligence' are you really risking it by spending time getting to know people who are less intelligent than you? If one of your values is 'behaving properly' consider this. Who is to say what proper behaviour is? It varies from culture to culture and you could benefit a lot by learning about other behaviour patterns. This doesn't mean that, necessarily, you have to change your own, but do, if you want to avoid loneliness, be open to others.

It is very easy to confuse values with prejudices or intolerances. It is very easy to claim a value as an excuse for having a prejudice. Take care to establish your own values and to know the difference between them and your prejudices. One way to do this is to go through the Values Elicitation process described earlier (and more fully in the Appendix). Then ask yourself the question 'what would happen if the opposite . . .?'

One of your values might be 'To be with people who share my interests.' When you ask yourself, 'What would happen if *I spent time with people who didn't share my interests?*' you might realise that you could learn a lot about different subjects to the ones that currently interest you. Another value might be 'To be with people who are popular and have a large circle of friends.' The question, 'What would happen if *I spent time with people who are alone and isolated?*' might bring the answer, 'I could find people who had more time to share with me.' Similarly if your values are prejudices related to being with people of your own class, race, religion, politics and so forth, this question, 'What would happen if . . .?' will show you that there are some acceptable outcomes, some benefits, to recognising that the value has elements of being a prejudice.

On the other hand, one of your values may be 'To be around people who are honest.' When you ask yourself, 'What would happen if *I spent time with people who were dishonest?*' you might answer that this would be a most unpleasant situation since you could not trust what they were saying. You could then ascribe this to the values group rather than the prejudice group, and stay away from such people.

This is not the time to try to justify your actions of the past and present, it is time to make appropriate changes so you can enter a less lonely future.

Chapter Thirteen

Learn to Forgive – Stop Holding Grudges

Grudges have been the cause of split families. Failing to forgive has ruined friendships. Are there people in your life who used to be friends and to whom you now refuse to speak? Are there people in your family who you feel have behaved so badly that you won't have them in your home any more? Are there people you refuse to acknowledge when you walk past them in the street or see them in a crowd? Is there someone who has let you down and who you'll have nothing more to do with? There are parents who are lonely because they have told their children 'not to darken their doorstep again', relationships that have ended unnecessarily and inappropriately because one participant has refused to forgive the other, and friendships that have foundered on a misunderstanding or a single misdemeanour and a refusal to forgive.

Friends and family are precious. Few people are evil. Few people set out to do you harm. Many of the things people fail to forgive stem from misunderstandings or from failures in communication. Furthermore, to reach the point of failing to forgive you first have to criticise and to judge and we have already seen the problems that these two steps can cause on their own.

It's You That Suffers

In many ways a decision to refuse to forgive someone is also a decision to go on causing yourself pain. When you are in pain and holding a grudge you may well find that you spend a lot of time chewing over the situation, and since the situation was presumably painful or unpleasant this cannot be a joyful experience. At worst it can turn you sour. In addition, as you mull over the situation, you possibly talk about it to other people. Few people want to hear your problems, few people want to hear you judging and criticising other people. Other people may even like the person or people about whom you are complaining and who you are refusing to forgive. You could be creating new problems for yourself, further losses of friendship and more loneliness.

The sad thing about holding grudges or failing to forgive other people is that it is often you that suffers more than them. Did someone ignore you, fail to include you in a social situation or forget an appointment? Did someone keep something you leant them or fail to repay a debt? If you refuse to speak to them as a result, you will lose their friendship and be that much more lonely. Not only that but you will feel bad inside as you mull over the perceived injustice. While you are feeling resentful what is happening to them? They may be totally unaware of the situation, blithely getting on with their life and feeling no pain. It is you that are suffering, not them. So, if for no other reason than for your own sake, forgive.

I recall an elderly widower, Joseph. His wife had died some years earlier. He had let his daughter know that, after the marriage of her brother, he expected her to look after him, at least until she married. When she had insisted on moving out and living with a boyfriend he called her selfish and unprincipled and told her she could stay away. Any comment I made about other friends resulted in muttered and angry comments such as 'Too busy with their own families,' 'No loyalty,' 'Can't rely on anyone,' and 'You just have to look after yourself.' One by one his friends had done something he took to be selfish or to his own detriment and he had refused to forgive them, turned down invitations and declined to communicate. As a result he was living on his own and lonely. He totally refused to make any moves, saying they should be the ones to contact him and apologise. In the meantime his resentment was eating into him, while they, almost certainly, were happily getting on with their lives, unaware of, or not concerned by, Joseph's moods and his broodings.

Forgiving the Forgivable

Few people set out to do you harm on purpose. You may argue that they did something that they knew would cause you pain. They may have cheated so they would get the job instead of you (or anyone else). They may have taken money or some possession from you. They may have told lies about a situation so they avoided being blamed, even though it meant the blame fell on you. They may have consciously neglected to invite you to a party. All these and a thousand other situations like them are possible.

In none of these situations did the other person set out to harm you, that was almost certainly not their primary goal. They set out to benefit themselves. They may not have realised that what they did would cause you pain. They probably cheated to get the job, perhaps one they desperately needed, after a series of failures to be accepted, not to hurt you specifically. They may have stolen out of desperation, out of a need to provide for a child or out of thwarted desire and personal hurt. They lied to avoid blame, not to harm you. They could have multiple reasons for not inviting you to a party.

Rosemary had, for years, invited Christine to events in her house. For a long time she had regularly invited her as part of 'the crowd', even though Christine had not, in all that time, invited her back. Gradually Rosemary was coming to resent the situation. Then by chance, one day she had reason to drop in on Christine and, during casual comments as Christine showed her around, she learnt that the reason for lack of invitations from Christine was that she felt Rosemary had such an elegant house that she was reluctant to show her own and that Rosemary was such an excellent cook that she was nervous of cooking for her. Understanding that, Rosemary forgave, and let go of the resentment she had felt when she interpreted Christine's lack of invitations either as based on selfishness and an unwillingness to share or a refusal to include Rosemary in her circle of close friends.

So many such deeds, and more, are done not, as the recipient might feel, to hurt them, but to benefit the doer, either by positive benefit or by avoiding situations in which they would feel uncomfortable. The fact that you got hurt in the process is secondary.

When you are willing to forgive you can resume more pleasant relationships. When you do this you may well learn, in time, of other circumstances that explained the situation in a different way, as Rosemary found. You may then be glad that you 'forgave' and sad that you let your assessment and interpretation of the situation spoil the relationship in the interim.

What you do, ultimately, with regard to the relationship with that particular person, is often less important than the fact of forgiving and letting go of the resentment and the effect it is having on the rest of your life.

Forgiving the Unforgivable

There are some misdemeanours you may feel are simply too heinous to forgive. The deed was too horrible. The disloyalty was too great. You may feel you can never trust the other person again, you may feel absolutely certain that you never want to see them again. Then at least let them, and the situation, go. If you hold on to a resentment it comes out in your life in other ways.

The better way is to 'Let go and let God.' What goes out has a way of coming round. Karma has a way of working out. If the person truly did you harm then that is the sort of person they are and you cannot be sure that they are not aware of it, are not suffering in some other way or finding that their actions are coming home to roost. This is not an argument for revenge, that too is a useless emotion if you are seeking friends, wanting to avoid loneliness and wanting to be truly comfortable with yourself. But it is not necessarily your job to 'right the wrong' that you perceive was done to you, fate will take care of that, in the grand scheme of things.

What you can know is that your brooding and resentment is making you unhappy and so the *most useful* action is for you to put the situation behind you. Don't just bury it, that still leaves it as a canker in your soul, more deeply buried than before but none the less capable of causing you harm. It is important that you let the situation go completely.

To start with, recognise that in everything that befalls you in life you had some input. You played a role in the situation. You could have chosen to play a different role. You could have chosen not to trust the person in the first place. You could have behaved differently, in such a way that they might not have done what they did. You could have avoided the situation altogether. Perhaps just by being there you got caught up in the situation. This is not to say that *you* are to blame. There is no question of apportioning blame here. Nor is it a question of taking away the responsibility of the other person for their own actions. It is a question of healing your own pain, of enabling you to let the situation go and of preventing it poisoning other aspects of your own life.

When you recognise that, inevitably, you have a degree of responsibility for everything that happens to you, it is easier to stop blaming the other person, easier to stop feeling resentful, and easier to move on to the future. Recognise that you did the best you could at the time, you did what you felt was right at the time. You don't blame yourself now for not knowing the answers to simple arithmetic when you were a child. You didn't know then, you made a mistake, you learnt, and you have moved on. Life is like that. When you look back on the situation you may be saying, 'Had I known then what I know now . . .' Indeed that is true, indeed things might have been different. But you did not know then what you know now. That is part of life, of learning, of growing and developing. One of the biggest mistakes anyone can make is not the original mistake but failing to learn from it. Look back on the past incident as an important learning experience.

If you continue to fail to learn from your experience and change your behaviour then learn, instead, what that says about you. You may repeatedly trust people and get hurt. Each time you may castigate yourself for 'doing it again' as well as for refusing to forgive the person you feel betrayed you. Andrew was like that.

Andrew came to see me because, in his own words, he was 'stressed out, fed up and pissed off.'

'I run a small printing business and inevitably I get asked to give credit. And I do.'

He frowned as he said it and waved a hand at me as

if to say, 'I know, I know if I didn't give credit I wouldn't lose money, then I wouldn't be in financial difficulties and I wouldn't be under such pressure from the bank and feeling so stressed.'

'Each time I hear the hard-luck story, that they can't pay me now but they will be able to in the future, I believe them. Then when they continue to say they can't pay I get cross, then I get angry, and I tell them I won't do any work for them in the future. Sometimes they do pay, sometimes they don't, but even when they do pay they don't come back as customers, I won't have them.'

'I just don't seem to learn.'

Andrew, it seemed, was resentful of the customers who had, as he saw it, let him down. He refused to forgive them when they did, and was progressively losing accounts as a result. And he was berating himself for refusing to learn from what he saw to be his mistakes.

When I asked him to complete 'The reason I give my customers credit in the first place is . . .' I first got such logical and practical completions as 'You have to,' 'It's expected when you run a business like mine,' and 'If I don't they'll go somewhere else.' I chose not to comment that if non-paying customers went elsewhere he could actually be better off. As I pushed further, and suggested to him that some printing businesses don't give credit he came out again with 'They'll go elsewhere.'

It finally transpired that it was not a case of failing to learn by his mistakes. What he came to understand was that he had indeed learnt from his mistakes, he did know and recognise, each time he did it, that giving credit could mean the person might not return and pay the bill. What he was doing, however, was hiding a bigger fear, the fear that they might go elsewhere. He also, as we worked, came to recognise that this, in turn, hid an even deeper fear, that his work was not good enough, that other and bigger printing companies could do a better job.

Either learn from your mistakes or find out the underlying reason why you choose to continue making them, learn from this and make the appropriate changes. Either way, do not give yourself a hard time for your role in the past, in the events that led to this situation where you feel you cannot forgive someone. Continue to recognise that you had a role in the situation, that you did the very best you could at the time, that there is nothing to be gained by continuing the resentment. Either do whatever you can to right the situation, whatever that may be, or forgive and let go.

Forgiving is not Condoning

Many people have said to me that they cannot forgive someone for something, it would be like letting them 'get away with it'.

> *Mrs P, who insisted on the formality and barrier of surnames, had breast cancer. It had been diagnosed towards the end of a five-year period during which time her husband, who travelled extensively with his work, had been having an affair with another woman. She had known of the affair towards the end and her husband had known she had known, in fact they had had arguments about it. They still did, as she was still suspicious that it was going on although he assured her it wasn't, that it had stopped, of necessity, when he retired.*
>
> *As we worked together she admitted that she was glad, in a way, that she had cancer. 'It shows my husband the stress he put me under. I wouldn't have got cancer or been ill at all if he hadn't done that to me.' In spite of her recognition of the fact that her state of mind had affected her health*[1] *and that the disease she had could kill her, she refused to let go. She had also refused any therapy for the problem other than surgery. Surgery, she said,*

would show him the damage he had caused; chemotherapy and radiation would be unpleasant only for her and she wasn't having that, nor was she willing to take any vitamins. Nor, finally, was she willing to make any changes in her mental and emotional attitude, all because if she got better her husband would know he had 'got away with' his adultery. In the meantime she was running up medical bills in all directions as she consulted one practitioner after another, even though she didn't follow through with any of the suggested treatments. This too, she felt, was a suitable punishment for her husband. So strong was her determination to continue with this grudge that she was even willing to allow the cancer to get the better of her, and to risk her own life.

Being willing to forgive doesn't condone the act. You are not the ultimate judge and jury. Even if you, absolutely and totally, in your heart of hearts, feel that the other person was at fault you cannot be sure. There may be other circumstances of which you are unaware that could change the perspective of the whole situation. Being willing to forgive means letting go, fully, of the situation. It means being able to get on with your life without resentment holding you back and souring your nature. It means being able to look or think back over the past without getting stirred up emotionally.

Forgiving does not mean that you have to do so to the other person, to their face. You have to do it inside you. Forgiving does not mean that you have to restore relationships with the other person. You may still feel that, however right the other person may have felt their behaviour was, you cannot agree with it. You may feel you want to have nothing more to do with that person. That is fine. Some people write a 'forgiveness letter' to get the whole situation out of their system, then tear it up and drop it in the waste-paper basket. Some people do the whole process internally. But, for your own sake, do forgive them. Do stop holding the resentment and letting it interfere, directly or indirectly, with the rest of your life.

It comes back to the bottom line. If you don't forgive and let go, far from continuing to prove them wrong, you harm yourself, spoil your nature, lose friends and become lonely and unhappy. Forgive, for your own sake.

Finally

Finally, the issue of forgiving, at all, requires comment. The concept of forgiving implies that you have some jurisdiction over the other person, that you have the right to judge and pardon. You don't. The act of forgiving is much more an act of letting go, of choosing a more appropriate state of mind for yourself than that of resentment or than of making a comment on the person, people or situation. Forgiving has little to do with the outside event, much more to do with your own inner environment. So, again forgive, for your own sake.

[1] Xandria Williams, *Choosing Health Intentionally*, Letts Publishing, 1990.

Chapter Fourteen

Being Impatient

Do you get impatient? You may think people should do things more quickly, that they should understand what you are saying more readily, or respond more rapidly to your needs, but *they* may not see it that way. Certainly it is unlikely that they will enjoy being told that they are slow. Nor will they enjoy your company if you are tapping your foot in impatient frustration. People operate at different speeds and if you show, by your impatience, that your speed is different from theirs, they may decide to look elsewhere for their friends, people more in tune with their rhythm.

You may not take your impatience out on your friends, but on a third person. Yet this is another way to lose their companionship. If you go out to a restaurant or to shops with friends and become impatient with the service, with the waiter or the waitress, you may well find that your friends become embarrassed by your behaviour and prefer to leave you out next time.

Even if they don't mind you getting impatient with other people they will be all too well aware that, if you get impatient with other people and express this behind their backs, you may well be doing the same to them.

Carol and Mary were good friends, but Carol was the more dynamic of the two. She would grit her teeth when things didn't happen fast enough for her and mutter to Mary such phrases as 'Inept idiots,' or 'If they worked for me I'd sack them,' or 'Stupid incompetents.' The first few times this happened Mary laughed, but in the end she began to wonder if this was the sort of thing Carol was saying about her, to other people. As a result she became uncomfortable in Carol's company, suspecting she was being silently criticised, and the friendship gradually cooled.

If you get impatient there may be many reasons for it. You may indeed be short of time. Perhaps you are in a queue and in a hurry to get somewhere. Perhaps you do need to have something done and wish the other person would do it more quickly. However there may also be a number of less obvious, underlying reasons, behind your impatience. In fact the reason is rarely as obvious as it might at first appear to be. Consider some of the following scenarios:

Barbara is five years old and wants her mother to help her with the puzzle she's doing. Mother, on the other hand, is busy dealing with the twins, eighteen months old, learning to walk, and constantly getting into mischief. Barbara says, 'Now, come and help me now,*' and when her mother doesn't, she gets impatient, bangs on the floor shouting, 'Now, now, help me* now.*' Mother tells her not to be so impatient, she's busy at the moment and she'll come in a minute, and wonders why Barbara has suddenly become so irritable. If asked, Barbara could not explain. She would, at five, not have the words and concepts with which to articulate her feelings. All she knows is fear, a nebulous fear that she cannot define.*

If she did understand what she was feeling and could articulate it Barbara would explain that the answer lies in her fear of not being wanted any more. Whereas she was once an only child and the focus of her parents' attention, a situation she took as normal, she is suddenly being pushed into the background. The twins have arrived. They are boys and she has overheard her mother saying to her father, 'Now you have sons, as you've always wanted . . .' Heard out of context Barbara has taken this to mean that she, as a daughter, may not be wanted and that she may be abandoned, a fear that worsens and makes her irritable and impatient when she doesn't get the attention she wants, and get it instantly. As she grows up, since the underlying fears are never addressed, impatience becomes a part of her nature, each delay in getting the attention she needs reinforcing her fear that people she knows may be demonstrating that she is not important to them and that they may suddenly abandon her. By demanding their immediate attention she is, unconsciously, demanding they show her that they do still care and will continue to do so. Sadly, her behaviour is unlikely to achieve the outcome she is after.

Gerald is in a hurry to get to school. His father normally drops him off, early, on his way to work but this morning Dad is running late. He brought work home last night and is taking extra time to make sure he has everything back in his briefcase. Meanwhile Gerald is hopping up and down, getting impatient and saying, 'Come on Dad, don't take so long, I have to get to school.' His father, knowing there is time to spare before the deadline when Gerald actually has to be there, and knowing it is important that he gathers everything he needs, still doesn't appear and Gerald gets more impatient and cross. When Dad is finally ready he takes Gerald to task for his manners and says, accurately, 'Stop being so impatient, you'll be in plenty of time for class,' to which Gerald replies, 'That's not the point,' as he slams the front door, earning another rebuke and further delaying their departure. The drive to the school is tense.

When Dad comes home that evening he is heard to mutter to his wife that he wishes Gerald would learn some patience, and they wonder why they have such a difficult son. As a disciplinary action Gerald is not allowed to visit friends after tea and stays alone in his room.

What was behind Gerald's impatience? Gerald had plenty of time to get to school before class. If it was simply a question of time, a logical discussion with Dad would have resolved the situation. The problem was more complex. Gerald knew that if he didn't get there early, in time to link up with his three friends, they would be doing their usual planning for the day without him. Again, logic would have dictated that he could catch up and join in with their plans when he did arrive. Deep down, however, was the fear that they didn't really want him as part of their group, that if he arrived late they would exclude him for the rest of the day and that, if this pattern repeated, he would be cast out of the group altogether. As I worked with Gerald it became obvious that nearly all his outbursts of impatience, nearly all his tantrums, came not because of the immediate time issue but because, deep down, he was afraid of being left out of things.

Andrew's visit to me was triggered by a girlfriend who had said to him, 'You know, going out with you really can be quite uncomfortable. Why do you always get so impatient with waitresses and so forth?'

'It's true too,' Andrew admitted as he sat in the office with me. 'Once I thought about it I realised what she meant. If I don't get instant attention from waiters, barmen, shop assistants etc. I do get impatient.'

As we talked he suddenly realised that it happened

mostly when he was with people. On his own he was rarely quite so demanding. Working through it he began to recognise that, in his eyes, the speed with which he got attention was a measure of his own stature and, he assumed, would be so perceived by the people with him. In other words, the attention he got was his way of letting the people he was with realise that he was respected. His demand that he receive, and demonstrate to his friends that he was worthy of, instant attention, was his way of saying, 'Look, people respect me, I am worthy of your admiration so please like and admire me too.'

Betty got impatient when she was kept waiting in a queue, picked the slowest moving queue or got an assistant who, in Betty's view, took too long to deal with the situation. She came to realise that her underlying assumption, and the reason she got impatient, was that when this happened she felt as if she wasn't important. As she was kept waiting she would start to feel insulted, then angry and finally this would erupt in a show of impatience.

Deirdre's impatience occurred in similar situations to those of Betty but had a different cause. Deirdre would get impatient if she had picked a slow-moving queue in a supermarket or a slow lane in heavy traffic. As she stood or sat there, watching the other queues or lanes moving ahead of her, she would get more and more angry and frustrated. As we worked together she realised that her unconscious assumption was that she had been stupid to pick the slow lane, that other people would notice and that they too would consider her to be stupid. This belief stemmed from a childhood where her older sister, already able to do the things that Deirdre was just learning, repeatedly called her stupid for being slow. This was further aggravated by the fact that her sister was good at intellectual subjects whereas Deirdre showed particular flair in arts and music. Each year, as Deirdre's marks in class fell below those her sister had achieved the year before, her sense of being stupid deepened.

In Barbara's case her impatience stemmed from a fear of suddenly being rejected and replaced in the lives of her parents and friends, even though she had once felt totally secure. Gerald's impatience came from the fear that other people didn't really want him to be part of their group, that he would be an outsider and not one of the chosen élite. Andrew's impatience came from a desire or need to demonstrate to people around him that he was respected. Betty's impatience came from an underlying belief that she wasn't important, and Deirdre's from a belief that she was stupid.

Notice that in all these cases the person involved is not impatient because they are short of time. They are impatient because of some other, underlying, belief about their own inadequacy in some way, or by a deeply buried fear that is being triggered by whatever *seems* to be making them impatient, one of which they are unconscious and for which they have not sought. After all, it is easy to justify the impatience on the basis of the time that is being lost. There is no obvious prompt to look for an underlying cause. To the outsider, however, conscious that there is no real need for impatience in the situation in question, this type of impatience and irritability is unpleasant. It is the type of impatience that drives people away, that causes you to lose friends, that leaves you feeling lonely.

The type of impatience that comes from a love of life and a desire to do everything *now,* because the enthusiasm is there, now, not later, because the desire is there to experience the result; this does not leave you feeling lonely. This is a positive and exuberant impatience, others will go along with you in this because it will lead to a positive result all the sooner. It is based on a positive enthusiasm, not a sense of negative criticism or inner inadequacy. The worst that can happen if it is positive impatience is that other people may feel breathless as you rush headlong through life.

If, on the other hand, your impatience is of the negative variety, the type that drives people away, then it is important that you address the problem. There is little point in gritting your teeth and willing yourself to remain calm, the underlying tension will still show, it will still, sometimes, erupt, and you will suffer as the tension builds up inside. You may even get an ulcer. You cannot live on will-power, the time inevitably comes when you don't have enough of it.

The First Step

The first step in dealing with this negative type of impatience is to search for and find the underlying cause. Put aside the part of your brain that is rationalising the situation, that is justifying your patience on logical grounds. You've been listening to that for too long already.

Instead you are in search of the deeper cause. To find this use the technique of Running a Phrase already described. It is one of the easiest ways of finding the subconscious causes of what you are feeling and doing. Run a lot of phrases, such as 'A reason I am feeling impatient is . . .' 'Another reason I am feeling impatient is . . .' 'What I am afraid of is . . .' 'What I am feeling beside impatience is . . .' 'The *real* reason I am impatient is . . .' You will also think of phrases of your own to run.

If there is a part of your mind insisting that the problem is not your fault, is not of your creating, stop being a victim, ignore the temptation to play the victim role and be willing to do the exercise with an open mind. It is all too easy to say, 'It is not my fault, I didn't choose this situation.' Yet you are where you are because you played a role in being or getting there. Keep in mind that, as discussed elsewhere (*Stress*[1], *Beating the Blues*[2]), you have created what is happening in your life. Your life didn't just happen to you. You had a part in creating all aspects of it. Sometimes this may have been a major part, sometimes a minor part. Simply being in a situation means you chose to get into it. You could have acted differently. You chose this queue, these friends, the timing of your actions, the assumptions you made about what other people would and wouldn't do, should and shouldn't do.

Given this fact then consider the next questions. Do you really want people to know you have created a situation that frustrates you? Almost certainly you don't. So go ahead, act positively, search for the deeper meaning behind the situation. Refuse to believe the obvious reason; after all, other people don't necessarily get impatient in the same situations as you. Be willing to delve deeper and opt for greater self-knowledge and another step in your growth and development rather than justification and staying as you are.

Running a phrase is one of the easiest ways to find the underlying cause of your mood, particularly if the conscious part of your mind is insisting that the mood was legitimate, but there are others. You could try simply asking yourself what you were saying to yourself at the time, what was causing the pain. I have had clients who got impatient when things didn't go their way for a variety of reasons; they felt out of control, they felt stupid, they felt they were not being given the credit or courtesy due to them, they wanted someone to pay more attention to them and to care about them, they felt superior to other people, their prejudices were showing (as in 'those bloody xxxxxxxs'). While you are doing this keep in mind that no blame is being attached. This is simply a useful time and opportunity to learn more about yourself, to learn things that you can work on to your positive benefit. It is a glorious opportunity.

When you have done all you can to uncover the underlying cause of your mood you will probably have found some aspect of yourself and your emotional panorama that you would like to work on and change. If you feel you have uncovered nothing of significance, or that you have not uncovered the real cause, then you might want to find someone who can help you in this search. There is almost certainly an underlying cause, particularly if it is a relatively common experience with you. (If it only happens occasionally, if it does not affect your relationships with people, be they friends or strangers, then it is unlikely to be a significant problem.)

Once you know your real fear or concern you can start to do something about it. If it relates to some other topic covered in this book then turn to that. If not, then find another book that can help you or go for appropriate counselling. It will be resolving this deep-seated cause of your impatience that will help you to resolve your impatience and then, through it, your loneliness.

At the more practical level, ask yourself what you could have done to avoid the situation.

David was a busy advertising executive. He worked long hours, arriving at work before the rush hour and going home late in the evening. Part of his job included taking clients out to business lunches which he enjoyed. He was a sociable chap and enjoyed the company of his clients, he enjoyed the food and the wine, and he enjoyed being waited on. However, he frequently found the service was not to his satisfaction and would berate the waiters for being tardy. When one of his clients said, 'Hold on there old chap, if you get frustrated like that you'll give yourself an ulcer,' he realised that not only was that true but that he was beginning to lose the goodwill of his guests.

We worked together on the underlying cause but I also asked him what he could do to prevent the troublesome situations happening in the future. He now has a standing order with each of the restaurants that he frequents, that he wants drinks served the minute he sits down, the food order can be taken later. In a new restaurant he makes a point of telling the person who sees him to his table that he wants a drink immediately. This way he can feel pampered, can relax and have his first drink without working up a lather.

Another Step

Dealing with this deep-seated cause is an excellent long-term solution. However, it will not necessarily help at the point of immediate frustration once the situation is under way. When your blood is beginning to boil, your temper is rising and your impatience is about to explode you are unlikely to sit back, run a few phrases and make commitments about making changes in your life. You need a more immediate tool. Here is one immediate habit you can develop that can help you to deal with the frustration on the spot.

As you stand in the queue, muttering about the woman in front who has lost her purse in the bottom of a capacious handbag full of three months' accumulated goodies, ask yourself, 'What is good about this?' After the initial scream of 'Nothing', ask yourself again, with a deep intent to find a positive answer, 'What is good about this?'

This process does a number of things. It changes your focus from a negative event to a positive outcome. It takes your mind off the immediate problem. It forces you to think of something different and it may produce some surprising side-benefits.

Once you ask yourself such a question your brain is diverted to searching for an answer. Whereas a few seconds ago you had tunnel vision, focusing totally on what was wrong, what was not happening and what was holding you back, you now have to open up your mind, look around, and find something else to notice, to think about, to learn from and to concentrate on. At once your impatience will start to subside. In addition, instead of focusing on something negative, the (surface) cause of your impatience, you have now directed your mind, specifically, to think of something positive and you may make a significant gain from the situation.

If, instead of using this technique, you had said to yourself, 'Think about something different. Don't think about what is annoying you, just think of something else,' you would have experienced very little change. Try it for yourself. It is hard to 'think about something else' when all the time half of your mind is harking back to what is making you impatient. The instruction 'Don't think about a green jumper' sets your mind thinking about a green jumper, not about something else. Your mind is thrown on to its own resources, and it will quickly turn back to the immediate problem.

When you ask it to solve the question, 'What is good about this?' your mind has to turn outside itself and search for the answer to the question. Not only that but it has to come up with something positive and good. This means that the answer will actually provide you with pleasure.

Margaret had a tight schedule for the whole day followed by friends coming for dinner. Early in the morning she had gone back to her old flat to meet the removals men who were to bring one larger piece of furniture to her new flat. When they arrived at the old flat they realised they had not brought all the tools they needed. As a result they would have to return later in the day. Margaret was impatient to get her new flat organised and see everything in place and, at the delay, she was ready to blow a gasket. She could see her entire day being ruined, she called them idiots, but deep down she knew that she could have been more specific as to what had to be done and she felt stupid. She was also afraid that her friends, when they heard, would laugh at her for not having been properly organised.

Eventually she agreed to give the men the key and they said they would return later and bring the piece along in the afternoon. As she stomped out of the building cursing since she now had to walk home instead of getting a lift in the van, she recalled my suggestion and asked herself, 'What is good about this?' As she thought, she realised she had left the old flat sooner than if she had waited for them to load the van, she could do the shopping on the way home instead of going out again and, though she would have less time to arrange the furniture, she might actually have more time in the day to do other tasks.

'It was amazing,' she said as she recounted the experience to me. 'I suddenly started to feel quite happy and light-hearted about the whole situation. In fact I actually became pleased at the way things had turned out. If I had kept focusing on what had gone wrong I would have failed to recognise the benefits and been in a bad mood for ages. In fact I'd probably have recounted the whole irritating story to my friends in the evening and still *have been in a bad mood. I might even have managed to spoil the dinner party as a result.'*

If you are in a queue and ask yourself, 'What's good about this?' you may look around and learn something new, read a poster that gives you an idea, notice an outfit that gives you an idea of what you could do with one of yours, or see a holiday poster that appeals to you. If you're not served fast enough in a restaurant you might ask yourself, 'What's good about this?' and you might conclude you will only have time to eat one course instead of two and will be the healthier as a result. In a shop you may recognise that you will spend less.

Getting impatient can make you unpleasant company and if people don't want to share your company you will be lonely.

[1] Xandria Williams, *Stress – recognise and resolve*, Charles Letts & Co. Ltd, 1993.
[2] Xandria Williams, *Beating the Blues*, Cedar, 1995.

Chapter Fifteen

Your Expression Says It All

Do you go round looking sad and downcast? Are you frowning? Do you look cross, angry or irritable? Where are your eyes, do you look at the ground or in other ways avoid people's gaze, avoid making direct eye contact? Are you, by your expression, giving the impression that you are not happy with your life, not having fun and, above all, will not be much fun to get to know or to be with?

Next time you are in a public place surrounded by strangers look around you at the people, in particular look at the expressions on their faces. Then consider which ones, based on the expression you see, you would like to get to know. Are you drawn to the sad and unhappy people, the ones who look as if they are lost and lonely? Or are you drawn to the smiling happy faces, to the people that look as if they have an inner secret you would like to share, who are happy with their life and who could be fun to be with?

If you are drawn to the people who look lost, lonely and sad consider why this could be. Are you drawn to them because they feel like you do and together you can both be unhappy? If so it is definitely time you consider what your reasons are for choosing to stay lonely, what hidden agenda you are following. Now might be a good time to read Chapter Seven again.

On the other hand you may be drawn to these sad-looking people because you would like to help them. If this is so, if you are a Melancholic by temperament[1] and you feel best when you are helping people, then this will give you a clue as to your way out of loneliness. First recognise that being with a group of happy positive people may not be the solution for you. Then look for ways you can play a positive role in a caring capacity. Use this role both to help other people and to enable you to meet people and make friends. You might want to offer your services to a charity or a community service, to do voluntary work, or deliver meals on wheels, to help out at the school canteen or at your local church. If this seems like a good idea to you you're on your way. If this seems a depressing thing to do then you are not a true Melancholic so read on.

If you are typical of the majority of people, you will be drawn to, and feel you would like to get to know, those people who are happy and smiling, the people who look as if they have an inner secret of happiness, people who by their expression seem to say, 'My life is fun. I do lots of exciting things. I have great friends and stimulating and enjoyable things are happening for me.' This may or not be true, of course. Some people just smile anyway, but the fact remains, they are the people you are drawn to.

Consider the posture and movements of the people you are drawn to, the people you feel you would like to get to know. Are they standing straight or slouched over? Are their arms crossed, as if in self-protection, cutting them off from others, or are they relaxed with their limbs spread casually and invitingly? Are their hands held firmly in their lap with their knees close together or do they look at ease? Are they facing the people to whom they are talking or are they looking to the side, or up, or down at the ground, or are they looking awkward?

A great way to find out how people feel is for you to imitate their posture and their movements. Try this for yourself. As an example sit straight in your chair, feet and knees together. Put your hands together and in the centre of your lap, hunch your back and shoulders over, bend your head down and look at your hands. How do you feel? Do you feel like being the life and soul of the party? Almost certainly not. Now, stand up, give yourself a shake and sit down again. This time lean back in the chair, drape one arm along the back, the other out at right angles. Cross your legs or arrange them in some other casual way. Put your shoulders back, head up and survey the room. Now smile. How do you feel? It is certain that you do not feel the same as you did in the previous position. You are also probably a lot more inclined to speak to people and to welcome their attention and company.

So, eye contact, your facial expression and your body position all affect the way you feel. Use this now to find out how other people feel. Consider again those people you were drawn to in a crowd, the people that looked as if they would be fun to be with and who you would like to have befriend you. Now imitate their posture and find how they (probably) feel. If that feels a lot better than the way you feel in the posture you commonly adopt, stick to it, make it your new habit.

We know a lot of the above instinctively, yet often that knowledge is unconscious and is only used unconsciously. You're with someone and you get the feeling they would really rather be somewhere else. You may not know exactly why, it may be nothing they are saying, but the message comes across. If you were more observant you might notice slight changes in their posture, their breathing or their eye movements. You do get the message and you do respond to it. Yet we do not often make positive use of this knowledge, we don't often act on it. The problem is that, while you are admiring the group of people you would like to join, as the result of the way they act and look, they have seen your posture, looked at your expression and possibly decided that you are not a lot of fun. You cannot refuse to communicate in this way, it is happening all the time, whether you like it or not. So be wise, make good use of your body language.

To quote a much used expression, 'For things to change you have to change.' This is the time for you to change the way you use your body. Find someone who is happy, popular and who you envy, someone you would like to be like, someone who has the number of friends and close relationships you would like. If you do not know someone like that then look at someone, even a stranger, who seems to be the way you would like to be and seems to feel the way you would like to feel. Copy them. Imitate them. Mirror them. If they look welcoming then adopt their position and find out how open you feel to other people. If they are moving in a particular way then copy that. If their expression is smiling and happy, create a similar expression on your face and find out how that feels. If they look as if they have just asked a question and are vitally interested in the other person's answer, then copy their gestures and discover how it feels.

The first step is to find out how they feel, by doing this mirroring, and to enjoy the feeling of being happy and positive. Use it in your daily life to adopt positions and expressions that will attract to you the sort of people you would like to have as friends.

Now you may be saying to yourself, 'But that is false, that is not the sort of person I am.' Indeed it isn't, not at the moment anyway. But do you want to continue being the sort of person you are at the moment? If you are lonely then you do, presumably, want to change and this change has to start somewhere. It might as well be here.

If you choose to continue to be the sort of person you are now then you will continue to be lonely. If you choose to make changes then you can change your life and create one with which you are a lot happier.

You may not be interested in other people but in that case they are unlikely to be interested in you and you will continue to be lonely. So change your posture, change your expression and look interested. Fake it till you make it. Either the change in your posture and attitude *will* make a change and you *will* become interested in other people rather than yourself or the effort will seem too great, you will stop and nothing much will have changed. Yet remember this, you can make more friends in a week by showing an interest in them than you can in a year by trying to make them be interested in you.

The next step comes about when other people see you and respond to the changes.

All this has to be done somewhat subtly of course. Yet you will be amazed at how closely you can imitate someone, even the person you are talking to, gesture for gesture, without them realising what you are doing. In fact all they are likely to feel is a growing rapport with you, a growing sense of comfort and familiarity as they begin to recognise in you a kindred spirit. So go ahead and practise this.

By now you will have realised that you communicate a lot of your thoughts and feelings through the way you look. In fact some studies have indicated that as little as seven per cent of the messages you convey comes from the words you speak, the rest comes from the way you say them and, above all, how you look. In other words for the receiver, the visual input is often dominant, it is certainly a large part of the message.

You may not be a warm and outgoing person but in that case it is unlikely that warm and outgoing people are going to be drawn to you and you will continue to be lonely. So again, change your posture, change your expression and look as if you are a warm and friendly person. As this changes the way people respond to you you will make new friends, people with whom you can let your warmth show in a more relaxed way.

You may not be happy, you may, in fact, feel sad, lonely and miserable, but if you look like that you already know the type of response you get. So smile, and change your posture – yes, your posture, it is difficult to be sad when your head is up and your shoulders back. Try it for yourself. Stand up, put your shoulders back, tilt your head back so you are looking directly at the ceiling, put a smile on your face and grin. Now, try to feel sad – don't move. Did you find that you moved when you tried to feel sad? Almost certainly you did. Hold that posture, fully, then try to feel sad. It's difficult, isn't it?

Now do the opposite. Sit down, slouch, look at the ground, frown, turn the corners of your mouth down. Now try to feel happy – don't move. You did, didn't you; the moment you tried to feel happy some part of you, however small, moved into a position more consistent with feeling happy.

Remember, right now you may not be a happy person, the sort of person that adopts the happy body language, but you want your life to change, don't you? So you must change. Smile – it takes a lot less energy and uses a lot fewer muscles than does frowning.

[1] See *Love, Health and Happiness* by Xandria Williams, Hodder and Stoughton, 1995.

Chapter Sixteen

Spiritual and Religious Beliefs

It is not for me to tell you what to believe, in a spiritual sense. I do, of course, tell you to believe in yourself. I think that that is of vital importance for everyone. In all other senses I believe that everyone has the total right to choose their own beliefs, their own experience and that everyone should respect the beliefs and experience of every other human being as being real and being true for them.

You may have no spiritual or religious belief. If you believe that this is the only life you have, that there is no hereafter and no god, or higher being then you're like the gambler, staking all on one throw of the dice. In that case, if you are alone and unhappy there is a sense of urgency. Time is running out and you had better get this life right. If this is your belief system then the rest of this book, both before and after this chapter, is for you, but you may want to skip the next few pages.

I do not want to attack or criticise any religion, far from it. I have total respect for the 'reality' of each individual and that includes, of course, their thoughts, ideas and beliefs. In fact it seems to me that there is no such thing as an objective reality, one that is true for all people, or even true for two people. The only true reality is the experience each individual has within themselves. Two people may be at the same event, they may describe it similarly, yet their inner experience will be different, and not only subtly. Each of them will interpret the happenings in a different way, they will each focus on different aspects of the occasion. They will each experience the event against the background of their own, different, lives and past experiences.

This is also true for their beliefs. Even two people, of the same faith and going to the same church, temple, ashram or meeting will experience their faith, their god, their leader and their religion in a different way. They may hold to the same creed yet one may expect their god to make more allowances for the individual's weakness, while another will expect to be punished more severely. One may hold that their god demands obedience yet they may each argue, if only slightly, as to what they should be obedient to. Should they move towards telling the absolute truth, for instance, in favour of avoiding hurting someone or should their love for another individual come ahead of a slight fudging of the truth?

There are many such examples and the religious fights, wars and conflicts through the years demonstrate this most fully. The fights and arguments occur not only between different religions but between different branches of the same religion, between different sects, within different parishes and between individual churches or places of worship. They even occur between different groups within the one church (or its equivalent), between families and, of course, between individuals.

Your own beliefs will inevitably be influenced very considerably by what you were told as a child and the way you grew up, yet children from the same family can find that, as adults, they have very different beliefs, possibly even different religions. All this means, ultimately, that what *you* choose to believe is just that, what *you* choose to believe.

It is also worth considering the word 'belief'. Firstly, it can be a very gentle word, lacking in conviction. When you say, 'I believe so' about a situation you may mean no more than, 'I think so.' Your belief may be simply a faint hope. Secondly, it may be a strong belief, that, for instance, after this life, certain things will happen. Yet in this life it is just that, a blind belief about something that you feel you cannot know for absolute certainty, at least not right now. Yet you are willing to put your trust in it for some point in the future. Thirdly, it can be a conviction, an absolute conviction, one on which you would stake your life as readily as you stake it, for instance, on relying on a piece of equipment such as your car, or the lift up to your office. Fourthly, and beyond that, it can be an absolute experience. You may *know* and *experience* the spiritual aspects of your reality as totally and clearly as you know and experience what you do physically. You may, for instance, recall past lives or other spiritual or out-of-body experiences with the same clarity and certainty as you recall things you did in your childhood.

So there we have it, your belief can be a think/wish, a strong belief, a strong conviction or an absolute certainty of the experience.

I would like to add at this point that I hope, in this chapter in particular, I will not offend against anyone's convictions, beliefs or views. I do not mean to. I only ask that you consider the situation logically as we continue.

If you have a belief, and that belief is not adding to the quality of your life, is not making you happy, or is not fulfilling a positive purpose with which you are in agreement, then is it not perhaps time that you take another look at that belief? Perhaps the belief is not as strong as you think it is and that is why it is not supporting and sustaining you and why you still feel lonely. Or perhaps it is a belief that is not in line with your own experience, one that you would like to change.

If, for instance, you believe that there is a god who is all-powerful, who has ordained all things, including your life on earth at this time, and who is aware of all things, then you cannot be lonely. S/he is with you. Provided you *truly* believe and are convinced of this as a reality, then you have, at all times, your god for your companion. What's more, if you believe your god is all-powerful, has ordained your life and has the power and the right to do so then, if you are on your own, or lonely, that is the will of your god and you may not want to argue with him/her. In which case, be happy that things are as they should be.

You may believe in a benevolent god and that all will be well in the end if you simply go along with what that god has ordained for you in this lifetime. If you believe in a god who is not benevolent you might want to consider why you choose to believe in such a god. After all, no one is making you. No one else is insisting that you believe in a particular way. Although most of us, in this century and in the western world, have religious freedom, there are, it is true, places and situations in the world where this is not possible. You may, as a result of your present circumstances, have to conform outwardly to a particular form of belief, but no one can insist on or control what you think and what you believe inwardly.

In other words, check out your beliefs. If they are of a nature that should leave you feeling supported and protected, cared for and watched over, how can you feel alone? If you do, perhaps this is the time to check the strength of these beliefs; are they convictions or only hope-like beliefs? They certainly won't be strong experiences in the sense of the word as used above.

This is quite a test of your beliefs. Being lonely often comes down to 'Nobody cares. Nobody loves me or is bothered about what happens to me, nobody is interested in me.' Yet if you have a true belief in your god then of course this is not the case and you need never be lonely. You can talk with your god, share your day, discuss your hopes and fears.

To Hold or to Change Your Beliefs – Are They Serving You?

There are many, many belief systems in the world today, many different gods that people believe in, even a huge number of people who claim that their god is the one and only true god. Yet clearly this cannot be so. If there is indeed only one god and everyone else has it wrong then the majority of the world is dealing with a god that is not the real thing. In other words, if indeed there is only one true god then the chances are high that your belief is the wrong one. The odds against you having picked the right god, of all the ones that are available, are long.

A more likely possibility is that the various belief systems, the various views of a god or a supreme spiritual being are indeed just that, different views of the same god, rather like the many and different views you get of Mount Everest, depending on the point from which the photo is taken, which face is being looked at. If your view of god is one that is supporting you and leading to a happy and fulfilling life for you, fine. If it is not, if you are unhappy, sad and lonely, and can take no comfort in the path you are on, then perhaps this is time to look at your god from a different point of view.

Another possibility is that all the various gods are lesser gods and that none of them are the supreme being, should such a one exist, but rather a step along the way. To continue our analogy, it would be as if you were looking at a variety of minor peaks, not at the ultimate summit. Again, if the belief system you have chosen to adopt is not serving you, if it is not leading to a happy and fulfilling life, then perhaps you should question the value of this belief, and aim for the summit by a different route.

You may argue that, in this latter instance, there is indeed one true god, and that the others are all lesser gods, and that your god is that god, but then we are back to the long odds of before.

Note that I am not, here, opting for a whimsical or flighty view of a god, and a butterfly-like change of belief system. Rather, it seems likely that, if you are not happy, content and at peace with yourself, yet you profess to some higher faith, then, given that there are innumerable other faiths you could have chosen, it would be more sensible to choose one in line with your own underlying beliefs, one that is in harmony with you and your spirit?

Other Lives

There is one belief that can have a major impact on whether or not you feel lonely and how you handle the situation, and that is the belief in reincarnation. It changes your perspective on your current situation and state of mind. It also changes your level of responsibility and control in relation to your present situation since there is usually the associated belief that you had at least some input into the nature of this lifetime. Let's explore this concept and its implications a little further.

Perhaps you don't believe in a specific god at all. Perhaps you do believe in a spiritual world but not in a specific deity. Perhaps you believe in reincarnation. It may even be a definite experience for you, a real memory, as real as the memory of your childhood. If this is so, if you *know* you have lived in a physical body before, and will do so again, then you are aware that this current life is just one of many lives. Furthermore this life, in your present physical body, is only a part of your experience, since much of your time will be spent out of body. Thus if things are not perfect right now it is not such a serious situation. The present is a smaller part of the whole and you can fret about it less. A year is a much smaller percentage of your time when several lifetimes are involved than when you only have the standard 'three score years and ten'. This does not mean that you stop trying to solve the problem of loneliness, but it does mean that your perspective changes.

Most people who believe in several lives also believe that they chose the details of their birth into this lifetime, either as a conscious choice and decision or as a consequence of things they have done in the past, prior to this lifetime. They believe they chose their parents, their sex, the place and the situation into which they were born, their genes and thus their physical and genetic make-up. If this is your belief you can feel less of a victim – if you claim your life, right now, is not the way you want it to be – and more in control. This in turn means you have the power to make changes now, changes that could have long-lasting benefits, not only in this lifetime but in the future; so even if you are elderly now, it is worth making the effort, making the changes.

Most people of this persuasion also believe they have brought with them, into this lifetime, their own soul, their own emotions. They no longer say, 'I can't help it, it is the way I am,' but instead say, 'This is the personality I have developed thus far, and I am in the process of developing it further.'

Since, at some higher level, they have chosen the circumstances of this lifetime they have also chosen their particular situation. Many people trust that, while out of body, they made the appropriate choices for themselves in this lifetime and take comfort in the fact that, as such, their present situation is not only of their own choosing but to their own, ultimate, benefit.

These concepts are important, as they influence how you deal with your present loneliness. They also influence the way you incorporate the ideas of previous chapters into your thinking. For some people, who truly believe in reincarnation, the change in perspective is enough to reduce the magnitude of their problem, their loneliness.

In other words, if reincarnation is really your belief system, you can reap several major benefits. Being alone at this time in your life is what you had planned for the next learning step. This makes it all the more important that you learn what you can from your present situation and then make any changes that may be appropriate.

PART III

Practicalities

Chapter Seventeen

Leaving Home for the First Time

Leaving home for the first time can be scary, yet everyone does it. Even if you had an unhappy time and are glad to get away from the problems there may still be times when you feel lonely, even though, in the long run, it may be well worth the price.

Alternatively you may have had a happy home, one in which you interacted comfortably with parents and other siblings. It is likely that you planned some of your time, some of the things you would do independently. It is equally likely that much of the time you became involved in whatever the rest of the family was doing. When you move out and live on your own this latter component will be missing. When you lived at home, with other people, you could say, 'I feel like going to a movie, who feels like coming with me?' If you want to go to a film when you live alone you have to make the arrangements ahead of time with one or more of your friends. The same is true if you feel like a game of cards, someone with whom to share a pizza or company on a walk. It is wise to recognise this ahead of time and plan accordingly.

Mary was seeing me because she was unhappy in just this situation.

'I had been so looking forward to leaving home,' she said. 'Much as I love my family I kept thinking of the peace and quiet I would have, and the reading I could do, without my two brothers arguing and playing loud music, without the inevitable television going and without the parents telling me what to do all the time. I do love them, but I feel I'm old enough now to make my own decisions.'

'So what's the problem?'

'Well, I know it sounds odd, but I find I miss them. I miss them for the sort of automatic company they provided. Now I find I go home after work and wonder what to do. I actually get lonely. I mean, reading is great, but I'm not too keen on going to a movie or a restaurant on my own.'

The answer was for Mary to plan her evenings. At first I suggested that she plan every single segment of spare time.

'Gosh,' she said, 'won't that be a bit rigid? There won't be any spontaneity.'

'Not at all. Some of the things you plan will involve other people, others won't. But each evening you will know what you will be doing, you'll have a plan. Then you can deviate from it if you choose.'

Her first plan looked like this:

Monday evening: *Change library books, clean the flat and do my washing – omelette and salad for dinner.*
Tuesday evening: *Go to a movie – talk to people at work and find someone to go with.*

Wednesday: *Arrange to call in on the parents.*
Thursday night: *Go to the gym – then finish sewing blue skirt.*
Friday night: *Visit Barbara for coffee, do my nails.*
Saturday morning: *Food shopping for the week – check out the CD shop.*
Saturday afternoon: *Bush walking with the group advertising in the library, pub afterwards.*
Sunday: *Invite friends in for lunch – evening free for reading.*

When I saw her on Monday her comments were interesting.

'It's almost as if you are making arrangements with yourself. When I first did it I thought it would be a grind. But then I found I had things to look forward to. I realised that while I was doing the chores on Monday I was also looking forward to the movie I had arranged for the next evening. When I got impatient with my younger brother on Wednesday I could look forward to seeing Barbara on Friday. If I wanted to change things at the last minute I could, for instance I didn't go bush walking because I met up with some other friends, but I didn't once go home and think, "What now, I'm all alone and have nothing to do?" It was great.'

A few weeks later she reported a further benefit.

'You know what's great about this? Because I plan things during the day, when I am with people at work and so forth, I find I'm actually being more social, making more of an effort, meeting more people and making new friends.'

In time Mary may become comfortable going home to an empty flat with nothing planned. But in the meantime she has found a way to stop feeling lonely.

Mary particularly wanted to live on her own. Michael didn't. He simply wanted to leave the family and stretch his wings. He didn't want peace and quiet; on the contrary, he wanted fun and people, but people of his own age. For him the answer was to share a house with several others. Some of them he liked, some got on his nerves, but he was never on his own.

For many people leaving home coincides with leaving school or college. The possible problem is then compounded since it is generally easier to make friends at school or in college, where a large group of people start at once and spend a lot of time together, than it is when you start in a new job, possibly as the only new person among a group who already know each other and have established relationships.

If your job and new home are some way away from your old home, school or college, and so at some distance from your friends, the problem may be even more acute. Many people report going to their job each day and going back to their flat or bedsit and having nothing to do and no one to talk to until it is time to go to work the next day. This is all the more reason to make plans, and there are many ideas for this in Part IV.

Chapter Eighteen

Changing Jobs

Just as in the last chapter when leaving school, college and home resulted in a new isolation, you can feel cut off from your friends when you change jobs. You may have thought, in the old job, that you had lots of friends there, good friends, even friends that you saw after work, and assumed you would go on seeing them after you had left. Yet this may not have turned out to be the case.

You may well find that much of the social life surrounding your old job evolved out of spontaneous decisions taken at work and, now that you are no longer there, you are no longer included. You may feel rejected as a result. Yet often it is not because they don't want you, not that they don't care. It is simply that you are not there when the idea is conceived – to go out for a meal, to a movie or to have a party.

You may also find that, even when you do make the effort to keep in touch, you have less in common with them than you thought, now that you are no longer involved in the same work activities and office politics.

If you definitely do want to keep in touch it is wise to realise ahead of time that some additional effort will be required. Otherwise you may look back in a year's time and regret the loss of old friendships as you let people you had seen regularly drift gradually out of your life.

It takes time to make new friends, it also takes effort. So plan your time ahead, week by week, as suggested earlier. Make additional efforts to organise specific events. As in earlier chapters, if you would like people to invite you out, invite them out. If you would like to be asked round for the evening, ask someone to visit you for the evening. If you would like to go to a party, hold a party and invite others. Life is a mirror. Whatever it is you are wanting others to do in relation to you, start doing it in relation to them. You will be pleasantly surprised at the result.

In the new job it is up to you to make the effort to make friends. You are the new person on the block, the others have their established routines and relationships. It is also up to you to give, there is no point in sitting around insisting that they should make friends with you, as the new person. If that is not getting you what you want then change tactics. You issue the invitations, you offer to contribute, you make the moves that show the others you would like to be friendly and join in. Find out what their shared interests are and, if necessary, learn something about them so you can join in. I learnt to do cryptic crosswords simply because everyone else did at my first job and I wanted to be able to join in the activity at the tea breaks. I've since had enormous fun as a result, doing them over the years.

Do not be concerned that, at first, the initiative seems to be all yours. In time you will find that the invitations are returned. Again, there are many practical suggestions elsewhere in this book as to what you can do.

Chapter Nineteen

Lacking Friends

We have already spoken about having and making friends. We won't be covering the same ground here, this is intended to be a more practical section. Nevertheless it is still appropriate to repeat, 'Life is a mirror.' If you do not have friends ask yourself, 'Have I been friendly to people?' Stop thinking of yourself. Think about ways you can give friendship to others.

There are many practical things you can do. Look for people in need, people who are unhappy, people who are lonely. Go out of your way to invite them to things, to include them in what you are doing, to ask for their company. You may not like them particularly, but they, like you, may be wanting to have more friends. And you never know who you might meet through them.

If you want to have friends with your specific interests then go to where these people might be.

If you are interested in the arts go to art galleries and talk to the people there. Sign up for talks and discussion groups.

If you would like friends with whom you can discuss politics, join the local group of whichever party to which you feel most drawn. Go to events, talk with people, offer your time and effort in helping them achieve their goals – 'Give before ye shall receive' – then take a real and genuine interest in the people you meet and take it from there.

If you are interested in a particular country go to evening classes to learn the language, or go to where classes are held to help people from that country learn your language and offer to spend time with them helping them with your language.

If you are interested in things historical go to the historical museums, look for historical societies.

If you are interested in things scientific go to science museums, go to talks on the sciences.

If you are interested in the local community go to the local library, offer your help at the council, ask to go on committees. Do not feel that you have to wait to be invited. There is a lot to be done in a community and there are often too few people willing to give of their time and energy.

If you are interested in anything, go to where you might find the appropriate people.

And . . . having done all that, *talk to the people that are there*. I have had many clients who have done the first part, they have gone to events and situations where they might meet like-minded people and come back to report that 'nobody spoke to me.' Of course not. For the same reasons that you didn't speak to people, other people didn't speak to you. But if you want to make friends you have to *speak to people*. The other people may well have felt just as lonely as you, they may have been just as shy as you. You may have looked as self-assured and independent to them as they did to you. Someone has to breach the gap, it might as well be you. What have you to lose – except your loneliness?

There are many other ways to make new friends.

Have a party; even if you only know one or two people, invite them and insist that they each bring five people you don't know. When I first suggested this to

George, a client in his early thirties, quiet and bookish, who had suddenly realised that his friends from college days were gradually marrying and leaving the city, he said he would be ashamed to do that, to let people (who? – since he said he 'knew nobody') know that he had so few friends of his own. Not a problem. If you don't know many people and don't have enough friends then dream up a reason. In the end George announced at his work place that he had just finished some research that had taken all his free time for the past two years and now he intended to socialise, he was having a party, would they please each bring three guests to his home on Saturday. He did the same thing with the neighbours and anyone else he knew even slightly. The result was such a success that he repeated it – and so did some of his friends.

If you're into astrology have a 'zodiac sign' party on the twenty-second of each month. Ask everyone you know who they know who is a Virgo, a Libran, and so forth. Tell them to bring people of that sign. Set the theme accordingly.

Have a singles night. Invite all your friends who are single and tell them to bring someone of the opposite sex who is also single and with whom they are not in a relationship. That way you and the guests will know that everyone is 'free'.

Kill two birds with one stone and go to a fitness centre. Play whatever sport you choose, play it and keep fit in addition to using the place as a source of new friends.

Life is easier if you are male, you can hang around in bars, pubs, cafés etc. and strike up a conversation with whoever you choose. A woman *can* do that but she has to be more careful, and although the sexes are claiming to be equal, there are still women who are reluctant to be seen 'hanging out' on their own.

Your local town hall may well be a source of information on activities. Churches are another possibility, so are libraries and the various community centres.

The real problem, as will be becoming obvious, is not any lack of sources of information on ways to meet people, lack of places you can go or lack of things you can do to meet people. The real problem, as often as not, is the person's own lack of initiative, motivation or drive to actually do what is required. Most people who are lonely are lonely because they have sat back and waited for new 'friends' to search them out and come to them. It doesn't work like that. If you want new friends you have to go out and make them.

Chapter Twenty

Are You Shy?

Are you shy? Do you avoid situations where there are lots of people, afraid of what they will think of you? In a crowd, do you remain silent and avoid contributing to a discussion? If someone talks to you do you blush and become flustered?

Many people are shy and, when pressed, are willing to admit it and even use it as an excuse for not doing a variety of things involving other people. Yet what does shyness really mean? Generally the person who is shy is unsure of their own worth, of their own abilities or their own value within a group of people. Secondly, the shy person is focused on what the other person or people will think of them. The shy person is often convinced, as we have already seen so many people are, particularly those inclined to think negatively, that they can read the other person's mind and that the result is unsatisfactory.

The solution, therefore, involves dealing with these situations. Firstly, build up your own opinion of yourself, recognise your own value and learn to love and accept yourself, just the way you are, without judging, comparisons or self-criticism, by all the methods we have already discussed.

Secondly, stop trying to second-guess what they are thinking of you. In Chapter Eight, Dealing with Other People's Negative Comments, there is a step-by-step process (p. 99) you can use to change your own internal experience in response to what they say. You can also use this process for dealing with what you think they are thinking.

Thirdly, stop focusing your attention on yourself, focus instead on other people, be more interested in what they have to say than in what you are imagining. We have covered this, too, in earlier sections. This is possibly the easiest step to start with, it is certainly one that will win you friends.

Ultimately shyness is a non-productive emotion. It interferes with your enjoyment of and interaction with other people. It also blocks your own growth and development since you are likely to remain quiet and closed off from many forms of communication that could be beneficial as well as enjoyable.

Fortunately, shyness and the thoughts and emotions associated with it are all things you can change, since you are in control of what you think, say and do, so this is not an unalterable attribute or one that need stand in the way of you resolving your loneliness.

Chapter Twenty-One

Losing Friends

Perhaps you have had friends, only to find that they have suddenly all drifted away, suddenly you are receiving less invitations, suddenly you are feeling isolated, alone and lonely. In general there are two reasons for this. Either things have happened in the life of your friends that has caused the separation, or it is something you have done.

If you are lonely and feeling in a negative frame of mind you may be blaming yourself, asking yourself what you have done, what is wrong with you, what you said or did that upset them. This may be the time to realise that it is only your world that revolves around you. Their world is affected by many factors, of which you are only one. There are many many reasons why they may have less time for you and, in general, it is far more likely to be due to other situations and events, nothing to do with you at all. How amazing, possibly even self-centred it was of you, to think it was – at least that is a different perspective for you to have!

So, firstly, do not assume it is all your fault and you have become some sort of a pariah. It is probably not true and it is certainly not constructive to think along these lines. There may well be good reasons for it. Perhaps your friends have, one by one, married, had children, moved house or changed job and, for reasons related to their own lives, their interests and preoccupations, they have changed. If your interests and occupations have not changed and headed in a direction similar to theirs then it may be your diverging lifestyles that have caused the separations.

You can probably recall school friends with whom you swore undying affection and yet with whom, even a few years later, you found you had very little in common any more. You may have been part of a men's drinking group in the pub, but as each man married or settled into a relationship you found yourself part of a diminishing group and eventually, possibly, on your own. When you shared a common boss and common work politics you may have had lots to share with some people, but when you moved to a different department, job or part of town, you found that you are less inclined to meet up with them.

You may still want to be friends with someone and find you cannot understand their reluctance to go out for a meal with you. Perhaps they are short of funds and don't like to admit it. Perhaps they are having an affair and wanting to keep it quiet. Perhaps they have not been well, have family worries they don't want to make public or perhaps some new demand is being made on their time. All these reasons are the result of something going on in their lives, not of something wrong that you have done.

These and hundreds of similar situations can account for the loss of friendships. It's all very well to say, 'If they were true friends they wouldn't have drifted away, they wouldn't have stopped phoning or inviting me round.' There's no point in arguing with that. If that is your definition of true friends then they obviously weren't. However, through and through, till death do us part, true friends are few and far between. They are to be treasured when you have them. A far greater number of friendships are based on common circumstances and should be recognised and valued as such.

When, on this basis, you find yourself being more and more alone, it is time to make new friends. Do not sit back and become despondent. Don't soul-search to find what you did wrong. Don't blame yourself. If you do you greatly reduce your confidence and your chance of going out and making new friends. Even if your old friends did decide not to go on seeing you there is nothing wrong with you, it is simply that their tastes have changed.

Remember that strangers are only friends you haven't yet met and this is the time to go out and meet them. As long as you recognise the problem for what it is and do not start to think that no one likes you, or that because one person doesn't like you no one in the future will like you, then this can be the beginning of some exciting new relationships. There are more than enough practical tips for meeting and making these new, replacement, friends at the end of the book.

If, on the other hand, you really are sure that it is you that has changed, then this may be the time for some personal development. Have you changed, and for the worse? Have you become more irritable, more critical, more argumentative? Are you more self-engrossed and less giving and caring than you used to be? If you truly are sure that it is you that has changed and for the worse and that that has led to your present loneliness then this is the time to go back to Part II of this book. Remember that no one is inherently bad or nasty. You are a wonderful person, you may simply be doing certain things that are not popular. Change them. There is very little you cannot change if you set your mind to it.

The road back to friendships will be twofold. Firstly you will want to make the necessary changes in yourself. Then you will want to reconnect with your old friends and let them know about or see the changes, that the old character they used to know and like is still there and has resurfaced.

Michael had been one of a large circle of friends. They met up after work and often during the weekends. They'd go to parties, movies, include their various girlfriends and so forth, drop in on each other, sure of their welcome, and generally hang out together. Then Michael was promoted. He was given some authority on the factory floor and, slowly but steadily, started to think of himself, inappropriately, as better than his old friends. In time they came to regard him as one of the 'others', one of the bosses who could get them into trouble or cause them to lose their job. When Michael realised what was happening he not only had to change, he also had to go back to them and acknowledge what had been happening and demonstrate that he was still their friend, still, underneath, the same person. It was just that he now had charge of their productivity records.

A similar thing happened to Susan, at school, when she was one of the first in her class to be made a prefect. She started to put on airs and lost a lot of friends, before she recognised what was happening. In her case she decided to make new friends with the more senior girls but she also tried to build the bridges with some of her old friends.

In Anne's case it was different. She lost her job, went on the dole and just managed to make ends meet. At first she continued seeing her friends, then she started complaining every time they did something she couldn't afford. They were happy to go on being friends, even to make allowances when she couldn't pay her share, but they got tired of the complaining. Even when she did find a job she had some rebuilding to do since it wasn't the money difference that had bothered them but the way she complained.

So if you suddenly find you have fewer friends than you used to have, it might be time to do some careful thinking. Don't assume, at the start, that it is your fault. Instead sit down and list all the other possible reasons that could be behind the situation, factors affecting their life and factors affecting your own. Then take an honest look at yourself. Have you outgrown them or have you changed for the worse? Decide how you should alter the latter and then put your ideas into practice. Become a nicer person again, someone people want as a friend. Be a friend.

Chapter Twenty-Two

Rejection

As a child, when you had done something wrong you probably heard a parent or teacher say, 'That's naughty, you're bad,' when what they really meant was, 'You in yourself are a wonderful child and I love you dearly, but what you have just done is very bad.' In other words, there was no differentiation made between the behaviour (bad) and the person (good). As a result a pattern was set. Any criticism was taken, not as a criticism of the act, of what you had done, but of the person, of you and your inherent worth.

Much the same pattern continues now, even though you are an adult. 'You are wrong,' is what you hear when you and a friend have a disagreement. Yet what your friend means may really be, 'You are a good friend and I like and admire you, but I think that what you have just said is wrong.' They may even have meant, 'You are a good friend but I disagree with what you have just said.' In other words they weren't even necessarily saying that what you were saying was wrong, but simply that the two of you have different opinions. Yet when you hear, 'You're wrong,' it tells your subconscious mind that you as a person are 'wrong' and therefore less likely to be wanted as a friend.

As these occasions accumulate, and if your subconscious interprets them against a background of decreasing self-confidence, they can all too easily add to a growing feeling that people don't want to have you around. Notice that it is the way your subconscious interprets the statements that counts, not whether or not, in an absolute sense, they are true. If, as a result of a variety of circumstances in your life, your self-confidence is at a low ebb, the times when someone disagrees with you or criticises you can cumulatively build up and lead to a growing feeling of not being popular, or not being wanted, of rejection.

This also happens when you issue an invitation and someone turns you down. Think of the following situation when you ask a new friend, 'Would you like to go to that new restaurant one evening for dinner?' and hear them say, 'No thank you, I really can't, I'm just too busy.' This can all too easily be received by you as a message that they don't want to spend time with you, particularly since you haven't even specified a time or a date so that they're giving you a general and blanket 'No' to any day or to any time in the future. Yet their reason for saying 'No' may have had nothing to do with you specifically. They may really be too busy, perhaps they can't afford it but don't want to have to admit this, or perhaps they didn't like that particular restaurant but don't want to be rude by saying they think your choice is poor.

Lesley was feeling miserable one weekend and wanted company. She phoned a couple of friends and asked them round but both of them were busy. Then she phoned someone else and suggested a movie, only to be turned down because they had seen it. Finally, in desperation, she phoned a friend she knew was planning to go out and offered to babysit but was told they already had a babysitter. That was the last straw, she sat down and howled, feeling not only lonely now, but rejected and unwanted as well. Later, when talking to the friend who had seen the movie, she said, 'I really wish you hadn't already seen that movie. I was feeling thoroughly miserable that day and wanted someone to do something with.'

'Why ever didn't you say so? I was feeling a bit low too and would have loved to see you, but I thought you particularly wanted to see the movie and I didn't feel like sitting through it a second time.'

It is very important to be clear on your goals, at the very least to yourself, but preferably also to other people, and to articulate them. You can then avoid this type of spurious but painful rejection. All you achieve by issuing a roundabout invitation is the chance of rejection and of not getting your needs met. By issuing the direct invitation or request, such as, 'I'm feeling lonely and I'd like your company, how about us doing something together. Would you like to go to a movie, or what about coming round here for a meal?' You have a much better chance of achieving the goal you are after.

When you want company, ask for company. When you want to see a movie invite a friend to join you at a movie. The problem is that people often prefer to hide the fact that they are lonely, hence the indirect invitation, the one that carries with it the greater risk of a rejection.

When you do get a rejection there are two possibilities. You can shrug it off as a rejection of that particular offer or you can take it on board as a rejection of yourself personally. The chances are good that if you are a happy and confident extrovert you will shrug it off. If, however, you are feeling lonely and so somewhat low on self-confidence, you will assume it to be a rejection of yourself and this will compound your problem.

I was impressed recently when I saw a friend handing out leaflets outside a railway station. In general she got about an equal number of knock-backs as acceptances but suddenly for a spell everyone to whom she offered a leaflet refused to accept it. One of the cab drivers in the line of waiting taxis saw this and called out to her, 'Never mind, luv, we luv ye.' To this her unthinking and immediate response was, 'It's all right, it's the opportunity they're rejecting, not me.' With an attitude like that her self-confidence is well in place. Not only that but she has clearly learnt to distinguish between the specific situation and herself as a person.

I have another friend who is never ruffled when someone is grumpy, irritable or rude to him. His usual response is something like, 'I'm sorry you're having such a bad day.' It rarely occurs to him that the other person is specifically being antagonistic to him. If it is a criticism he will consider this on its merits and, if he feels it is warranted he will do something about it, if not, he mentally sidelines it, attributing it to some problem the speaker is having. Again, he refuses to accept the comments or criticisms as rejection, in fact I suspect it never occurs to him that they could be, yet he is not aggressively self-confident, nor does he ignore other people's opinions or comments. He simply has a quiet sense of his own worth, tries to sort out the wheat from the chaff and then makes his own decision. Needless to say he is rarely lonely, being content with his own company when he is alone and enjoying that of his friends and other people when he is with them.

Do you often feel rejected? Here again is the six-step method we used before (see p. 99), applied this time to dealing with these situations involving rejection:

1. Clearly define in your own mind the situation that makes you feel rejected.
2. Find out what assumptions you have made about the situation and what conclusions you have drawn.

3 Specify in detail how you feel as a result of drawing these conclusions.
4 Ask yourself what other assumptions or conclusions you could have come to and write them all down.
5 Find out how you would feel if you chose to change your belief from the old assumptions to the new.
6 Decide which way you choose to feel and make the appropriate assumptions.

Consider the example of Lesley given above. Lesley issued an invitation to a movie (Step 1) and it was refused. Her assumption (Step 2) was that this meant her friend did not want to spend the evening with her. As a result (Step 3) she felt miserable and her loneliness increased. Had she stopped to ask herself what other reason there could have been for the refusal (Step 4) she might have come up with a list, including such things as that her friend couldn't afford the ticket, had indeed seen the movie and didn't think it was worth seeing twice, was relaxed in old clothes and couldn't be bothered to dress up, or was hoping a man she had met at a recent party would phone her. Lesley could then (Step 5 and 6) have recognised that none of these reasons reflected on her own popularity and felt better about it, still lonely, possibly, but certainly not rejected. In fact, as we know, had she phrased her invitation differently she could easily have had the company she was after.

In the case of my friend with the leaflets it was pretty clear to me, as well as to her (Step 2), that the people pouring out of the station were rejecting the leaflet, not her. They didn't look at her and think, 'I don't like the look of her, I don't want to have anything to do with such a person. I'll refuse to take her leaflet to show her how I feel about her.' It was much more likely, as she assumed (Step 2 again) that they were thinking that they couldn't be bothered to lift a hand, already full of shopping, or that they didn't want to have to deal with scrap paper, that they weren't interested in learning about something new, or it may even have been that they were tired at the end of the day and couldn't be bothered with anything more.

Many people in this situation, however, would have felt embarrassed at the rejections, interpreting them (Step 2) in ways more destructive to their own self-confidence, such as, 'They're not taking them because they don't like the look of me,' or 'They're not taking them because they don't think they can trust anything I offer them,' or 'They're not taking them so I'm stupid to have thought they would and an idiot for choosing this place, and other people are laughing at me as a result.'

Could she know the truth? Did she really know the exact reason why some of the people refused her leaflets? Of course not. There was no way she could be sure if, when they refused them, it was because of something she was doing or if it was because of some other reason unconnected to her. She had simply decided, consciously or subconsciously, to choose a conclusion that was constructive from her point of view rather than destructive. After all, she wanted to hand out the leaflets, she was pretty determined to do so, she could either do it and enjoy it, or at least come away from the experience unscathed, or she could do it and allow every rejection (of the leaflet) to make her feel miserable.

The irony of so many situations is that, although you simply cannot know the real reason behind the other person's words or actions, people that tend towards a destructive interpretation are convinced that they *do* know why they were rejected, they *do* know that it is *their* fault and they will argue this case passionately.

If you want to be able to feel better about yourself, be open-minded, be willing to go through the six-step process above. Be willing to let yourself take one of the more positive conclusions and beliefs. After all, if you cannot know for sure exactly what the other person is thinking (and you can't) then why not choose the *most useful belief*. You might as well live in a fool's paradise (by assuming a belief that is positive and to your benefit) as in a fool's hell (by assuming a belief that is negative and destructive to you). Life has a way of fulfilling your expectations.

You can apply the same process to any type of rejection. Even to rejections that are not actually rejections of you as much as they are preferences for some other person. Take a job application for instance. Lots of people apply, only one is chosen. Keep in mind that the selectors have nothing against you, their selection of some other applicant is not a rejection of you personally. It is merely a statement that the other person, the candidate they chose, was particularly suited to the requirements of that particular job. It may also indicate that the job was not the right one for you and for your particular skills. If you keep that in mind you can continue to apply for jobs with enthusiasm, until you find one that is perfect for you.

If you choose to believe that the rejections, to your invitations, to your company, to your application or whatever, are rejections of you personally then it is likely that, over time, you will shrink from people, be more quiet and retiring in their presence, or alternatively over-compensate by being aggressively confident. In either case it is likely that the invitations will come less frequently. You can then say, 'See, I *was* right, it is me that is at fault, they *don't* want me.'

If you choose to believe that there are other outside reasons behind the things that happen in your life that you don't like, and that fundamentally you are a worthwhile person, this message is transmitted, in all sorts of subtle ways, to other people and you are taken at face value, at your own interpretation of yourself, and much more likely to have company when you want it. You too can then say, 'See, I was right, they do like me.'

Either way you can 'prove' your belief. You do this not because the belief was correct but because, by your words and behaviour, you bring about the result you expect.

Chapter Twenty-Three

When Your Lover or Close Friend Leaves You

There is a particular pain when your lover, partner or spouse leaves you, the person who has been your confidant, the person with whom you have shared some of the most intimate moments possible, to whom you have spoken about aspects of yourself and your life that you would share with very few people, the person you have trusted. They were an integral part of your life, now they have suddenly gone. For whatever reason, they have walked out, turned their back on you and left.

There is also a particular pain when a very close friend leaves you, ends the friendship, or in some way betrays the trust you had placed in them and your relationship with them. For many people it can, in its own way, be as painful as being jilted. After all, for a friend it was not, as in the instance of a lover or spouse, a case of only being allowed one partner. A friend can have other friends too. For them to leave you or end the friendship it is not a matter of saying, 'I have met someone else and, since I have to choose between the two of you, since I have chosen them, I must leave you,' but rather a case of saying, 'I simply don't want to count you as a friend any more even though that wouldn't mean giving up another friend I had.'

Rejection is such a loaded word. Someone else or some people don't want you. Yet in fact no one can reject you except yourself. All another person can say is that for them personally, at that moment, you are not their first choice for a partner, friend, or whatever. Remember, 'What Peter says about Paul tells me more about Peter than about Paul.'

If your lover, be they someone you have just met and felt an attraction with, an ongoing girlfriend or boyfriend, a live-in partner, or your spouse, decides you are not the person they want, this does not make you a lesser person. If they choose to leave you and be on their own or if they choose to leave you for someone else, it does not diminish you by comparison. In fact it says nothing about you. It does say a lot about the preferences of your ex-lover.

If you were a strong woman and your partner finally leaves saying that he wants to wear the trousers, he is tired of you making all the decisions, that doesn't mean you have suddenly become hard and unfeminine. The fact that someone doesn't like bright reds and oranges doesn't define them as hard, strident and unpleasant colours, it does tell you that the observer preferred pastels. That, in turn, does not mean that pastels are 'better' colours than the bright tones. Find yourself a partner who appreciates your strengths.

Other Perspectives

Think about this from the alternative perspective. Think about each of the people you know and like. Does the fact that you do not choose them as your partner, that you are not in love with them, that you do not want to live with them or have them share your life with you at the closest possible level, diminish them, is it a rejection of them? Of course not. You may like them, admire them, respect them, enjoy their company, value them as a friend, but not be in love with them. They are still terrific people. There is no criticism of them, they are not inadequate because you have not chosen them to be your partner.

Take it a step further. Think about the people you don't particularly like, people you can 'take or leave', people who are pleasant enough but who you don't choose to spend a lot of time with or with whom you have little in common. Does the fact that you feel this way about them, that you are not choosing to include them in your circle of close friends, never mind the fact that you aren't about to choose them to be your lover, diminish them? Is it a rejection of them as a worthwhile individual? Is it an objective criticism of them and should they feel bad about it? Of course not. All that your choice says is that they are not the person for you.

Finally think about people you dislike, people who annoy you, people who have views different to your own, people with whom you are definitely not compatible. Obviously you are not going to choose one of them as your lover. Yet does this make them a lesser person? Does this tell the world they are somehow inadequate and not worthwhile? Of course not. All it says is that they and you are not compatible.

From this angle it seems obvious, doesn't it? So someone thought about having you as their partner, so they gave the relationship a try, so they invested some time in it, be that measured in days, weeks, months or even years, so they finally decided against it. It is not a negative reflection on you. It is a demonstration of *their* choices, of what *they* want in life. Nowhere is it written that you should be the person to fulfil those expectations, to satisfy those desires, to be their perfect partner. Nor is it written that, if you do not fulfil these criteria, then it is you who is lacking or inadequate.

So often you hear, 'We were getting along so well, really getting to know each other. Then s/he lost interest. It's as if when they really got to know the real me, the person inside, they didn't like what they found. That's what makes the rejection so hard to take.' Nonsense, all aspects of you are the real you, even the surface parts you choose to display, after all the fact of choosing to display them is a reflection of the inner you anyway. We are back to the first point. The person doing the rejecting is simply showing their preferences. They are not, and cannot be unless you let them, diminishing you.

To feel good about yourself, is it essential that *all* people like you? Of course not. If it were that would be an impossible situation. When it comes to finding your partner, someone with whom you can feel close, with whom you can share your life in a way that is even closer, in many respects, than the way you shared with your parents or will share with your children, the wonder is that anyone is successful. It is a huge task. That you should need several attempts to find such a person is hardly surprising. After all, you try out shoes before you buy, you drive several cars before choosing, and those, by comparison, are easy choices to make, easy optimums to find. Just as you need to try out several options, so do other people.

Easing the Pain

In any situation involving people there are three positions. In the first position you are the one undergoing the experience. In the second position you are the one applying the experience to or acting upon the first person, and in the third position you are observing the second person acting upon the first person. From the second or third position, as you observe what is happening to the first person, the situation has an entirely different perspective to that of the first person.

Whenever you are in a position that is uncomfortable you will find the following exercise to be helpful. If you feel unhappy, rejected, criticised, unwanted, or that the world is unfair, that you have been badly treated or if, in any other way, you find yourself in a situation you don't like and that is painful, then it can be very helpful to 'get outside yourself' to take up either the second position or the third position in relation to the situation. This is what you do:

1. Find Yourself a Quiet 'Space'

Ideally you should find somewhere you can be on your own, be quiet, relax, close your eyes and focus on the exercise. You should also be able to feel confident that you will not be disturbed. However this is not always possible, nor is it always necessary, not once you have practised the process a few times. You can often do it while you are travelling on a bus, being driven in a car, waiting in a queue or anywhere you can allow your mind to wander for a few minutes. If you are surrounded by people, even at home, an interval spent in the bathroom is excellent; it is also, surprisingly, a time when your mind can most easily go into a state of creative imagination. If no other time is appropriate then do it when you go to bed at night. This is an excellent time as once you have completed the process you can go to sleep and allow the positive benefits to affect you subconsciously while you sleep. In the morning the entire situation may have taken on a new perspective.

2. Identify the situation

Get the situation, the total situation, clearly in your mind. In this case it may be that your lover recently told you that s/he was leaving and didn't want to be with you any more. As a result you are feeling unhappy, rejected, unwanted, miserable and lonely. Feel and acknowledge the emotions. Then move on.

3. Second position

(a) Preparation

Mentally put yourself in the position of your ex-partner. You know them well, after all you have been close, so get 'inside their head' and look back at yourself. What are they thinking as you observe from this perspective? You may well come to realise that they are not rejecting you out of hand, that they do still care but, for some reason, not enough to stay with you, that they do not want to inflict pain but they do need to leave the relationship, that there may be things they do not like, things they have probably told you, but that there are also things they still like about you.

Avoid any tendency to judge. Remember, in most situations there is no such thing as right and wrong, and this is particularly true in this one. There are simply the preferences of the individuals concerned.

Then create another second-position experience. Think of someone that you might have had a relationship with, possibly an old lover, one that you left, or possibly a lover in the abstract, someone you are 'making up' for this exercise. Imagine that you have known them for a similar length of time, that you have been in a relationship with them and that you have now found them to be unsuitable in whatever way your ex-partner has told you they feel about you.

(b) Assessment

In both these instances notice how you feel.

Firstly, when you mentally put yourself in the position of your ex-lover notice how you felt. What did you learn? There is a good chance that you found yourself saying something like, 'They are fine [after all, at some point you did choose them, at one time you were in love], but just not for me,' or 'They have lots of good points, I just feel stifled, I need some time to be on my own,' or 'There's nothing wrong with them, but so-and-so is the one I really want,' or 'There's nothing wrong with them, it's just that we've grown apart, we just don't have much in common any more.'

You are almost certainly not saying, 'They are horrible and revolting, they are totally inadequate, and they should really feel bad about themselves, unwanted and unworthy and they should recognise that no one will ever want them again.' Yet if you think about it, when you feel rejected and unhappy in such a situation, when you feel jilted, that, or at least some part of that, is often just exactly what you *are* saying to yourself, about yourself, isn't it?

You may well, from this perspective of second position, find yourself recognising that, however much your partner has come to have negative feelings about you, they are also aware of the fact that there are other people, out there, who do not feel the same way about you, who do like you. You are aware that s/he recognises that you do have friends, that you do have positive attributes and that someone else may well meet and come to love you.

If, when you do this, you still feel uncomfortable it still isn't a valid criticism of you, it is only a comment on the way your ex-partner has come to feel. So move on to the second part of this step of the exercise.

Go into the other second position, that where you

have told someone, either in your remembered past, or in your imagination, that you want to break off your relationship with them. How does it feel? You probably don't hate them or have powerful feelings against them. You are almost certainly focused on your own needs and wants, the alternative goals you now want to pursue. In all probability you will find that you are feeling warmer to them than you have been imagining your departed lover feels about you.

Already, by getting into this second position, you will have a different perspective on the situation compared to the 'fish-bowl' perspective you had when you were, in a sense, drowning in the situation, in the middle of the pain of it, *feeling* jilted, and feeling lonely.

4. Third position

(a) Preparation

Now it is time to move on to the third position, that where you are outside *both* people concerned, and watching them from a distance. To do this, close your eyes and mentally float up above the situation. Imagine you are up on the ceiling, look down and see what is happening below you. For many people it helps if you actually tip your head forward so that your eyes, although closed, are facing the ground. Notice how things look from this position. If there is still pain, if you are still too close to the situation, if you still feel involved, then float up higher, to a point where you are removed from the situation and can feel detached about it, an uninvolved observer watching the two people below you. In this way you can watch the scene playing out as if you were the proverbial fly on the wall, or a cloud in the sky, observing him, observing her, noticing the strengths and weaknesses of each, the needs of each, and noticing the lives and relationships the two people have with other friends in their individual lives.

(b) Assessment

Notice how you feel looking at the situation from this new perspective. If you are not doing the exercise, but are simply reading these pages, STOP. Do the exercise. The reality of doing it is totally different from the way you feel when you simply read about it. Sit back now, relax, and go through the steps to this point.

You will find you have learnt a lot from this position. You will almost certainly feel better about the you that you are observing down there than you felt about yourself when you were inside your body, less inadequate, less criticised, less rejected etc. You will see the things your partner has done and is doing in a totally different way to the way you view them when in first position. You can learn an enormous amount in this way, you can develop much more understanding of the other person, you can see yourself in a different light. You develop an entirely new perspective on the situation, on the other person or people involved and on yourself. Find out as much as you can, then learn from this and acknowledge and appreciate the feelings. Take this knowledge with you as you float back down into your own body.

Running a Phrase

There is another process you can apply, both to learning what is going on for you at a deeper level and to improving your present situation, and that is 'Running a Phrase'. It was described earlier, but it is so important that we will go through it again.

The process is designed to get to information held in the unconscious part of your mind. For this reason you do not ask yourself logical questions and then endeavour to provide the answers to these questions. If you did, your conscious, analytical mind would take over and work out logical, analytical and 'sensible' answers. In doing this it would automatically assess and filter in the way it has learned to do, leaving you with a contrived answer, one that you have reached before, and one that is of little help in unravelling the unconscious aspects of what is going on.

Instead, you start with a phrase that keeps the conscious mind busy, you then leave a gap for the unconscious mind to fill and, since the unconscious mind hates a vacuum, it immediately tries to fill it. You allow it only to complete the phrase with a few words, then you repeat the first phrase, then complete it again, and do this over and over until you feel you have exhausted all possible completions. Then you keep running it again, and yet again. When you have totally and completely dried up you move on to the next phrase.

There is an inbuilt assumption in the fact that you are not asking a yes/no type question, you are assuming that there *is* an 'answer', more accurately a 'completion' that can be accessed. Secondly, the phrase is structured in a way that facilitates the process, quietens the surface chatter of your logical mind and focuses your subconscious mind in such a way that the real reasons can pop up. This process is important in that it enables you to (**a**) access the (subconscious) core reason behind your present emotional state (**b**) learn about other aspects of the situation that had been hidden from your conscious mind and (**c**) find ways out of your present emotional state. Let's take an example.

If you asked yourself, 'Why do I feel miserable?' you would probably answer, 'Because so-and-so has walked out on me, I knew there was something wrong, I've been worried for a long time and now I know I was right.' When you run the phrase, 'A reason I'm feeling miserable is . . .' you immediately bypass the usual analytical or intellectual responses. You may come up initially with a similar completion:

' . . . So-and-so has left me.' But stop, don't go on chattering. Instead, repeat the phrase and find out what else you get. Your growing list of completions might include:

' . . . I feel lonely.'

' . . . I've got no one to talk to.'

' . . . I feel stupid.'

When you come up with a completion that is less logical and that is interesting then you might want to follow it. In this example it would mean following up with a second phrase that develops out of the somewhat surprising completion, ' . . . I feel stupid.' So your next phrase would be:

'A reason I feel stupid is . . .' and you might get something like:

' . . . I should have known.'

' . . . I'm sure my friends are laughing at me.'

Did you really think your friends were laughing at you when your lover jilted you? You might never have unearthed this had you simply asked logical questions.

The value of this process is that you can focus on the real problem. In this example it was only partly the loss of the lover that was causing you pain. The other aspect was the way you felt among your friends which, in turn, was sparked off by your own sense of self-esteem. The answer to the pain of this jilting would be to work on these aspects of the situation.

By Running a Phrase you have bypassed all the chatter and set your unconscious mind searching for a due. Ninety-nine times out of a hundred, it will find not only one but many. If at the start it rebels then let it know that it doesn't matter how outrageous the completions are, you will accept them all. You might even pretend, at the start, and make some up. Even this has value, because you can then ponder on them and wonder at their significance; after all, you chose to make up those particular ones, didn't you, and not some other equally unlikely completions.

If They Don't Want You – Do You Want Them?

This is another aspect of rejection. If your partner has decided that you are not the person they want to be with in the future then are they the person you want? Perhaps they are simply highlighting the fact that the two of you do not have as much in common as you thought. There is another aspect to this. Do you honestly want to share your life with someone who doesn't want to be with you? No matter how you feel about them, it is surely a form of masochism if you do. It could only be uncomfortable at best and downright self-destructive at worst, to want to be with them when all the time you would feel and know at some level, be it conscious or subconscious, that they are not happy with the relationship.

I have a friend whose attitude to such questions as, 'What would you do if Jeremy [her very-much loved lover of three years] was ever unfaithful to you?' is immediate. 'I'd tell him to go. If he doesn't recognise what I have to offer then he doesn't deserve me, and he's not the man I want to have around.' In the face of such inner confidence and clear-thinking does Jeremy play around? No, of course not. If he ever did would she weep? Possibly, but only briefly for she would immediately see that what she thought they had didn't exist.

Many clients have said, 'If only . . .' 'If only s/he'd come back. I'd do anything.' Why? What most people mean when they say this is that they want to put back the clock. There is the assumption that if the partner comes back into the relationship things will be as they were before. Yet the very fact of them having left tells you that it won't be. The way forward involves recognising this and moving on.

Generalising

Be careful what you say to yourself in the aftermath of a jilting. There is a common tendency to take one experience and generalise from it. This has its beneficial aspects in many circumstances. Once you learnt to drive a car, for instance, you generalised that driving any car would be pretty much the same. You do this automatically, generalising is a subconscious process. Unfortunately there is also a negative side to this tendency to generalise.

It is just as easy to take an adverse situation and make similar generalisations. It's easy to say so-and-so left me, therefore *all* men/women leave me. Not true. No two people are ever the same and, just as there is an infinite variety of people, so too is there an infinite variety of responses to you and what you have to offer in a relationship. You will greatly reduce the pain and the loneliness if you stick to the facts, namely, 'One person has left me.' You may even say, 'Three people have left me.' That still does not mean that '*Everybody* leaves me.'

Being Alone

The pain of being jilted has three components. The first part is the self-inflicted pain we have discussed above, the pain imposed by what *you* choose to say to yourself, by the interpretation *you* choose to put on the situation, by the self-criticisms, self-doubts and self-recriminations and the 'if onlys' you apply. And it's true, much of this pain is indeed self-inflicted. You now have a couple of techniques for dealing with that pain. One involves changing your perspective on the situation, the other involves learning some deeper aspect of the problem, one on which you can work and in which you can, by your own actions and words, make a difference.

The second part is the pain of missing that specific individual, someone you have liked, loved, cared for, someone with whom you have had fun and companionship, someone whom you may have envisaged as a desirable part of your future. If they decide to go, if they decide to do something you would have said was out of character, then it is time to recognise that they are not the person you thought they were and the relationship does not have the characteristics that you thought it did. Better to find out now, rather than later.

The third component is the pain of being alone, and since this is a book about loneliness and how to deal with it, it is now time to turn to this aspect of being jilted. For some people, possibly for you, the major distress in this situation is not so much the loss of the particular person – perhaps the relationship had been wearing thin for you too – but the fact of being on your own again, of being lonely. This can be true of long- or short-term relationships.

Barry had been twenty-five when he'd married. He was a quiet chap, working on his own all day doing computer graphics and relating far more to his equipment than he ever did to his colleagues. He had a group of friends that he had grown up with and one day, he told me, he had looked around and realised that he was the only one still single. His friends, male and female, were all married.

'I guess I panicked. I had always taken their easy companionship for granted and now, suddenly, they were all busy with their families. I had this sudden fear that

I'd be left on my own. I knew I wasn't very exciting to be with, I thought perhaps no one would ever want to marry me, or if I did fall in love with someone I'd find that they were already married, so I proposed to the girl I was going out with at the time.'

'And how was the marriage?'

'It was fine, she was quiet too. She kept the house well, had her own job as well. We'd settled into a routine that suited both of us. We were just coming up for our fourth wedding anniversary. Then suddenly two months ago she announced she was leaving me. I feel devastated, I don't know what to do. I guess I had grown to love her a lot more than I had realised.'

It took a while but gradually Barry came to realise the main problem for him was that of loneliness. He had not been passionately in love with Jane, nor had he grown to feel passionately about her. He was not actually devastated that she had spurned him or that she had gone out of his life. His real fear was that of being lonely, he was afraid that he'd never marry again, that no one would marry him and that he'd be alone forever. He had assumed that his distress was the loss of Jane, whereas it was the loss of 'a companion'. Once he realised this we could start to work on ways for him to deal with the loneliness and find other forms of companionship, rather than working on how to deal with grief over the loss of Jane specifically.

Margaret's situation was different. She had been in a difficult marriage; her husband, Tom, had been dictatorial, expecting Margaret to fit in with his ways, keep house for him, entertain his friends, fit her social life round his, have things at home the way he liked them. His reasoning was that he was earning most of their joint income; she had time during much of the week to do what she wanted, so when they were together he deserved to choose. Then he told her he was leaving her, that he was going to live with another woman.

Margaret had said, during her first visit, that she needed to learn to deal with her feelings of loss, of being rejected, of being jilted. As we worked together, however, it became obvious that she was really quite glad to be able to live her own life without Tom instructing her every move. In particular it was a relief not to have to have sex with him whenever he demanded it.

'It's a bit like getting your own body back again,' was how she put it.

Nor, when we analysed it, did she mind that he had chosen someone else. However, she did come to realise that she also found her new freedom hard to take and she was, as we discovered, hating the fact of being on her own.

'We always used to entertain, as a couple of course. I guess I haven't really stopped to think how many fewer invitations I get now that he isn't with me. I'm suddenly realising that that is what is making me feel so depressed.'

If you focus on what you expect to feel, the loss and rejection of the jilting, you may miss the real cause of your pain. In both of these situations, and many others like them, what was really required was a way out of the loneliness that resulted.

Time to Grieve

The period after being jilted can indeed be a lonely time. If you cared, and they left, it is bound to be a time of pain. You will also feel lonely in the sense that there is no one to fill the particular gap left by your lover, spouse or partner. Give yourself the time to grieve. This may be time spent on your own, or it may be time spent with people who you select to help you through the process.

However, every process, including this one, has its own time span. Only you will know what that is for you, but be careful not to prolong it inappropriately. It is possible, consciously or unconsciously, to use any adverse situation, and particularly this one, to get sympathy or to get attention. You may, since the jilting, have found that friends were being particularly considerate, that your family were making a fuss of you, that people were thinking up people to whom they could introduce you as alternative partners. You may fear that, if you let it be known that you are now over the situation, this additional attention and concern may stop and that you may then really start to feel lonely. Don't prolong the grieving. It is no long-term solution. When the appropriate time for the grieving is over it is time to get on with your life, to go out and make new friends and develop new relationships.

Avoiding Loneliness

It is no use sitting at home wishing things were different. Once you have dealt with the immediate problems of the separation you do have to go out and make a new life for yourself. If you want company, go out and find it. Your friends do not owe you anything. The fact that your partner has gone does not mean that your friends have a duty to make up the shortfall, to provide the companionship that you now lack. Even if they did so initially, it is not up to them to do this forever. They are not less good friends just because they don't know exactly what you want from a relationship, they don't know who would be your ideal partner and they don't, magically, provide that person for you. It is up to you to get on with your life.

If you want companionship then go out and ask for it. Invite friends in, arrange social situations, do some of the many things suggested throughout this book. But be wary of that trap of the recently jilted, especially if you were still in love with the person involved. Do not judge new people you meet for their similarity to the ideal goal you are after, for their replacement value for the person you have lost. If someone invites you out for the day and is less than the perfect companion it is not their fault. It is not their fault that they are not like the partner that has left you, that they do not fill in the same gaps in your activities, that they do not make you feel the way your ex-partner did. On the face of it this is an obvious statement, but so often I hear clients saying such things as 'I went out with this chap that invited me to go for a drive with him. It was OK, I guess, but it wasn't the way it was with Bill.' Of course it wasn't. That is like trying to compare apples to carrots. He is not auditioning for the part of the ex-lover but for the part of a new friend. He should be considered as such.

If friends invite you round for a lunch or a dinner and you don't meet the perfect new partner, do not, as one client did, come away crying and thinking, 'If they were really good friends they would have invited someone special for me.' Not true. They are good friends, they did invite you. People are worth taking an interest in even if they do not exactly fill the hole in your life.

As in all forms of loneliness, ultimately, you are in control of your mood and emotional state. You are in charge of what you are saying to yourself. If you do not like your mood and you do not like to hear what you are saying to yourself, then change your mood, say different things to yourself, go out and create changes in your life. There *are* ways to do it, it is up to you to put them into action.

Chapter Twenty-Four

Lonely Within a Relationship

One of the loneliest feelings you can have is being lonely within a relationship. You should have it all, yet you don't. Other people see you as part of a couple. Other people assume you are not lonely, that you are happy, that since you have a partner, even a family, you must have someone who cares; you certainly have someone to do things with when doing things together as part of a couple is mandatory, or virtually so. It can be lonely within a poor relationship even if you have close friends to share your problems with; it can be even more lonely if you are putting a brave face on things or are afraid of acknowledging the situation, leaving and then being even more lonely.

There are many people like that, people in a loveless or unhappy relationship who stay there because, for a variety of reasons, they fear being lonely if they make a change. There are two problems with this. Firstly, you stay in the relationship and remain unhappy because of the inherent problems. Secondly, by telling yourself you do not have any choice, that you are trapped and powerless, you make yourself into a victim. As a consequence you probably take your unhappiness out on the situation you are in, causing it to deteriorate further.

Anne was unhappily married, bored and feeling trapped.

The children had left home and were independent, her husband had his work to occupy him during the day and when he came home he was too tired to do much in the evenings except watch television. If they went out to visit friends he drank and became argumentative. When she wanted to do things he told her they couldn't afford it. Anne told herself she was unhappy at home, yet she couldn't leave, that if she did she wouldn't have sufficient money to live on and certainly would not have enough to be able to make a life where she could meet people and have friends. As she said, she was afraid of landing up in a tiny flat, lonely, miserable and with no chance of meeting people.

As a result of this situation and of her attitude she took her unhappiness out on her husband. In their frequent arguments she told him he was inadequate for not earning enough so they could have a decent life, that he was selfish in not agreeing to do things she wanted them to do, that he was boring when he slumped in front of the television each evening and that she was ashamed of him when they went out with friends and he drank too much. Inevitably, of course, the relationship deteriorated as a result.

As we worked together she came to realise that she had two options. She could stay with him, recognising that that was her *choice and not one foisted on her by him. Whether or not there was sufficient money was not the point. It was her choice whether she left or stayed regardless of the basis on which she made such a decision. Even without much money there would be ways she could create a life for herself, she did have choices. She also began to realise that she might indeed be able to do sufficient things to avoid feeling lonely and that she could leave in the realistic hope of creating a new life for herself.*

Together we went through a list of her values (see Appendix) and determined what was important to her in her life. We then ranked them according to the priorities she gave them. As a result she decided, somewhat to her surprise, that staying put was probably the better of the two options. Having made this decision consciously she stopped blaming her husband for everything and gradually started to improve the relationship. However with time, as her confidence grew, she came to realise that her actions and decision had still been motivated by the fear of being lonely if she left. Her developing confidence gave her the strength to realise that she, and probably he, would be happier if they separated and she was also able to move her focus from the fear of loneliness to the anticipation of the activities she could do, the new friends she could make and the peace she could have in her new home when she could create her own life and do what she wanted.

'The thing that's interesting,' she told me, some time later, 'is that I used to fear that if I left him I wouldn't find another man, and that if I didn't I'd inevitably be lonely. But that's not really true, is it? After all, I don't have much interest in sex any more, for years it's been more of a bore than a pleasure. What I want is companionship and I certainly didn't have that with my husband. I've now realised that I can have that with a man or a woman. It's just society that says if you are single, if you don't have a man, you must be lonely, unwanted, unhappy, and even somehow inadequate. Since I've been on my own I've realised that women are actually much more interesting than men, we have so much more in common.'

It does not always work out like this. One client had remained in a loveless and unhappy marriage for forty years because she was afraid that if she left it she would be lonely. She had married in her late teens only a year after she had left home and during which time she had shared a flat with two girlfriends. Within a couple of years she had realised her mistake but felt ashamed to admit it and so stayed, telling herself she should give the marriage more of a chance. Then there had been children and so for twenty years she had felt she had no option but to remain. After that, as she told me, she had wanted to leave – there had seemed little point in staying together as the children were independent – but she was afraid that if she did she would find herself living alone, with few friends, and in any case, she felt she'd left it too late to find someone else to marry.

When she was sixty-five her husband died and she simply had to start building an independent life for herself. Since she was essentially a gentle and friendly person she soon made friends. This she did by joining some local groups, doing things in which she took an interest, and making more of an effort to see the friends she had. Instead of being lonely she blossomed. To my knowledge she hasn't married again but last I heard she had a good 'friend' with whom she shared a lot of activities. One of her comments to me had been, 'If only I'd had the courage to separate twenty years ago my life would have been so different, think what I've missed.'

It is commonly women that fear this type of loneliness, particularly as they get older, and so tend to hang on to worn-out relationships. Men generally feel that they will have sufficient options, both for friendships and for relationships, after a separation. None the less there are men who also stay in painful situations out of a fear of loneliness. They may stay because they feel they couldn't look after themselves domestically, or because they like the quiet family life, as well as for many of the same reasons that women stay.

You are not powerless. You do have choices. You can make a significant change to your emotional state by recognising and acknowledging this. You could leave, any time. The fact that you choose to stay actually says, 'I can go or stay. I have assessed the consequences of both actions and I have decided that staying is the better of the two options.' When you say this to yourself, when you acknowledge this and stop telling yourself you are a victim, you can then stop blaming your partner or your circumstances, you take away the negative, blaming, energy you have been putting into the relationship. This in itself can make you less unhappy.

If you decide not to leave a relationship, for whatever reason, yet you feel intensely lonely within it, then some solutions are possible. There may be children, there may be too much to risk financially or practically. There may be too many other people who would get hurt. You may have any number of reasons for staying where you are, yet you may still want to have more of a life for yourself. There is no reason why this cannot happen.

Alternatively, it may be that such compelling reasons for staying do not exist, yet you are still in the relationship and feeling lonely. If you have decided you have nothing in common with your partner, be it someone with whom you are going out, someone with whom you live, or your spouse, then you have some serious thinking to do. Whilst it is true that the grass always *seems* greener on the other side of the fence, when you get there it is often disappointing. The problem with leaving one relationship, with its attendant inadequacies, and looking for another, is that you take yourself with you. In other words, if you want the next relationship to be better than the one you are in you should do some work on yourself.

After all, you chose your present partner. You did this whether this was an active choice on your part, or a passive acceptance of his or her suggestion that the two of you should become involved. At the time it must have seemed a good idea to you. If you don't make some changes in yourself and in your attitudes and thinking, you could well make a similar mistake again. How often have you seen a second marriage follow the same road to destruction as a first one?

Statistics show that the majority of people that divorce or break up a serious relationship are no happier, five years later, than they were when they split. At one time you did like your present partner, so your most likely option is to see whether or not the present relationship can be revived. Recall the experience Marian went through with Colin (Chapter Four, p. 45). Experiment, give yourself a week of relating to your existing partner as if s/he were a total stranger. Stop thinking that they owe you something, that they have a duty to behave to you in a certain way simply because you *are* a couple, because of the things you have done for them. No one knows better than the two of you how to press each other's buttons, how to find each other's weaknesses and work on them. Don't do this. Each time you are about to say or do something ask yourself if this is something you would say or do with a stranger or with a new friend. There are obvious exceptions here, in terms of immediate sexual activity and so forth, but in general I'm sure you get the idea. It is surprising how often someone treats their partner, especially in a failing relationship, in a far worse way than they would treat anyone else, including a total stranger.

Now, you may be saying, that's all very well, but s/he should be doing this or that, then things between us would be better. Maybe, but can you make them? Can you force them to change? Have you already tried that? Probably. Have you succeeded? Probably not, or you wouldn't still be unhappy in the relationship. You cannot make the other person change, but you *can* change yourself. That's not fair, you may be saying, why should I change and not them? But ask yourself this. Is what you are presently doing working? If it isn't, would you be willing to change what you are doing? If your answer to that is yes, then go ahead and make the changes. If your answer to that is no, then ask yourself why not. Are you trying to get even with the other person? Are you trying to prove them wrong? What other motive have you for insisting that they should change and not you? Is there any chance that these motives will turn the relationship back into one that you can enjoy? Unlikely.

The amazing thing is that most people are basically nice. If you treat them well they will usually treat you well. If you change the way you behave to someone you may well be surprised, even very surprised indeed, at the changes they make in response. Who knows, you may well be able to resurrect the old relationship that you started with. After all, as we said, you did like them once, and you already have a head start on any new relationship, both physically/materially and emotionally. You have already made an investment of yourself in this relationship. It would be exciting to see this grow.

If nothing else, look at it this way, you owe it to yourself to find out whether or not there is anything you can do to build on what you have rather than destroy it. You haven't done this until you have made all the changes you can possibly make, within yourself. If, having done that, you still feel lonely and separate within the relationship and want a change then maybe that is what is needed.

At the very least, you can use this relationship as a chance to experiment, to practice some of the exercises and suggestions made throughout the book. If you really don't like the relationship it can hardly matter if some of the things you do don't work, and if they do, you can look on it as a bonus.

Fear of Leaving

Perhaps you have now decided that you want to make a change, but don't know how to. You may have recognised that you are indeed in a relationship that you would like to end and replace, yet still feel that what you have is better than nothing, a bit like a non-swimmer, unwilling to let go with one hand, until they can find another hold with the other one.

Yet for as long as you are seen to be in a relationship with your existing partner, certain options are either closed to you or are more difficult. You may meet someone you like, they may even like you, but, thinking you are already involved, they may not show any interest in you or invite you out. You are in a dilemma. If, for instance, you are married, you can hardly announce that you are on the lookout for a new partner. If you do start to go out with someone else while you are in a relationship they may well wonder just how faithful you would be to them if they got into a serious relationship with you.

Whatever the details and consequences, the fact remains that you would love to leave but are stopped by the fear of being lonely if you do. The devil you know may be deemed to be better than the unknown of loneliness. Yet this initial state, that of being on your own, alone, and possibly lonely, could be the essential hurdle over which you must leap to find a much happier and more satisfying situation. It may seem like an insurmountable hurdle, yet it may turn out to be have been composed of an empty fear.

A step in the process is for you to come to terms with being on your own. After all, if you do decide to leave your present relationship, there is no guarantee that you will find another one. You may well be on your own for a while, certainly in terms of a one-to-one relationship, there are no guarantees as to if or when you will find your next and perfect partner. However, if you are truly lonely and unhappy within your present relationship and feel you may have more options when you have separated, that is a risk you have to take. Work on all that is said throughout this book so that you can come to feel comfortable at the idea of being on your own, at least for a while. Then you will not feel as if you are leaping off a cliff into the unknown but you can be reasonably confident that you will be able to create a new life for yourself.

If, after all this, you do decide to stay in your present relationship, you can use all the ideas covered in this book to work at improving the situation. You will want to apply all the ideas that have been given to you as means of improving your relationship with yourself. Then take the ideas that cover improving your relationships with other people and apply them to your partner. Finally, use these and other suggestions, including the practical ones given later, for going out and making friends outside the relationship. If your partner does not fill a particular need, find someone else that does. If, for instance, they are not interested in football or cooking, classical music or pop, politics or the latest movie, find someone else that is and focus on what you can share with your partner.

Chapter Twenty-Five

When Your Lover/Partner/Friend Dies

The ending of a relationship by the death of your partner inevitably makes a huge change in your life. If the relationship was a good one and you were close, the ending involves a great deal of pain, pain over the loss of someone you loved, pain over the loss of the companionship and shared activities, pain over the loss of having your needs met in the particular way that they did it and many other forms of pain. You may have lost a close friend, one who you had been close to for years, with whom you had shared and done many things. How you deal with grief is a whole subject in itself, here we are concerned with how you deal with the situation afterwards and avoid or deal with the loneliness.

If the relationship was not a good one there is still pain. Few people like to see another person die, whatever the relationship. The fact that you stayed together means there was *something* in the relationship.

You now have to consider what you are going to do about the new situation. You can either remain alone or you can build anew. You may decide to remain alone and try to be content, not feeling the need for a new partner, or not wanting someone else to take the place of the old, and filling the void with friends and family, or with memories and your own company. On the other hand you may want to be part of a relationship again.

At the end of any such close relationship, particularly if it has been a long one, spanning many years, even decades, some people seem to feel that this is the end. They may be lonely, yet decide to stay on their own and put up with or accept the situation. You hear such phrases as 'I couldn't marry again,' 'I'd never find anyone else like him/her,' 'I couldn't betray them by finding someone else,' 'They wouldn't want me to marry again,' 'The family wouldn't like it, or approve,' 'What would people think if I married again, it would look as if I hadn't loved him/her.' Let's address some of these issues.

No-One Else Like Them

Of course you won't find anyone just like the partner or friend you have just lost, for several reasons. Firstly people are different, *no* two people are alike, however similar they may seem, and so it would be totally impossible for you to find someone else exactly like your previous partner. Secondly, by the time your partner died you had come to know each other intimately. You knew, without thinking, how they would react in a particular situation, what they would say and how they would respond to your words and actions. They also knew you, how you would react and respond, what you liked and didn't like. This type of knowing takes time. Thirdly, the relationship you had was built up over many years. It had a history, you could share memories and the relationships with friends, family and places. This same history can never be part of the new relationship.

The mistake is to try to repeat what you had. If you decide to find a new partner, be they a new companion or a new lover, take it as just that, a *new* experience.

Otherwise you can torpedo the developing relationship from the start.

Penelope came to see me saying she was tired, depressed, bored and lonely and was there anything I could do to help. She'd been widowed in her late forties after nearly thirty years of a marriage that she described as, 'Good, generally, though of course we had our ups and downs, like everyone else, who doesn't.'

'So now you're on your own and you're lonely, is that it?'

'Oh no, I've had several men friends since my husband died, but it's not the same somehow.'

Of course not, I thought to myself, but let's find out what is going on.

'Tell me about them.'

'Well, there was Bob, I met him a couple of years after my husband died. He was a friend of one of the neighbours. He was nice, but he kept telling me what to do, making decisions for me, expecting me to fit in with what he wanted. I began to feel trapped. David would never have done that. We used to make decisions together. He said we were equal partners and he cared about what I wanted. After a while I began to feel that Bob didn't love me otherwise he'd be more concerned to find out what I wanted to do. Maybe he also felt that what I thought was unimportant.'

'So, what happened?'

'I'd tell him to stop being so domineering. He'd say he wasn't, he was just trying to take care of me because he loved me. I'd say he had a funny way of showing it, telling me what to do all the time. Then it would build up into a row. Eventually we split up.'

'And after that?'

'After that there was Gerald. He was nice, but he never seemed to want to do anything. At least he didn't tell me

what to do the way Bob had. But he'd drop round at the weekend and hang around the house, never suggesting that we go out or anything. I began to feel he was just making use of the place, letting me cook his meals and things, perhaps just because he was lonely. It wasn't any sort of partnership.'

'How did it end?'

'Well, I didn't want to hurt him by telling him not to come round any more so I'd arrange to do things and be out. After a while he just stopped coming. I did miss him, in fact I missed both of them in their way, but they just weren't a substitute for David.'

Of course not, no one could be a substitute for David. She had married him when they were both young. They had done much of their growing up together, they had learnt to deal with the adult world together. They had also built up a relationship that had developed over the years and suited both of them. Although Penelope had now forgotten it they would, at the start, have kept doing things, having misunderstandings, sorting them out and then finding out what each other meant by their actions. The process of easy and silent communication that she had developed with David over thirty years of marriage was something she had come to take for granted and the origins of which she had forgotten about. She had then applied these same criteria to Bob and then Gerald, but it was entirely likely that her conclusions were not valid. That was one point that Penelope came to understand as we worked together, the other was the value of communication.

When Bob said, 'I've arranged for us to spend Sunday with Jane and Charles,' and Penelope responded with, 'That's all very well for you, but I've got things round the house I want to do and the garden's becoming a mess, why are you so selfish, why don't you ever bother to find out what I want?' Bob felt criticised and went on the defensive. He would do this by attacking her in turn, saying, 'You know I don't like gardening, and we haven't seen Jane and Charles for ages, and they're good friends of mine.' The row grew from there.

I suggested a way for Penelope to test out her conclusions, in any future relationship and to improve communication. Instead of criticising, or, as she saw it, standing up for her rights, she was to use the following phrase, or something similar: 'When you say/do . . . . . ., I feel . . . . . ., is that what you mean?'

In the situation with Bob the conversation might have gone like this:

Penelope: 'When you plan our Sunday for us, without asking me what I want to do, I feel that you want to do things your way and that you don't care what I want, is that what you think?'

Bob: 'No, of course not, I thought that by planning a day out it would give you a nice change from being at home and doing the housework.'

In this scenario Penelope would have learnt that Bob was actually trying to please her, not steamroll her into doing what he wanted. She could then either accept his positive intention as a sign of affection and enjoy what he had planned or, if she really didn't like what he suggested, she could express her appreciation for what he was trying to accomplish for her but explain that she did enjoy staying at home and gardening. Either way, they could both have learnt a lot more about each other and about how to build a positive relationship together.

On the other hand Bob's reply might have been different, something like:

Bob: 'I do want to do things my way, I'm used to it, I work hard all week and I like to see my friends at the weekend. My first wife cared enough to fit in with me, why can't you?'

Penelope would then have had to decide if this was a

relationship with which she wanted to continue, but at least she would have known accurately where she stood, not just made assumptions. Further, she would have found that out without a row and Bob too would recall what he had said and on what premise she had based her decision.

There's another important strategy when you are building a new relationship. Recall the six-step process mentioned earlier and adapt it to include extra steps, if helpful. When your new partner, or potential new partner, does something, check out your conclusions.

James had met Rowena a few months earlier but was still unsure of her and the way she felt about him.

'She's very quiet, we like each other a lot, but if we go out for a meal she doesn't talk much. I can't help feeling that she doesn't think I'm sufficiently intelligent or interesting for her.'

I put him through the process, with a slight variation, and this was the result:

1 'What does she do that concerns you?'

'She says very little when we go out together.'

2 'What assumptions are you making about the meaning of this?'

'That she doesn't think I'm sufficiently interesting to have a serious conversation with.'

3 'How does that make you feel?'

'Pretty depressed, and sort of inadequate. Maybe I should leave her alone.'

4 'Why are you making that assumption?'

'Because when my first wife went all quiet it meant she was cross and in a bad mood. She was normally so chatty and she said that sharing ideas was an important part of our compatibility.'

5 'What alternative assumption could you make?'

'I guess I could assume that she felt comfortable and relaxed with me and that she didn't have to make conversation all the time.'

6 'How would you feel then?'

'Happy of course, that's the way I feel about her.'

7 'Which way would you like to feel, which assumption is the most useful?'

To this James nominated the new assumption saying, 'I like her a lot, and I'd like the relationship to continue, it's just so hard to know what she's thinking and what she wants.'

When someone is relatively uncommunicative, and you feel you can't know what they want, then the most constructive move to make involves making the most useful assumption, the one that leads to the more pleasant experience, rather than the more destructive assumption.

The slight variation I used in this case was to ask one more question, number 4, namely 'Why are you making that assumption?' and the answer, 'Because my wife was so chatty, she said that sharing ideas was an important part of our compatibility,' gave him the clue he needed.

Many misunderstandings in a new relationship can come about when you make the assumption that what your new partner means when they do something is the same as what your past partner would have meant had they done the same thing. This is rarely true. Yet the assumption is often there, and it is usually unconscious, it is simply something you take for granted. It can also lead to a great number of misunderstandings and a great deal of unhappiness.

If you are having trouble finding a satisfactory new relationship to replace the old one do this exercise. Go through this six- (or seven-) step process with every situation where your new partner, or potential partner, does or says, or doesn't do or doesn't say anything that doesn't please or satisfy you. You may be surprised at the result.

It is a natural and understandable tendency, if you have been close to your first partner, to look for someone else who is similar to them. Yet, as we have seen, the attempt is doomed to failure. Instead of looking for someone to take their place this may be the time in your life for you to move on, to explore a new relationship, to look for the differences, for new experiences. Comparisons can be so destructive, the new can be interesting. Don't judge by the old but look for what experiences new relationships can bring you.

Betrayal

Some people will claim, 'Of course I could never love anyone else, it would be a betrayal.' Or 'It would show disrespect,' or 'It wouldn't be right, what would the rest of the family think.' I suggest to you that if you truly do want to have a new relationship then you should just have one. It doesn't mean that you loved your previous partner any the less, or respected them less simply because you are capable of finding someone else to love. It just means that you want a new relationship.

The reason you want a new relationship could well be that, since the past one was so wonderful you would rather search for another than remain single. It could mean that you do not like being on your own. It could mean that you are a warm and loving person and that, without someone to love, someone to give to and to share with, you feel stifled and unfulfilled. It could mean a number of things. One of the things it is least likely to mean is that you are, or want to be, betraying the person who has died.

It is your life and it is for you to decide how you want to live it. Don't live your life to fulfil the expectations of others and tell yourself that you have no choice. When you do so, and when things don't turn out the way you want them to you then turn on these other people, either overtly or in your mind, and blame them for the outcome, a situation that is not healthy and is not conducive to having a good relationship with the people concerned. Do what you want. If you want to please them, fine, but acknowledge that that is what you want to do, don't lay the blame of the outcome at their door.

Joanna's husband, Peter, had died of an unexpected heart attack in his early fifties about a year before she came to see me.

'I'm so lonely,' was her opening remark. 'I'm still relatively young, I miss Peter badly, but I'm lonely and I do want another companion. Yet I can't marry again, my daughter was absolutely horrified when I suggested I might find someone else, some time in the future of course. I can't upset her, yet I hate living alone. I just don't know what to do.'

'So what's happening now?'

'I'm feeling more and more resentful of my Shirley. After all, if it wasn't for her, I would look for another partner. I'd go to one of these clubs for divorced or widowed people. There's a very nice one attached to our church.'

'How do you feel about this?'

'Cross, resentful. She's getting over her father's death, but I'm supposed to stay the same, she's stopping me from doing what I want to do. I'm beginning to feel it's all her fault that I'm so lonely, yet there's nothing else I can do.'

'Of course there is.'

I went on to point out that by what she was currently doing she was not only creating an ongoing situation of loneliness for herself but, by firstly behaving as her daughter, Shirley, wanted her to and, secondly, by blaming her for the outcome, she was also damaging the relationship she had with her daughter.

'You're right,' was her response, 'but what can I do?'

I suggested she do one of two things. She could decide that her life was her own and make the decision she wanted about finding a new relationship. After all, I suggested, it was unlikely that Shirley had let her mother choose her own husband. Joanna could go ahead and plan her life in the way she deemed desirable. She would then, of course, have to learn to live with the consequences whatever they turned out to be, that's the way life is.

The second possibility was that Joanna sat down and said to herself, 'Right, I would rather do what Shirley thinks is right and have a good relationship with her, even if it means being alone for the rest of my life, than lose that close relationship.' If she chose this option I suggested she should then also say to herself, when she felt lonely and unhappy that she didn't have a partner, not, 'I'm lonely and it's all Shirley's fault,' but 'I'm lonely but I made the decision to live my life this way so I could have a closer relationship with Shirley.'

By taking responsibility for her own actions, she could reduce the chance of spoiling other relationships, something that almost inevitably happens when you claim to have done things because 'Someone else made you.'

Note that in either case, and whether you acknowledge it or not, you have actually done what you want. In this case Joanna either remarried because she chose to or she stayed single and conformed with Shirley's ideals because she, Joanna, wanted to do that. The difference is that when she chose to blame Shirley for the outcome rather than recognising the fact that she had made her own choices, she risked spoiling a second relationship.

Acknowledge that you do what you do, for whatever

> *reason,* for yourself. *This applies whether your chosen actions are what society would call selfish or unselfish.*
>
> *In this case, as it turned out, Joanna decided to look for another partner and the consequences were, in fact, only minor. Shirley soon came to accept Joanna's new friend and less harm was done to the mother–daughter relationship than had been occurring in the past when Joanna acted to conform with what Shirley said she thought was right.*

This same type of thinking applies also, of course, to some of the other objections, voiced at the start of this chapter, such objections as 'The family wouldn't like it, or approve,' 'What would people think if I married again, it would look as if I hadn't loved him/her.' You have to live your life by your own rules, whether the rule is doing what you want or doing what you think other people want you to do. If you are wise you will recognise this, stop blaming other people, decide what you really want to do, and get on with it, whatever it may be.

Staying Single

Recognise your real aim. Often it is to avoid being lonely, not, specifically, to find a new mate. You may recognise this, or you may not. So don't count your efforts a failure when you make new friends, develop new interests but don't find someone to replace the person you have lost. That may be part of your requirement but it may not be and it is certainly not the only way to resolve the loneliness that results from a partner's death.

We are such a Noah's Ark society that there is often the general assumption that if you are single, particularly if you are young, that if you live on your own and don't have a partner, you must be lonely. Many people look for a partner to avoid the feeling that other people are commenting unfavourably on the fact that they are single and thus portraying a type of inadequacy. Nonsense. If you need or want time on your own, have it. If you are lonely doing this there are plenty of other ways to solve the problem.

To recapitulate, when you lose someone there is pain; there is general loneliness as well as specific loneliness. The pain and the loss of the individual are things you have to deal with and are beyond our scope here. Look for a new partner if that is what you want. If not, if it is a more general loneliness, you can deal with this using many of the tools in this book.

Chapter Twenty-Six

Tied to the House

There are many reasons why you may be tied to your home, unable to go out and meet people, socialise with friends, wander round the shops or have any sort of social life. You may be able to invite people into your home or even that too may be difficult. The type of constraints that result in these situations can leave you feeling very lonely indeed.

Let's start with the most difficult situation. You are alone, except for the possible people who constitute the reason for you being tied to the house. You are certainly feeling lonely. What can you do?

Again it's up to you; and because it's up to you there is something you can do. You can stay at home and mope, or you can find creative things to do, things that bring you into contact with people.

I know one man whose wife could not be left alone in the house. A nurse came in for an hour a day during which time he did the outside things he simply had to do. Full-time nursing cost more than his total income so it was cheaper to give up his job than employ a nurse. He then had to find some occupation he could do from home. He chose network marketing, normally thought of as a people business, one in which you go out and meet people and interest them in either your product or the business opportunity, and one involving regular meetings and trainings two or three times a week. He could do none of these things. He could, however, place ads, respond over the phone, have products delivered to his house and parcels picked up from his house and take care of his clients by getting to know them over the phone. In the end he built up not only a very successful business that more than paid the bills but also a large circle of friends all over the country. Inevitably some of them started to call on him at home, but the nature of his wife's illness made this difficult. Was he lonely? Certainly there were times when he wished he could go out to functions but compared to what his life might have been he said he had found a wonderful way to have a full, rewarding, interesting and satisfying life while still looking after the person he loved.

Another friend had a somewhat similar problem which they solved by enrolling in a Lifeline training programme and then working on the phone from home, helping people in distress and being there to talk to when people needed a sympathetic ear.

What about pets? They may not be human but you can talk to them. They are also there to be loved and loving is an enriching experience. Studies done in old people's homes have shown that having a dog around lowered people's blood pressure, stopped arguments and reduced the level of complaints. Having a pet to love can open up your heart chakra and make you more loving and caring to the people with whom you do come in contact. As a result you can add to their enjoyment of the experience and may well find this leads to new friends among the people who do call in to see you.

If you are tied to the house but can have people in to visit, then start running groups from home. They can be hobby groups, such as sewing, crafts, cooking, they can be games groups such as bridge, or they can be groups revolving around other interests such as music, films (built round a video), art. I was recently asked to speak at a women's group. Twenty-five years earlier a group of young mothers tied to the house with young children, had started by meeting for coffee one morning a week. Taking their children with them they rotated the event between the homes of the different members of the group. They soon added an evening a week at which they had a guest speaker and on which occasions they asked the husbands to babysit. For fifteen years I had an opera group. Friends came round once a month, bringing a plate of food and a bottle of wine. We started with tapes and videos of the operas that had originally been produced from 1590 onwards.

If you are tied to your home it is likely that there are other people in the same situation. Make the effort, go out and find them, then offer to share. This could be as simple as babysitting in turns so that you, and they, could get out and meet people. If there are several elderly people to be looked after perhaps you could arrange a regular party for them, which they would enjoy, run by half the minders and leaving the other half free to go out and socialise etc.

More and more people are actually choosing to stay at home to 'cocoon', to coin a term that is becoming popular. This means that more and more activities are happening around the home. With the advent of interactive television as well as computers, modems and the internet, communication is still possible in a variety of ways. As before though, it is you that have to make the effort. These things are available, but you have to tap in to them, though you may be surprised at how little effort is necessary once you start. When you do, you may well be surprised at the rich world of possibilities that exists.

Chapter Twenty-Seven

Retirement

Only two or three generations ago people expected to leave school or university, find a job and work at it until they reached the retirement age of sixty or sixty-five, then relax and take things easy. By then, it was assumed, they would have married and settled down, had children and watched them marry and have children in turn, and become the matriarch or patriarch of an extended family. They had possibly been in the one job, rising in seniority with the years, possibly two or three but probably not more. They may have remained in the same town or local area, almost certainly in the same country. They would probably still be married, and to their first partner. They would have children and grandchildren visiting them. They might have worked for forty years or more and only received a watch at the end of it, instead of a golden handshake, but they had their pension, on which they could live comfortably, if not well, and they had family support and the circle of friends and relations they had built up over the preceding fifty or so years, for company. Even if widowed, they would have friends and family around them, people they had known for decades.

This may be a somewhat rosy-eyed view of things. After all, there was certainly much misery and loneliness at the time too. None the less, it is often the view people have when they retire, if they are alone and poor, as they look back, enviously, on the lives of their parents and grandparents.

Whether or not that picture of the past is accurate or romantic, nowadays the picture is very different. Sadly we know that in most western countries, by the age of seventy, over ninety per cent of the population is either dead or dead-broke, approximately eight per cent is comfortably off and only two per cent is wealthy. In other words, one of the problems you face when you retire is a drop in income, a drop that is sufficient, in most cases, to limit the opportunities for being with other people. The odds are, that if you are at retiring age now, you are probably not still married to your first partner. You may have gone through a divorce, been separated or widowed. You may have had more than one marriage. You have probably had several jobs, you may well have moved from town to town, city to city or even from country to country. If you haven't moved it is likely that many of your friends and family have.

With increasing urbanisation, the increased tendencies of families to break up and move apart, an increasing tendency for people to stay in their own homes rather than go out to church or clubs, especially after dark, retirement can be a lonely time. For younger generations isolation loneliness is often countered by increasing technology, such as television and videos, faxes and computers, all of which may be beyond the easy familiarity of someone brought up at a time when slide rules and log books were thought of as exciting arithmetic tools. The village green, the local community, the family network can no longer be relied on.

Many people know this, yet they do little about it. Many people head straight for retirement with blinkers on and no concept of what the reality will be like. Others can only think of the pleasure it will be not to have to get up and go to a job that they don't enjoy. Some people prepare for retirement. If you are already retired the time for preparation is passed, yet there is still a lot you can do. If you have not yet retired then this (if you're sufficiently interested to be reading this chapter) is the time to do something in that direction.

John and Elsie came to see me three years after John had retired. He was depressed and bored, she was increasingly irritated by his negative comments as he sat around the house during the day, and they both felt that, for the first time, their marriage was under threat. John had worked in a bank all his life, rising to the position of local manager. He hadn't much enjoyed the work, though he liked the status and the authority it gave him. She had been a secretary for a while after the children left home, and then worked part-time for a local charity until John retired.

John had looked forward to retirement as a time to give up the tedium of his job. Elsie looked forward to a time when they could do together many of the things they had wanted to do.

However, once John retired, and after the first sense of release had worn off, he found that they no longer received any of the social invitations appropriate to his work. He suddenly realised he was no longer a power within the town, but instead, gradually, was becoming regarded as an old man and of little consequence in the local business community. Since he had allowed his work and civic affairs to take up most of his time, as well as giving him his sense of importance and self-worth, he had developed few outside interests and now he had little to fall back on.

Elsie had not calculated on their reduced income and the way this would limit their ability to do all the things they had talked of. They were fortunate, their income had only reduced by twenty-five per cent, but their expenses remained the same. The 'spare' money they used to have had disappeared and now they barely had sufficient for their basic needs. Holidays, excursions and costly outings were out of the question.

Betty and Martin were in a similar situation. Their plan had been to go travelling once they retired but heavy expenses in relation to a mild heart attack Martin had suffered at fifty-nine, followed by a period off work, had cut into their budget and Betty's arthritis meant that getting about, cheaply, was a problem.

Both couples found that their children had moved away, had no space for guests to stay and, busy with their own lives, saw less of their parents than the parents would have liked. Even babysitting opportunities were limited, for John and Elsie as the distance was too great and for Betty and Martin as their health and their ability to go home on their own at night was questioned.

What Can You Do?

If the problem exists then there must be something you can do about it, and there is. The important thing is to prepare. Don't simply keep going until suddenly one day you wake up and find you no longer have a job to go to and you wonder what to do with your day. Many jobs and most careers today demand so much time that there is little left over for hobbies. Yet developing hobbies and interests before you retire is an excellent way to prevent boredom and loneliness stepping in when you do retire. There are many preparations you can make, and by making them you can make retirement an exciting phase of your life instead of a lonely and frustrating time.

Eileen was only fifty-three yet she told me her home was a retirement centre. She was a quiet woman, single and never married. She enjoyed her job as a social worker and the voluntary work she did for the homeless. She obviously liked caring for people. I asked why she had chosen to move into a retirement centre at such a relatively young age.

'It's not all that young,' she pointed out, 'I'll be retiring in another twelve years. I haven't married, I don't have children and my sister lives a long way away so I don't really have a family. This means that when I retire and don't have my work colleagues to see each day I could be all on my own.'

She had picked a centre in the middle of a busy shopping area. She had a space to park her car. She went to work and did all the things she would do if she lived independently.

'In addition there's all the things that are organised within the centre,' she continued. 'I may not feel like all of them yet, such as the bowls and some of the bingo sessions, but they organise theatre visits and many other things that I do enjoy. I want to stay in my job as long as I can, but it is government and there is a compulsory retirement age. However I do plan to continue the voluntary work. When I finally do retire it will be in stages and I think it will be very smooth. I'll have a bit more time and will do a few more of the activities that are organised here. I've made a few friends already and I'll make more. I quite like old people too, and I like helping them. I plan to travel a bit and that's another advantage. I'll know that people are keeping an eye on my home while I'm away since the staff do keep an eye on all the apartments in case anyone is unwell.'

Clearly Eileen had made her plans carefully. The down side was that she had, inevitably, paid more for her home than she would have for a flat or a small house and, if she changed her mind, it might be somewhat more difficult to sell it and get her money back. However, she seemed settled and very content with her plan. As yet she doesn't need the extra care that they could provide. However her retirement, when it comes, will, as she says, be smooth, there will be little disruption in her other activities, just more time for them. She will still have many of the same friends. Her plan would not suit everyone but the idea made a lot more sense once she had discussed it with me.

Harry and Arabella had made different arrangements. As with many couples, they had been short of money and space when their children were young and needing it. They had enlarged their home when they could afford to and as they needed the space but then soon after that the children had each left home. Instead of remaining in it and offering the occasional room for visiting grand-children, they had moved to a small home in an area where they felt they would be content to retire. It meant slightly more travelling for Harry while he was still working but it also meant that they could dispense with their mortgage, save up some funds and budget such that they could do the travelling they wanted to do when retirement came. In their case I watched their plan reach fruition and complimented them on their planning.

Another couple were in a similar situation although somewhat younger, since it had come about through early retrenchment. They stayed on in their large house but took in paying guests in the form of students to the local university visiting from overseas to do a variety of study courses. They filled the rooms, added to the couple's income and provided company and interest.

Life doesn't owe you a living and the community does not owe you a safe haven at the end of your working life. Your life is your responsibility and it is up to you to plan now for a time when you will have fewer resources and, perhaps, fewer capabilities. If you want to receive you must also give and even in retirement giving is still a part of the equation. Sadly, many people feel that by the time they retire they have done their job and that it is time for other people to look after them. It doesn't work like that. You keep giving. You just give in a different way.

By the time you retire you have had a lifetime of experience. There is a great deal you *can put back* into society. Sometimes you can give actively, with your time and your energy. At other times you can give passively. Give the gift of silence when you feel like complaining. Give the gift of your company when someone simply wants to talk, even if you are bored or irritated by them.

The same rules apply as when you were younger. If you would like to be taken to the theatre then arrange a theatre outing and organise it for other people. If you don't like going out late at night then choose a matinee. If you wish people would invite you in for coffee, invite people in for coffee. If you wish you had friends you could drop in on, have your own open day and tell people they can always drop in on you on, say, a Tuesday afternoon, you will be at home and you will serve tea. You need not make anything elaborate; remember, the goal is to stop feeling lonely, not to feed your neighbours. If you would like to see more of your family offer to help them, but find out first what sort of help they would appreciate and, probably even more difficult, be willing to help them their way, don't expect them to do things your way.

Study. Many people have spent their working life wishing they could study one subject or another and then decided, when they retire and do have time on their hands, that it's hardly worth it any more, saying what's the point, they won't use the knowledge now. The point of knowledge is not usage, it is the fun and interest of acquiring it. I know one dynamic man who is doing a Ph.D. in dentistry at seventy-eight. He will surely never go into practice, yet the subject interests him. It may not be possible for everyone to go to university at sixty-five, never mind at seventy-eight, but there are many other ways of studying. Local councils run a wide variety of courses, many of them at negligible cost. Local libraries have information on courses. They also have the books.

In many countries there is the University of the Third Age (based in London), or its equivalent where a variety of subjects can be studied for interest and enjoyment, in addition to the people you meet there. If you feel you have knowledge to impart you may also find an outlet and an interest here as many of them are grateful for voluntary teachers.

Look in the local papers. In most cities there are so many free things you can do that, provided you can get about, you need never be on your own. If you are single, for whatever reason, and live alone but don't like to be alone, then make appropriate plans. Making plans, creating your own social timetable, is just as important now as it was (Chapter Seventeen) when you first left home and confronted the possible loneliness that could come from having no automatic company provided by your family at home. Even if the plan comprises such simple things as 'Go shopping', 'Collect library books' or 'Clean the house', it gives structure to your day. Plan some event each day that takes you out of the house.

Emily hated to be alone. Her husband had died three years before she saw me and she herself had retired six months earlier. She was suffering from depression and claimed that her two sons were too busy to spend any time with her, she was lonely, miserable and hated it every time she went home and shut the door behind her.

'When I wake up and realise I have no reason to leave the house during the day I feel so depressed I simply want to curl up and hide under the covers.'

Getting out of the house was the clue for her so I told her to come to see me one Monday morning, bringing the weekend newspapers with her. She didn't like to go out in the evenings but didn't mind staying out if she was already out, at least until about seven or eight o'clock. After some discussion she did agree that, although it was not her normal routine, she could *do her housework in the evenings. We then found a variety of things she could do that she agreed she would quite enjoy and mapped out a week where there was some reason for her to go out every morning and every afternoon. The activities included shopping of course, and visits to the library when there were talks on as well as books to borrow, free lunchtime concerts and so forth. I suggested that on each occasion she either take someone with her – after all she would have loved an invitation so I was simply suggesting that she give what she would like to receive – or that she find someone to talk with when she was out, someone with whom she could feel comfortable and have a chat.*

We didn't have to fill the full week as she already had some things she did do; even so she skipped a few of them. After about three weeks she was more clear on what she did like to do and what she didn't and, as, time went on and she started seeing a few people regularly, she really began to enjoy herself and to agree that she was indeed making a new circle of friends and developing some new interests. She even found that by the time she got home, instead of feeling depressed, she was glad to have some peace and quiet on her own.

There's another potential pitfall when you retire. If you are still married you may see too much of your partner.

You have spent the last forty or more years (depending on the length of the marriage) seeing each other for a few fleeting hours in the day; now, suddenly, you're together for twenty-four hours. This may show strains in the relationship you hadn't realised were there. You may make changes that spoil other aspects of your life.

Bob and Janine had often said how much they looked forward to retiring, to a time when they could be together more, rather than leading the rushed life they had when Bob was working and Janine looking after the children.

As soon as Bob retired Janine felt that she too should stay at home since that is what they had dreamed of. However, this meant that she stopped doing a lot of the things she had been doing during the daytime. She stopped seeing her friends, women she had met for coffees during shopping time, women she had had lunch with from time to time, or played the occasional game of bridge with. Suddenly she felt desperately lonely for her friends. Even though she and Bob had some good times, there were many times when they found themselves at a loose end in each other's company, they both missed the friends they had had, yet both felt disinclined to discuss the matter.

It is not always a good idea to make drastic changes when you retire. Take things slowly and explore the changes you want to make and the results that come about. What you have been saying you wanted may not be what you want when the time comes. It is often very valuable if you both sit down and make plans for this new phase of your life.

PART IV

Specific Activities

Chapter Twenty-Eight

Practical Details and How-Tos

We will work now on the assumption that you have moved some way to recognising that loneliness really is a state of mind, and one that is created, ultimately, by yourself, and one that you can change. While recognising that there are, from person to person and situation to situation, more or less external inputs that affect you, your situation is your starting point. It is all very well for an Irishman to say, when asked how to get to Dublin, 'Well first of all, if I were you, I wouldn't start from here.' Where you are right now, is where you start. Where you are going is up to you.

The aim of this section is to provide you with a fairly extensive list of things you could do to put your new-found initiative and willingness to make changes, into practice. However, the list is by no means complete so add to it any ideas that occur to you. When you first read the lists of ideas put a tick or a mark beside *all* of them that you think might be interesting. Do *not* filter them. The moment you start to think, 'That would be nice, but the problem is . . .' you are setting limits to what you could accomplish. This list, with its ticks and marks, will serve, in the future, as a reference to which you can turn when you are looking for more ideas.

Anything can be done, provided you have the will to do it. There is no suggestion, given here, that someone has not acted upon, and very successfully too.

When you have your maxi-list (List 3) then go through that and mark off the things you feel you could do immediately, or that you could put into practice relatively easily (List 1). Then go through again and mark off the things you would like to do, but that might take a bit of time or some more involved planning (List 2).

The next step is vital. Get out your diary, your time-planner, your calendar or whatever you use. If you don't use anything of this sort then get one for yourself. This is the time to start planning.

Take each suggestion that you have selected in List 1. Mark appropriate dates and activities in your diary. If it is to phone a friend, see a movie or have a dinner party, then put that in your diary on the appropriate day. If some pre-planning is required, such as issuing invitations, then put those actions into your diary too.

Now take each selection on List 2 and do the same thing. However, since this list may involve things that needed greater and more careful planning, it is particularly important that you plan, and diarise, the entire strategy. For instance, if you intend to set up a home-based business there may have to be contacts made with a variety of local authorities or suppliers and thought given to advertising.

Find a pencil and let's get started. The pencil is essential for I hope you won't simply read the following suggestions but will consider each one and assess their potential value to you. The major thrust of all the suggestions is to help you to find ways to meet people, some of whom, in time, will become friends and companions and thus banish your loneliness. The other thrust of the suggestions is to help you to find new interests and activities that you find sufficiently interesting and exciting to achieve a similar effect. If you are successful in achieving both outcomes it is very unlikely that you will be lonely again.

There is one more very important, in fact vital, point. When you do the activities you have selected, *speak to people*. You might be amazed at how many clients have told me that they did join a walking club, go to art galleries or attend lectures and are still lonely, because they were too shy to talk to people when they got there. *Talk to people*. Many of them may turn out to be uninteresting to you after a while but in any search there is only a small amount of pay dirt and to find that you may indeed have to sift through a lot of dross. Equally, you may well be surprised to find just how interesting some of the seeming 'dross' can turn out to be, especially if you listen openly and with real interest, rather than with a what's-in-it-for-me attitude.

The ideas below are given in no particular order, although they are grouped in somewhat logical ways. The main thing is for you to read them all and make notes.

Clubs, Societies and Associations

All the clubs listed below exist, at least somewhere in the country. They may exist in your area or, if you live in a small town, you may have to travel some way to find them, but they are there somewhere. If they don't exist close to you and you would like to join one then think about starting one for yourself.

Useful sources of information are libraries, community centres, local churches and schools, local newspapers. Be honest with them. Say you are lonely, or that you have time on your hands, or that you don't know as many people as you would like. Tell them you are looking for things to do, people to meet and friends to make and ask for their advice.

The *Yellow Pages* phone book is an excellent source of ideas. Look at the listings under clubs, associations and societies. There is an endless variety of 'things' you can join and at which you can meet people. If you only went to one a week, as a guest, to find out what they do and if you would be interested, you would be very busy for a long time.

Singles clubs: Some are overtly for sex and marriage, others are designed for friendship and companionship among single people.

Parents-without-partners: A variant on the singles theme, but with the recognition that the individuals have constraints that involve their children and there is often an emphasis on two-generation activities such as picnics and family outings.

Once-married-now-single: Similar but with less emphasis on children.

Non-smoking clubs: Created in response to the growing dislike of non-smokers for being in smoky venues. Groups meet regularly and at a variety of restaurants or pubs where there is a strict 'smoke-free zone'. Start your own if you can't find one.

Political clubs: Whatever your political persuasion there is almost certainly a support group. If you are drawn to one of the major political parties there is bound to be a local group that meets regularly, and to which you can belong. They frequently hold meetings to which they invite interesting speakers, require volunteers for social and administrative tasks and give you the chance to get out, with others, and meet vast numbers of people.

Professional clubs or associations: Whatever profession you belong to it is bound to have an association and that, in turn, may have meetings or conferences to which you can go and at which you can meet people with whom you have your work as a shared interest. Even if such a meeting does come under the category of a 'busman's holiday', keep in mind that you are there to meet people as much as for the content of the meeting itself.

Sports/athletics clubs: If you play a sport, join a club. If it is a team sport all the better. If it is not and if it only involves one other person, such as a game of squash or tennis, don't fall into the trap of pairing up beforehand.

Search out clubs that have open sessions where you can play with strangers and try to play with someone new and different each time, as well, of course, as following up any other friendships you have already made.

Look for walking and cycling clubs. Cycling is a great way to explore your neighbourhood – and what a marvellous way to get and keep fit.

Join a gym. Young or old, there are classes to suit your level of energy and skill.

Hobby clubs: You may already have a hobby. If not, then start one. Library and shop book-shelves will give you lots of ideas. When choosing one it is not a question of asking yourself, 'Am I interested in that subject?' You probably aren't; if you were, you might well already have it as a hobby. Ask yourself, 'Could I be interested in that subject?' If you're not sure, find out more about it, until you get your answer, yes or no. In the process of doing this you will meet people.

If you do have a hobby, perhaps one that has languished, then dust it off and get started again. Perhaps you once collected stamps, you may even have an old collection from your school days. Dust it off, locate the local society and go along. Remember, the main aim is to meet people so use the opportunity to do this. You might also find that you really do resurrect the old hobby and acquire an interest.

There may be something you have meant to take up or learn about. Now is the time to do it.

Gardening clubs: If you garden you will enjoy it, if you don't you might learn something interesting and start a new hobby. Even if you don't have a garden you can grow things in boxes on patios or balconies, in window boxes, or even indoors. They may also have excursions to interesting gardens.

Historical societies: Learn something about your local neighbourhood and its history. Learn about other places of interest. Join the Natural Trust and visit interesting historical sites through the countryside.

Retirement clubs: These, and clubs by similar names, exist in many towns and are aimed specifically at people who have retired and may have more time on their hands than previously.

All nations clubs: In every large city there is almost certainly a number of clubs relating to specific nationalities. There may be an Irish club, a Norwegian club, a Brazilian club. If you are lonely because you are in a country where the language is unfamiliar then you may feel more at ease and less homesick if you find, at one of these clubs, a group of people from a similar background to yours.

In other towns there is an All Nations club, or some such title, that caters for people of all different nationalities. This is a wonderful way to get to know and understand people from different backgrounds – and what a great way to reduce prejudices stemming from the unknown and unfamiliar.

If there is no such club in your town and you would like one, start one. It need not be grand, initially it could meet at a coffee bar once a week, circulate among the homes of the members or meet at a local school or community centre. Once gathered you will doubtless be able to think of many interesting activities, from ethnic meals to slide shows, language classes or the sharing of local customs.

Bridge clubs: These deserve a mention on their own. Bridge, as a game, seems to be overwhelmingly popular wherever you are. No matter how large or small the community, you will find people who play bridge. It has entertained and saved people from boredom on ocean liners and in isolated communities, on rainy days when outdoor activities are limited and in the evenings when conversation languishes.

If there is any chance at all that you would enjoy bridge then learn to play it. If you are unsure, go to some beginners classes. Even if you don't like the game and give it up, you are sure to have met lots of people.

Others: There are women's clubs, men's clubs, flying clubs, a variety of musical clubs. Look for some that interest you.

Learn

Learn a language: This is a rewarding experience in itself. It also makes a possible holiday in that country particularly appealing and a greater source of new friendships. In addition it offers you a logical reason for joining the English–French club, or whatever language you have chosen.

Evening classes: You can do evening classes on almost any subject, from a craft to a profession, from sewing to painting, from ancient history to astronomy. And you will meet very interesting people both during the course and during activities you can engage in as a result of doing the course, to use your new skills.

University of the third age: Most towns and cities have some form of this, a study centre or study courses for people who have retired and want to learn one or more new subjects, without the threat of heavy exams, but with sufficient stimulus to keep them at it.

Teach: This is an invaluable form of learning. You may have a skill you would like to share. Offer to teach it. Ask, again at community centres, in your town hall, at libraries etc. to access the appropriate people or organisers.

Entertainment

Outings groups, including theatre, ballet, opera, music, jazz, discos etc.: These may be advertised in your local paper. Some towns have a theatre group that hires a bus once a week or once a month and goes to the nearest city to a preselected theatre. If not, and if you are interested, start your own. Put a notice in the local paper, library or school. Ask anyone who could be interested to contact you. Your first outings could be small and would need only a little planning. As it grows you will find people willing to help you. You could, perhaps, structure the costs so that the organiser went free as a recognition of the work they did.

This applies to theatre but obviously also applies to any similar form of advertised entertainment. To give the outings structure you might want to work your way from theatre to theatre, regardless of what is on. In this way you might see productions you would not otherwise have chosen and thus broaden your outlook.

Home (canned) entertainment: One of the best ways to do this is to hold an 'at-home' evening at the same place, possibly your home, on a regular basis. Then people who've been once know when it is on and don't need to be invited each time. To lighten the load you could ask each person who comes to bring a plate of food, a bottle of wine, or some other such contribution.

The theme could be built around videos, choosing films, certain types of plays, operas, ballets, jazz, or any other special-interest topic. If you simply ask people around for a video night the group may never build into a regular activity. If you give it a theme, such as working through the plays of Shakespeare, or some other common interest, then you will build a close-knit group with an interest in common, one that you can expand on outside the particular events – you might, for instance, get together and go to a Shakespeare play when it is on in town.

Home games nights: There is an element of the child still, in everyone. We liked playing games as kids and many people still do as adults. Whether it is Monopoly or Trivial Pursuit, Whist or Canasta, there are hundreds, probably thousands, to choose from. A quick look at a games shop, aimed at adults (but not sex-games – unless that's what you're after), will provide you with ideas you could not have dreamt of. One client found one called Mid-Life Crisis and said that most nights when she and friends played it they spent more time discussing the concepts that came up than actually playing the game. However, as she said, since preventing loneliness was the real aim of the game, and they certainly did that as they got to know the other players better and better, the evenings were generally considered to be highly successful.

Support the arts: A visit to your local art gallery or museum will provide you with a variety of leaflets listing talks and discussion groups, plus information on exhibitions and displays. Go to these. But remember, you are there to meet people, make friends and stop being lonely. The success of the venture, therefore, is twofold. **1)** Enjoy the particular art that is involved. **2)** Be willing to talk to the people near you. It is relatively easy, when standing beside someone who is admiring or studying the same painting as you, to make a comment such as, 'Interesting use of colour isn't it?' If they want to talk they will, if not they will simply smile and move off, no harm has been done. Keep in mind, though, that many of the people you see are just as lonely as you and would love it if someone else made the effort to be friendly. When you do this in a public place it is relatively safe and you need not invite people to your home until you know them a lot better.

Friends of the arts: The performing arts provide other opportunities. Most orchestras, ballets, opera companies, theatre companies have a 'friends' section. If you join this, for a small fee, you will be able to go to dress-rehearsals, get preferential seating, be invited to talks by special guests, and so forth. All of these are wonderful opportunities to meet people, provided, of course, that you take advantage of them in that way.

Voluntary work: Remember what was said about 'Be a nicer person' and 'Give what you would like to receive.' There are many people in difficulties. There are many organisations that need volunteer help. If you have some time to spare then offer this up. Contact your local hospital, nursing homes, blind society and others. They may be looking for people to visit the patients, people to read to those that have difficulties, people to do some shopping for those who cannot get about. There may be people living at home who would appreciate a visit from time to time, to see that they are all right and offer company. All sorts of services can be offered.

House-sitting and pet-minding: House-sitting can be a wonderful opportunity if you want brief respite from where you live. You may be sharing accommodation, you may be in a tiny flat. By offering to stay in someone's home and look after it while they are away, thus depriving possible burglars of an obviously empty house as a target, you could be doing them a favour, earning some pocket money (possibly) and having the pleasure of staying in lovely homes. You would, of course, need careful references and appropriate agreements if they are total strangers, but this sort of thing can often develop by word of mouth. The house may well be empty and so not a solution to loneliness, but you do meet interesting people this way.

Pet-minding can be fun too. You will need to be sure that you can have the pet at your home, if that is the plan, and know how to take care of the practical details. Alternatively it may mean going round to feed the goldfish while the owners are away. It could also mean watering their garden for them. An advertisement in the local newspaper should provide you with a start, as well, of course, as referrals from friends. You may be on your own while doing this but, in the establishing process, each time, you will meet new people, and the extra pocket money could give you enough to be able to afford some other activity you would like to do.

Running a business from home: There are many advantages to this. A growing number of people want to be their own boss. You may be short of funds and want an additional source of income. A home-based business gives you a chance to get started with limited overheads and, provided you choose an activity that brings you into contact with people, may also stop you feeling lonely. It will almost certainly stop you feeling bored. Your local library will have books listing hundreds of different possibilities.

Appendix

Eliciting Your Values

In the text (p. 29) we mentioned the process of eliciting your values, of finding out what is really important to you. This example will explain how it's done.

Some people want freedom, others look for security. Some want love, others want independence. You may value honesty or cleverness, peace or excitement, success or comfort, variety or routine. You may like to have people around you, people that depend on you; you may want possessions, children, money, partner, opportunity, skills. It is important to find out what *you* want, then to rank these values and to decide which of them are the most important. After that you can begin to shape your future in such a way that you no longer need to feel, or to be, lonely.

Listing Your Values

Start by taking pen and paper and making a list of what you value most in your life. Don't worry about which ones are the most important, just write down anything that comes into your head that you would like to have in life. It can be a quality, an emotion, an object; anything that you value should be written down.

Gerald Weeten was a bachelor in his early thirties, restlessly uneasy about his life and feeling depressed because when he looked around most of his friends were married with children and he felt he was missing out. When he was asked to list his values he produced the following list: Security, wealth, wife, children, nice house, being the boss, peace, good job, freedom to be with my own friends, time alone.

Ranking Your Values

The next step is to rank these values in order of their importance, a task that is not always as easy as it sounds. When Gerald first considered his list and I asked him which was the most important he was uncertain.

'Well, I'm tired of feeling lonely, so friends and family are important, then again, I want to be wealthy, but I think I want security more, yet security sometimes stops me being free and freedom is more important than wealth, yet I need money to be free, I think, then there's a family, I would like a good home life, they give you security and companionship . . .' and his voiced trailed away in some confusion.

There's a simple way of doing it. First, write the values down in a list. In Gerald's case the list looked like this, in the order he'd thought of them and written them down:

Security
Wealth
Wife
Children
Nice home
Being the boss
Peace
Good job
Freedom to be with friends
Time alone

I started off by putting a dot beside 'security', the value

at the top of the list, and asked him, 'Is security more important than wealth [The value below it]?' He answered, 'No.'

So I put a dot beside 'wealth' which was now the most important value we'd covered and asked, 'Is wealth more important than a wife?' He answered, 'Yes.' So I stayed with wealth and asked 'Is wealth more important than children?' 'Yes.' Again I moved on. 'Is wealth more important than a nice home?' 'Yes.' 'Is wealth more important than being the boss?' 'Yes.' When we got down to, 'Is wealth more important than freedom to be with friends?' he said, 'No.' So I put a dot beside 'freedom to be with friends' which was now his most important value to this point, and asked, 'Is freedom to be with friends more important than time alone?' 'Yes.'

Thus we established that 'Freedom to be with friends' was his most important value and I put a **1** beside it. By then the list looked like this:

• Security
• Wealth
Wife
Children
Nice home
Being the boss
Peace
Good job
1 • Freedom to be with friends
Time alone

The next step is to go back to the previous dot, which at this stage is the next most important value and find out how far down the list you can go with it, so I asked, 'Is wealth more important than time alone?' (We'd already checked it out against all the others.) 'Yes.' So I put a **2** beside 'wealth' and went back to 'security', checking that against each one as we went down the list asking, 'Is security more important than . . .' and proceeding down the list. He had trouble when we got to, 'Is security more important than being the boss?' but eventually decided it was and carried it down to the bottom so that 'security' became his third value.

The next free value, working down the list, was 'wife' so I put a dot beside that and asked, 'Is a wife more important than children?' 'No.' A dot went beside 'children' and I asked, 'Are children more important than a nice home?' 'No.' Another dot and I asked, 'Is a nice home more important than being the boss?' 'Yes.' This meant I could continue so I asked, 'Is a nice home more important than peace?' 'No.' A dot beside 'peace' and I asked, 'Is peace more important than a good job?' 'No.' A dot beside 'a good job'. 'Is a good job more important than time alone?' 'Yes.' A good job was his fourth value and the list looked like this:

3 • Security
2 • Wealth
• Wife
• Children
• Nice home
Being the boss
• Peace
4 • Good job
1 • Freedom to be with friends
Time alone

I went back up to the lowest unnumbered dot, 'peace', and asked, 'Is peace more important than time alone?' 'Yes.' So peace was marked as number **5**. Up again to the next highest unnumbered dot, 'nice home'. I'd already discovered that this was more important than 'being the boss' so I asked, 'Is a nice home more important than time alone?' 'Yes.' So that was number **6**. Up to 'children', the next dot up without a number.

'Are children more important than being the boss?' 'No.' Mark a dot.

'Is being the boss more important than time alone?' 'Yes.' So being the boss is number 7. And the list had changed again. It now looked like this:

3 • Security
2 • Wealth
• Wife
• Children
6 • Nice home
7 • Being the boss
5 • Peace
4 • Good job
1 • Freedom to be with friends
Time alone

By continuing in this vein we got the following list, ranked in sequence:

1 Freedom with friends
2 Wealth
3 Security
4 Good job
5 Peace
6 Nice home
7 Being the boss
8 Time alone
9 Children
10 Wife

Once he took a good look at that list Gerald relaxed visibly.

'You know that does make sense. My friends are very important to me. I guess I've been feeling lonely because they've been marrying and so have less time to spare for me as a bachelor. I don't really want to marry, I just thought I ought to, as a way to stop feeling lonely. And while I want to be wealthy I also want security; I'd rather be wealthy by not spending it on a wife and family than by getting a riskier and more stressful job. I guess what I really need is some new men friends.'

This may not be everyone's idea of the good life, but it suited Gerald. More importantly, by recognising consciously what he had been feeling at the unconscious level he was able to rationalise his emotions and start creating the life he wanted, without doubts and without being pulled in different directions. This is the benefit of sorting out your values.

By now I hope the method is clear and you can work on your own.[1] With a little practice you will realise that the method is not really complicated and it is a simple way to avoid going round in circles.

[1] For a more complete description, and for other variations on this process, see *Beating the Blues* by Xandria Williams, published by Cedar, 1995.

Also available from Cedar

XANDRIA WILLIAMS

Fatigue

Are you tired? Run down? Depressed? Listless?
Or are you totally exhausted?

Fatigue is an ailment of our times. It is also an ailment which manifests itself in many ways. In this book, Xandria Williams explains how your body generates energy and how these mechanisms can fail. She offers diagnoses and suggested cures for all aspects of tiredness, whether it be a mild condition or full Chronic Fatigue Syndrome, and asks:

- Does your diet supply sufficient energy?
- Is your environment holding you back?
- Are you suffering from stress, allergies, candida or hypoglycaemia?

From nutrition and exercise to emotional and spiritual dimensions, *Fatigue* is packed with information, case histories and day-to-day practical advice to help anybody struggling with tiredness or Chronic Fatigue Syndrome. It is an expert and easy to use handbook for anybody who wants to get their energy back.

XANDRIA WILLIAMS

Beating the Blues

A guide to avoiding and lifting depression

Depression is on the increase – more people than ever before are suffering. *Beating the Blues* is a practical guide for people, working on their own or with the help of a friend, who want to recognise and deal with depression without resorting to professional help or drug treatments.

Using real-life examples and case histories, Xandria Williams deals with depression, its causes and solutions in three clear sections:

- Personality, personal responsibility and personal power
- Specific techniques for dealing with depression and a variety of emotions and situations that can lead to or result from depression
- Creating a future without depression and in line with your own values and goals

There are ways to deal with depression. The techniques described in this book have been developed and refined over many years of clinical practice. They are specifically designed and selected that they can be applied by the individual with little or no help from other people.

JUDY TATELBAUM

The Courage to Grieve

Creative living, recovery and growth through grief

Profound loss and disappointment are emotions that each of us will experience at some point in our lives. Loss is one of the most difficult experiences to come to terms with. *The Courage to Grieve* explores how we can deal with every kind of grief and reveals:

- How grief manifests itself in many ways, ranging from anguish, exhaustion, emptiness, resentment, longing, tension, confusion, sleeplessness and sometimes the temporary loss of the will to live
- How we can help ourselves and others to cope with the immediate experience of death and the grief that follows
- How children and adults cope with grief in different ways
- What we should do mentally and physically to prepare ourselves for loss and bereavement
- How grief can transform our lives in unexpected ways, encouraging joy and growth

The Courage to Grieve offers spiritual, optimistic, creative and practical guidance and shows us how to live with courage, not fearing death.

ROBIN SKYNNER and JOHN CLEESE

Families and How to Survive Them

'It achieves what it set out to do – explaining in ordinary language to ordinary people just how relationships work' *Sun*

- How do people choose a partner?
- Why do they fall in love?
- What roles do they adopt or impose on one another?
- How do they behave towards their children?
- How does a child grow up into a healthy – or not so healthy – adult?

These are just some of the questions – vital to a happy healthy family life – explored by family therapist Dr Robin Skynner and his former patient, humorist John Cleese.

'A simple, down to earth book for those with family or marriage difficulties' *Scotsman*

'Unusual, demanding, potentially painful but often funny' *Ideal Home*

ROBIN SKYNNER and JOHN CLEESE

Life and How to Survive it

'Breathtaking . . . On every page you will find insights that will cut straight to the heart of your own life' *Daily Mail*

From religion to politics and from ethical principles to the process of change, this is an enlightening, fascinating and often amusing exploration of almost every aspect of human life.

'Enormously important . . . no literate person will any longer have an excuse to turn his or her back on psychotherapeutic evidence because of the jargon' *Weekend Telegraph*

'I wholeheartedly recommend it to everyone . . . masterly. It'll make you laugh too' *The Therapist*

'Who could understand life as well as these two . . . our lives are the richer for their struggle' *Modern Review*